## AND THE PRINCESSES ROYAL

To understand what it is to be a Princess Royal, through all the marvellous moments and other times too, read how 'that doyen of royal-book writers' Helen Cathcart skilfully handles the royal daughters from the days when princesses were 'ladyes', and the King's eldest son was styled Prince Royal, through to the present day.

Anne emerges from this background, casual and candid, quick-witted and quick-tempered, careless of speed limits in more ways than one, wilful yet self-questioning. A Princess for our times.

We meet the schoolgirl 'tagging along' to holiday camps; the teenager dreamily sailing along with 'someone you really care for', the debby Princess with meterioric enthusiasms, the intensive royal traveller, the European Champion rider . . . And, finally, with her characteristic charm and uniquely intimate knowledge, the author captures completely the love story of the Princess and the Dragoon.

A Star Book
Published in 1975
by W. H. Allen & Co. Ltd.
A division of Howard & Wyndham Ltd.
44, Hill Street, London W1X 8LB

First published in Great Britain by
W. H. Allen & Co. Ltd. 1973

Copyright © 1973 by Helen Cathcart

Printed in Great Britain by
Richard Clay (The Chaucer Press), Ltd., Bungay, Suffolk

ISBN 0 352 30048 5

# Contents

|  |  | page |
|---|---|---|
| Author's Note |  | vii |

A PRELUDE OF PRINCESSES

| 1 | The Style and Distinction | 3 |
| 2 | A Debut of Ladies | 7 |
| 3 | Scottish and French Marriages | 13 |
| 4 | Sisters of Henry VIII | 17 |
| 5 | The Tudor Daughters | 21 |

BOOK ONE—THE BYGONE PAGEANT

| 1 | In Stuart Times | 29 |
| 2 | The Princess Royal Anne | 51 |
| 3 | The Princess Royal Charlotte | 64 |
| 4 | Princess Royal, Empress of Prussia | 78 |
| 5 | The Princess Royal, Duchess of Fife | 91 |
| 6 | Princess Mary, Countess of Harewood | 107 |

BOOK TWO—PRINCESS ANNE

| 1 | The Noonday Child | 128 |
| 2 | Enthusiasms | 142 |
| 3 | Benenden | 152 |
| 4 | Hopeful Venture | 167 |
| 5 | Princess of the Seventies | 180 |

| Bibliography | 207 |

# Calendar

CHARLES I
|_____
              Princess Mary, 1631–1660
              Princess Royal, c.1642–1660

GEORGE II
|_____
              Princess Anne, 1709–1759
              Princess Royal, 1727–1759

GEORGE III
|_____
              Princess Charlotte, 1766–1828
              Princess Royal, 1789–1828

VICTORIA
|_____
              Princess Victoria, 1840–1901
              Princess Royal, 1840–1901

EDWARD VII
|_____
              Princess Louise, 1867–1931
              Princess Royal, 1905–1931

GEORGE V
|_____
              Princess Mary, 1897–1965
              Princess Royal, 1932–1965

ELIZABETH II
|_____
              Princess Anne, b. 1950

# Author's Note

This book originated in a quest for the first Princess Royal and all her successors, and an enquiry into the origin of the 'style and distinction', presenting as it does an enigmatic gap in the written records of the past. With this search there has been combined a personal biographical study of H.R.H. The Princess Anne of today, in the early years of married life.

In attempting to break new ground I have had to cut through thickets of the fast-growing shrub popularly known as 'taking-it-for-granted', planted by generations of authors who assumed that the eldest daughter of the monarch is automatically born to the title of Princess Royal. The assumption was indeed accepted by historians otherwise impeccable in research and profound in knowledge, but the precedents now sufficiently establish that the distinction of a Princess Royal is conferred at the discretion of the Sovereign and is not a birthright alone. The style and title has evolved with the ever-changing and yet timeless monarchy, as these pages may show.

My self-imposed task could not of course have been completed without help on specific points from many quarters, and I must particularly cite and thank Dr. E. Pelinck, director of the Royal House Archives at The Hague; Major-General P. B. Gillett of the Central Chancery of the Orders of Knighthood; Mr. J. G. Wickham of the Public Record Office; Sir Anthony Wagner, Garter King of Arms, and the sympathetic and ever-helpful staff of the London Library. The Earl of Harewood kindly enabled me to establish many hitherto unpublished facts concerning his mother, the late Princess Royal, the Princess Mary, and I am very much indebted to his brother, the Hon. Gerald Lascelles, both for his helpful advice and for furnishing basic family material. Miss Gwynedd Lloyd similarly contributed her great personal knowledge as a close friend and lady-in-waiting of Princess Mary over many years. The Duke of Fife was also good enough to enlighten me on the family records of his grandmother, the Princess Louise, Duchess of Fife. On other princesses of the past, I must naturally acknowledge the illumination of earlier authors, and a bibliography is appended.

By gracious permission of Her Majesty the Queen I have been enabled to reproduce the portraits of Princess Mary, daughter of Charles I; Anne, Princess Royal; Charlotte, Princess Royal; and of Victoria, Princess Royal, from the royal collection. My study of the Princess Anne of today could also not have been completed without much personal assistance. I am most grateful to those who so generously contributed their information and guidance, and I have to add that the copyright in quotations from royal letters, journals and associated material is reserved.

HELEN CATHCART

# A Prelude of Princesses

'Be not angry, most mighty princess that I have adventured To try your taking of a false report'

—*Cymbeline* Act 1, Scene 5.

# 1 The Style and Distinction

The style and dignity of Princess Royal is not a distinction of established tradition or ancient origin. In all the long rollcall of the dynasties since the Norman Conquest, one may count forty-five Queens of England and royal daughters innumerable, but only six Princesses Royal with an established definitive right to that title. The male Heir Apparent to the Throne automatically becomes Duke of Cornwall either at birth or upon his parents' accession, an inheritance ordained by Edward III in a charter of 1337, and twenty-one holders of the Duchy have been subsequently created Prince of Wales. Yet there has been no comparable system for princesses; and Princesses Royal are as rare within the royal scene as Queens Regnant. Their rights are unprescribed, their duties undefined, their additional status arbitrarily conferred. And within the past sixty years at least, their mysterious ennoblement has been not merely by the entitlement of birth as the eldest daughter of the Sovereign but as a symbol of the recognized respect or affection of the nation.

There is a story that when King Edward VII wished to appoint his own eldest daughter as the first Princess Royal of the twentieth century, he desired his close and expert friend, Sir Arthur Ellis, to explain the forms and precedents, and Ellis promptly replied, 'Sire, there are none!' As comptroller to the Lord Chamberlain, Ellis could call upon the historic lore of the Heralds' College and all the deep knowledge of Garter King of Arms. He was himself no mean authority, with 'an unrivalled knowledge of the way things were done', as the King's private secretary testified, but the required details on the ceremonial of a Princess Royal were not forthcoming. Sir Arthur Ellis found himself in a quandary. It appeared certain that any early documentation had been destroyed during the eleven years of Cromwell's republic, hardly a tactful loss to report to a choleric monarch.

Edward the Seventh was crowned and the niche of Princess Royal remained vacant for more than four years when, on the eve of his sixty-fourth birthday, the King declared his pleasure that his eldest daughter, Princess Louise, Duchess of Fife, should bear the style and title. The direction appeared in his Birthday Honours list, but that seems to have been the end of the matter. Apparently no document of Letters Patent was ever issued, and no hint can be found in the Patent Rolls of the reign. The new dignity gained no further mention in the *London Gazette*, and neither Letters Patent nor a Royal Warrant on his grandmother's enhancement can be found in the archives of the present Duke of Fife.

It has been more customary to decree the title by Royal Warrant under the Great Seal and so assure the position of the Princess Royal with courtly formality. Queen Victoria assumed that her first-born daughter and her first-born son became respectively Princess Royal and Prince of Wales at birth. She found herself mistaken, and there ensued a flurry to fulfil her wishful thinking, whereupon her daughter was 'granted arms as Princess Royal' when two months old, while her 'fine large Boy' had his necessary attestation rushed through within a month. The future Edward VII was thus created Prince of Wales seven weeks before being christened.

Closer to our own time, King George V conferred the title on his daughter, Princess Mary, Countess of Harewood, in his New Year Honours of 1932, less than a year after the death of the former Princess Royal, her aunt Princess Louise. The sequence was broken once again with the sudden death of Princess Mary—styled Her Royal Highness the Princess Royal—in 1965. Our own Princess Anne was then still a schoolgirl at Benenden, considered too young to undertake public duties, and expectations that the present Queen's only daughter might be declared Princess Royal in 1966—possibly as a corollary to the Queen's fortieth birthday—were not fulfilled. Nor was a similarly anticipated announcement made for the twenty-first anniversary of Princess Anne's birthday in 1971.

The delay enshrined tributes of family affection for the 'Aunt Mary' who, more than any of her predecessors, had brought to the dignity of Princess Royal significant attributes of genuine zeal for public duty. As the modern monarchy departs more and more from the pomp and flummery of old, the declaration of a Princess Royal becomes an evident exercise in public relations, requiring judicious timing. It cannot prudently seem to compensate for Olympic disappointments or to emphasize sporting honours.

More probably the Queen's daughter herself preferred to be known simply as the Princess Anne until, in fuller maturity, she might know she had earned the enhanced dignity by her own public merit.* But since her marriage to Mark Phillips, the conferment can be seen to be both appropriate and convenient. Taking her husband's name, the Princess has correctly become 'The Princess Anne, Mrs. Mark Phillips', and the single popular title 'The Princess Royal' would obviously be simpler. The bestowal requires no formal submission to the Prime Minister, Cabinet or Parliament, and can be made by the Queen at any time without consulting her advisers.

As with the Order of Merit, The Order of the Garter, the Family Order, the Thistle and the Royal Victorian Order, the distinction is a gift within the Queen's personal bestowal. Once declared, the status is conferred for life. Like the Garter, it could be withdrawn or relinquished, although the resignation or official retirement of a Princess Royal has never been known. This degree of permanence tends to give a prestige and seniority that can only be enhanced with the passage of time.

Since the title lies completely within the Queen's personal prerogative, there is also always the possibility that the Queen might prefer to establish a new precedent and declare Princess Margaret to be Princess Royal. The title has hitherto been conferred only upon the eldest daughter of a monarch, but five Princesses Royal have survived as eldest sisters of the Sovereign; and as the Queen's sister becomes farther removed from the Succession the stronger may be the desire to enhance her status in a more personal and individual manner. In the normal course of human life this departure might not prevent the title passing from the Queen's sister to the Queen's daughter at some future time.

In heraldry, the title of the Princess Royal does not change or amend her armorial bearings by a curlicue. The rank in itself establishes no fresh privileges and, unlike the investiture of a Prince of Wales, entails no admonitions, promises or vows. Princess Mary was given her enhanced rank five years before the abdication of her brother, Edward VIII—the late Duke of Windsor—but re-

* The reader's indulgence is sought if the Queen has made her wishes known while this book is in the press.

mained for another thirty years an aunt and mentor of a younger generation of royalty. Time transmutes its relationships at an inflexible yet leisured pace, so that the woman set apart in honour as the elder daughter of the Sovereign may find herself the adviser and aunt supreme of a later reign.

Adult maturity and responsibility have nevertheless rarely seemed prerequisites to a Princess Royal. When George II was summoned to the Throne in 1727, he lost no time at all in issuing a Royal Warrant, conferring armorial bearings on 'our eldest daughter the Princess Royal Anne', who was then only seventeen. No woman had been so styled for a century and a quarter, and when the title next became vacant in 1759, another thirty years elapsed before George II in fact accorded the dignity to his twenty-two-year-old eldest daughter, the Princess Royal Charlotte, who later became Queen of Wurttemberg and aunt to Queen Victoria.

The status goes back no farther indeed than the seventeenth century. It was an innovation at the time of Charles the First and an extravagant sequel, as we shall discover, to the marriage of a ten-year-old child in an era when kingship was stumbling into intense danger. Though mentioned in royal Netherlands documents of 1642, the first hint that the distinction had fully come into use appears in State Papers of the year 1646. Fourteen years later, the title formed an embellishment to the Restoration, setting Samuel Pepys and others 'crowding in' to see the Princess Royal and kiss her hand.

They found a plethoric middle-aged widow, overwrought at the change of fortune that shone upon her brother, Charles II. And yet the Royal magic persisted, a tincture of past times, of the age of chivalry of England's Edward III and the honourable Scottish heritage that stemmed from Robert the Bruce. Long before the prefix Royal ever graced a King's daughter, a masculine equivalent can be discovered in usage in Scotland. The legitimate heirs of the northern kingdom were commonly styled Prince Royal. The last Prince Royal, the son of James I (VI of Scotland) was also created Prince of Wales at the age of sixteen, and if this popular and talented Prince Henry had survived into manhood, there would have been a lively prospect that his younger brother, who later ruled as Charles I, might not have lost his head.

# 2   A Debut of Ladies

The style *Princess* is in itself a comparatively new ornament to the embroideries and splendour of the monarchy. King Henry VIII would have raised a sceptical eyebrow, if he could have heard his first bride, the widow of his elder brother, called Princess Katherine or even Princess of Wales. 'The high and noble lady Katherine', so she appeared in the heraldic pronouncement of the marriage. There are queens, royal daughters and royal ladies in Shakespeare's plays, but comparatively few princesses. The princesses of Tudor times whom we watch in television costume drama, had their ladies, their lute players, their maids of the bedchamber and mistresses of the kitchen, but for themselves there was not a 'royal highness' nor a 'ma'am' among them.

According to one authority, the daughter of Henry VIII by his Queen Katherine was the first to be formally proclaimed Princess of England and the first to sign herself 'Marie Princesse' to support and heighten her cause when at last named in the Succession. But in everyday life at Hampton Court and St. James's Palace, Mary and her younger half-sister were known as the Lady Mary and the Lady Elizabeth; and until Henry's only son, Edward VI, died of the poisonous effects of his doctors' physic, they are thus styled in the most resounding and ceremonious of Tudor records.

In the rougher courts of the Plantagenets, kings had scant time for daughters. The girl-children were bargaining counters on the market tables of diplomacy, betrothed in their cradles and frequently married into exile as tearful infants of eight or nine. Few otherwise impressed themselves on events for posterity, and few gained any personal lustre in their own day.

In 1066, when his ships in the harbours of Normandy were actively preparing to carry his archers to England, William the Conqueror dedicated his eldest daughter, Cecilia, to the services of God in the abbey he had founded in Caen. Whether this was intended to propitiate or gratify high providence was never made

7

plain, and in any event the gesture was a nominal one. William ceremoniously carried the child, then aged eleven, to the steps of the altar but she remained under the parental roof for seven more years before taking the veil. A novice so well connected, bringing a rich endowment, was not to be denied preferment. When elected abbess, she struck a royal bargain with her brother, the Duke Robert, and was awarded all the tolls of the town on days of markets, fairs or feastings. On the eve of these lucrative occasions, the lady abbess herself affixed her armorial bearings to each gate of the city. Her nuns collected the dues, and indeed the sisterhood was still in benefit seven centuries later.

Even earlier than William, we glimpse the inspiring and matri-archal figure of Ethelflaed, eldest daughter of Alfred the Great and wife of his friend and ally, the chieftain Ethelred. Her husband governed the vast and troubled realm of Mercia, which was con-stantly under attack, the prey of Danish marauders, and upon his death she found herself the sole ruler of a region extending nearly from London to York and from the Wash westwards to the Welsh border. Beyond the confines of Alfred's peaceful kingdom of Wessex, the Danish raids endangered the lives and fortunes of every family until Ethelflaed faced the threat with all her father's resource-ful intelligence and force of character. Fortifying towns and cities and strengthening defensive walls and dykes across the countryside, she substituted the tactics of siege for those of battle, confronted the enemy with a 'scorched-earth' policy and lived to defeat both the invaders and their insidious fifth columns. She merits immortality as the mother of England, which was to be unified within a genera-tion. Yet it illustrates the anonymity of royal daughters that the monkish historians recorded her leadership not in splendour as queen, princess or chieftainess, but merely in modest guise as 'the lady of Mercia'.

William's grand-daughter, Matilda, also rides in our procession as the first English princess of part-Scottish blood, the first to demonstrate to taxpayers the high cost of royal maidens, the first to win a crown by marrying into a foreign royal family and cer-tainly the only princess to avert a war when new-born from the womb. Her mother, a daughter of Malcolm Canmore, caused some scandal by emerging from a convent to wed her father, Henry I, and Matilda was born at Winchester with perfect timing and

English style on the very day when her uncle, Robert of Normandy, was marching on the city to assert his right to the sacrilege-shaken kingdom. Hearing of events, the Duke Robert abandoned his fight, saying that 'to wage war on a woman in such plight would be base indeed', and he rode to Winchester carrying gifts instead of arms.

At the age of eight the 'ladye Matilda' was married to the Emperor Henry V of Germany, a man thirty-seven years her senior. If we may trust the old scribes, her husband found her 'wise, valiant and beautiful', a child half-smothered in robes heavy and stiff with beads and jewels. A band of knights, headed by Roger Fitz Richard, accompanied the bride to Mainz, guarding not only the diminutive princess but, no doubt equally precious, the creaking bullion wagons containing her dowry, 10,000 pieces of silver exacted by a land-tax of three shillings upon every 100 farm acres of English soil. Matilda was crowned forthwith with the iron diadem of the Caesars and crowned yet again, at the age of fifteen, at St. Peter's in Rome.

The Emperor was a man of vindictive hates and caustic temper. One story is that he imprisoned his deposed father and forced him to eat his own boots in the pangs of starvation. He treated his wife with some kindness, but it seems just retribution that, although he desperately wanted a son, the marriage was childless. Matilda was only twenty-one at his death, and she returned home to England speaking more German than English or French. Her parents 'kept her straitly' within the claustrophobic walls of Windsor while they matured other future plans, and for her second husband she was espoused to a boy of eleven, the heir to the mighty Plantagenet earldom of Anjou. The marriage took place at Le Mans and the trumpeting of the heralds rang through the town that throbs in our own day to the roar of racing cars.

Meanwhile, in England, since King Henry I had no son, the prelates and barons accepted that Matilda, dowager empress and future countess, was heiress presumptive to the Crown, thus establishing the first English legal precedent that a woman could inherit the Throne. Four centuries, however, were to swing away before Mary Tudor was acclaimed and the first Queen Regnant became a fact of reality. Matilda was faced with private problems of her own. Her young husband, Geoffrey, though praised as 'a great knight and strong, handsome and valiant', was still a child and seven years passed before she had a son.

Then, as the poet Robert of Gloucester describes,

'Glad was kyng Henry when tydings him come
Of that child to be hys heir of hys kingdom
Then went he to Normandy, and all that year
For joye of the yonge child he remained there.'

As a highlight of the rejoicing, the silken birth couch was sold, and the money distributed to poor lepers, an early instance of royal charity. All unaware, Matilda had founded a dynasty which lasted through the Plantagenet strain for 200 years and through the quarrels of Lancaster and York to the dawn of the House of Tudor.

\*　　\*　　\*

Not that it was much of a life for those early princesses. The royal daughters who survived the hazards of infancy as baby brides then usually faced stern and austere years of convent discipline so that they might learn their lessons. The three sisters of Richard the Lion-heart—Matilda's grandson—should have counted themselves fortunate in being brought up by a worldly mama, the sophisticated Queen Eleanor of Aquitaine, who had been previously divorced from the French King Louis VII and fondly indulged their every wish. The fruit of this freedom was that the eldest girl, also named Matilda, went in exceptional splendour to her wedding with Henry, the Duke of Brunswick and Bavaria, her opulent bridal gifts, clothes and plate, sumptuously enclosed in fifty-six silver coffers. We know that her trousseau cost £63, exclusive of jewels, a fabulous sum for those days, that her seven ponies had saddles covered with scarlet and gold, with gilded reins, and her wedding-gown provides one of the earliest authentic fashion notes for regal brides. She must have looked enchanting, her young face framed in a full white frill, her brow garnished with a coronet of strawberry leaves and pearls, her robe full-waisted, very long and trimmed with fur. Her husband, also, wore a richly embroidered tunic to the ankles, surmounted by a scalloped cloak of white velvet, thrown open to reveal a satin apron, and upon his head a jewelled cap decked with three ostrich feathers. Undoubtedly, in this gear, they made a carefree and splendid couple.

They duly had a large family; and whenever the Duke and his Duchess journeyed between their castles, the children accompanied them in a glorious cavalcade of nursemaids and cot-makers, cooks and grooms, jesters, marshals, carters, courtiers and hangers-on. The Duke travelled one year as far as Ararat to greet the Turkish Sultan and, to the delight and alarm of his children returned with caged leopards and a lion, six camels laden with gifts and a train of slaves forming an astonishing retinue. The Duchess also had surprises for her husband. During his absence, she had created a pleasure park similar to the parkland of Woodstock, where she had spent much of her childhood, reproducing its charms complete to a maze, meandering streams and a romantic islet known as a lover's bower. Some of the menagerie beasts, proving rather unmanageable, were dispatched to the Duchess's father, who had recently inherited a family zoo, and the lion, it seems, was ultimately a troublesome wedding-gift to her younger sister, Eleanora, who married the King of Castille.

Yet the third sister, Joanna, must have been even more like her brother, Coeur-de-Lion. At the age of eleven she undertook a long and adventurous voyage to marry the King of Sicily, and her charms and lively personality made a considerable impression. Palermo was splendidly illuminated for her arrival, so that the city seemed on fire and 'the stars could scarcely be seen amid the profusion of lights'. The Sicilian lords 'looking upon her beauty were delighted beyond measure', as well they might be. Joanna presented her husband with an heir before she was seventeen. But her most remarkable adventure was still in store for her when, widowed and in her twenties, she accompanied her brother upon the Third Crusade. She witnessed the siege and surrender of Acre, and indeed slept amid the cushions and glowing tiles of its palace, her personal conquest so complete that she received a proposal of marriage from none other than the infidel Saladin's brother. Joanna's head was unturned. She accepted the Saracen's gifts of fruit and exotic birds, but put her foot down at becoming a harem bride as an accessory to a Moslem truce, and thereupon made her way safely home from the Holy Land in the care of the gallant and handsome Raimond, Count of Toulouse.

Whether this attractive and opportune escort was already married, and subsequently divorced, remains debatable, but he and the Lady

Joanna were married at Rouen shortly afterwards, with Richard Cœur-de-Lion giving his sister away. And there the story might have happily ended, except that Joanna died in childbirth, the tragic fate of many ladies, princesses and peasants, in the squalor and sickness of the Middle Ages.

# 3 Scottish and French Marriages

As long ago as the year 1221 princesses of the English blood royal established the sustained tradition of Scottish marriages. The first of these ladies (of legitimate descent) was another Joanna, eldest sister of Henry III, who was wedded to Alexander II of Scotland in a halfway ceremony staged at York. The expense-sheets of the journey, including a palfrey and saddle for Joanna's use, show that horsemanship was an accomplishment of princesses even then, and the sons of the farriers and saddlers on the route made handsome profits in their turn thirty years later, when her niece, Margaret, married King Alexander III. A thousand knights, we are told, rode in the lady Margaret's retinue, but this showy guard turned back at York, leaving her to the few hundred but 'decently enough dressed' Scotsmen. Margaret found Edinburgh Castle dismal, 'the sea air of Scotland' injurious to her health, and she eagerly seized an excuse to return home to have her first baby at Windsor.

This early Anglo-Scottish cycle of marriages extended over a century and came to an end when Joanna, the sister of Edward III, was wedded at the tender age of six to David II, the four-year-old son of Robert the Bruce. Crowned at Scone shortly afterwards, the two children spent most of the juvenile years of their marriage in exile in France at a safe remove from adult quarrels. But they had not long returned home when the young husband was taken a prisoner-of-war in some border skirmish, and spent eleven years in captivity; it is not surprising that the marriage was childless. The consequences were of importance, for the change in the direction of the dynasty saw the rise of the House of Stuart in Scotland.

In England, meanwhile, the winds of circumstance also blew darkly on the love and all too brief life of Edward III's daughter, Joan, the sister of the Black Prince.* In the year 1346, when the Prince returned victorious from the siege of Calais, the King

* Not to be confused with the Prince's cousin, Joan of Kent, whom he later married.

13

announced that twenty-five of the noblest of his knights would be honoured and united in the Order of the Garter and the rejoicings were blended with festivities for Joan's approaching marriage to Alfonso of Castille. Alas, this was also the year when the dreadful scourge of the Black Death carried off more than a million victims in England alone. The King's daughter fell sick with the pestilence and her hasty funeral occurred at the very hour planned for her wedding.

The French wars provided not only a prodigious booty of silks from Languedoc, furs and velvets for the English princesses, but also an unaccustomed choice of husbands from among the high-born French hostages and prisoners-of-war. Each new and successive military triumph saw a series of court entertainments held by the victors to welcome the vanquished. The revels often went on for days, 'the comfort inestimable, the pleasure without murmuring, the hilarity without care', as the cleric Adam de Murimuth enjoyably described it. In this indulgent atmosphere, the King thought it well to give some extra care to his wife and daughters, and an Act of 1350 declares it an act of treason 'si homme violast la compaigne le Roi on leisnesce fill le roi nient marie' (if any one shall violate the Queen, being the King's companion, or his eldest daughter unmarried).

This enactment of Edward III, in the old French phrasing, became the first to create a distinction between the eldest unmarried princess and her sisters, a precaution no doubt lest the eldest should inherit the Crown, and we are on the way to a precedent for the Princess Royal. When King John of France was captured at Poitiers, he was permitted to return to France pending arrangements for a ransom. The hostage who took his place, the personable de Courcy, Count of Soissons, was allowed, as deputy for his king, 'to hunt, hawk and take what other diversions he pleased'. The diversions, indeed, included falling in love with Edward III's eldest surviving daughter, Philippa, and they enjoyed an endearingly happy marriage.

The old annals also allow us a tantalising glimpse of another princess Elizabeth, who was not only the daughter of a King (Edward IV) but was also the bride of a King of England (Henry VII) as well as sister of the murdered princes in the Tower. This tragic mystery still lay in the future at the time when the Governor of Holland visited Windsor Castle, and the herald Bluemantle Pursuivant wrote an account still to be found in the present royal library. In the course of his entertainments, the visitor was conducted after supper to the Queen's salon where he found her with her daughters and ladies throwing balls at ivory ninepins, a diversion at which the seven-year-old Elizabeth shone with pleasurable skill. Then the minstrels arrived and dancing began, and the herald watched the King take his little daughter in his arms and swing her round the room, just as any young father might do today.

Next evening, the Lady Elizabeth was given leave to stay up late at a banquet, enjoying 'a great vue' of 'divers ladyes and certeyn nobles of the Kinges own courte', and no doubt especially relishing certain 'dishes of green ginger and sugared sweets'. A year or two later, we find Elizabeth betrothed to the infant Dauphin of France, only to be jilted—one of the few breaches of promise in British royal history—when Louis XI found the portents unfavourable and inconsiderately changed his mind. In her teens Elizabeth was then promised to Henry Tudor, who truly avenged her murdered brothers by defeating Richard III to the death on Bosworth Field. Although Henry was crowned alone in London, the long feuds of the houses of York and Lancaster could not be resolved until he had reassured the Privy Council that he was 'willing to take to wife and consort the lady Elizabeth'. At her wedding five months later she carried a symbolic 'posie wherein white and red roses were tied together' and the Wars of the Roses had come at last to a happy ending.

Elizabeth of York's crowning as Queen Consort was postponed by the discovery that she was to have a child and, while England rejoiced, preparations for the infant were made with the utmost elegance of state. The walls of the birth-chamber were hung, by order, with rich arras and the floors warmed by carpeting, to ward off draughts and protect both mother and babe against chill, while the maternity bed itself was decked with ermine and cloth of gold and arrayed with sheets of finest lawn.

As if encouraged by these rich and lavish signs of welcome a baby boy arrived a full month early. Two hundred torch-bearers illumined the brilliant procession to his christening in Winchester Cathedral. His chosen name 'Arthur' was intended to revive the legendary glory of the hero-king who had once held court at

Winchester. Unhappily for pomp and promise, Prince Arthur ironically caught his death of cold fifteen years later in the mortal chill of quite another castle—bleak, comfortless Ludlow—and the handsome younger brother who succeeded to the throne of England seven years later was the lusty and vigorous figure whom we all know as King Henry VIII.

# 4    Sisters of Henry VIII

The two sisters of Henry VIII were curiously to echo his marital vicissitudes in the matrimonial pattern of their own lives. The elder girl, the Lady Margaret, set out when fourteen years old to marry King James IV of Scotland. Broad of figure like her brother, her trousseau included 'a gown of tawny cloth-of-gold, another of purple velvet, and one furred with ermine', no fewer than 3,200 tails being used for the trimming of this garment, at the surprising cost of under six and eightpence. She was outfitted, in addition, with two petticoats, two hats, six pairs of woollen hose, three pairs of shoes, six pairs of slippers, two dozen pairs of gloves and, for the needs of the journey, a tentlike litter serviceable as 'a toilette at the wayside'. None of the Tudors lacked magnificence.

Margaret, who had never seen her bridegroom, took a dislike to his red beard on sight, at which the King, then aged just thirty, permitted her attendant lady, the Countess of Surrey, to cut it to the stub. With this proof of amity, the betrothed pair then rode into Edinburgh together, Margaret mounted pillion upon King James' horse. This day she had 'received him gladly and of good will kissed him'. But she privately wrote to her brother of 'this King here' and her disquiet crept into her concluding paragraph: 'God send me comfort to his pleasure that I, and mine that be left here with me, be well treated . . . I hold a wish that I might be with your Grace now!' To entertain his guests, the King arranged a tournament of his knights. One brilliantly successful competitor jousted honourably under the nom de guerre of 'the Savage Knight' and Margaret did not recognize, or at least pretended not to know, that this valiant contestant was none other than her husband.

Yet the marriage proved a happy one. When Queen Margaret recovered from an illness, she and James went on a pilgrimage of thankfulness together, the King 'in good patience', although the Queen's unstinted baggage train necessitated seventeen horses. Then the Scots renewed their old treaty with the French, and in 1513

James died among the abandoned Scottish guns on Flodden Field. And it was at this juncture that Margaret's impetuous Tudor blood warred with the prudence that until then had seemed her second nature.

The widowed Queen was appointed Regent for the new King, her seventeen-month-old son, provided she did not remarry. One of her first acts was to send 'loving letters' to her brother in England entreating him 'not to harm or oppress her little King, who was very small and tender'. Three Scottish nobles acted as her Regency advisers, the Earls of Huntley, Arran and Angus, and before her overtures to Henry could yield results she impulsively married Angus, youngest of her advisers but also head of the powerful Red Douglases, strongest and most headstrong of all the feuding Scottish families of that time.

Margaret was then twenty-four, her new husband only twenty. Legally, her marriage annulled the Regency, but she sought to keep the custody of the little King by hurrying with him to the security of Stirling Castle. It would be tedious to chronicle the varying intrigues by which either Angus or his rivals gained guardianship of the child (who was destined to father Mary Queen of Scots). At one stage, Angus was outlawed and in hiding, and Henry offered his sister sanctuary in England. She accepted but had been across the Border only a few days when Henry at Hampton Court received a letter from his warden, Lord Dacre. 'On the third day of the Queen her Grace's entry into your Grace's realm,' wrote Dacre, 'she was delivered and brought to bed of a fair young lady.'

This infant, Angus's daughter, Margaret Douglas, also ultimately traced a finger in history as the mother of Lord Darnley, husband of Mary Queen of Scots. Long before the 'fair young lady' could reach her teens, however, her parents' quarrels for power had reached the irreparable breaking-point of divorce. Ironically, Henry still considered himself firmly married to his first wife, Katherine of Aragon, and wrote that his sister's ideas of divorce were 'the veriest wicked delusions'. Katherine similarly advised her brother that matrimonial troubles should be borne in patience and, above all, never laid before the public.

Yet her marriage was no sooner annulled than Queen Margaret claimed that she had found 'a true man' in her third husband,

Henry Stewart, sometime Lord Treasurer of Scotland. Others with clearer insight declared that he 'filled the court with bragging and brawling', and in time Margaret, too, became disillusioned and we find her soon proposing yet another marriage, this time to the second of her Regency advisers, the Earl of Arran. It was for complicity in this affair that Lady Glamis, an ancestress of today's Queen Mother, was burned as a witch. It is not an illuminating tale. At the age of fifty-two, Margaret was still wallowing in 'four and forty proofs' of divorce against her third husband when she suddenly died, a Queen who established the unusual precedent of leaving 'two widowers'.

\*     \*     \*

Henry VIII's younger sister, Mary, five years his junior, was educated with her brothers at the little royal palace at Eltham. The more thorough education of princesses had gained favour and, like her brothers, she was set to studying French and Latin, as well as music and the more feminine accomplishments of dancing and embroidery. In the Eltham household accounts are tiny references to twenty pence paid to a tailor for 'a gown of black satyn for the Ladye Marye' and twopence for 'a letter of pardon', perhaps a fine for some juvenile misdemeanour. At twelve, married by proxy to the ten-year-old Prince Charles of Castille, she clearly and calmly recited her marriage vows in a ceremony at Greenwich: 'I, Mary, take thee Lord Charles to my husband and spouse. Henceforward, during my natural life, I will have, hold and repute him as my husband.' Within seven years, Charles nevertheless sufficiently disregarded his own vows to propose marriage to quite a different lady, and it was in vain that King Henry protested and sought to heal the breach with a most unlikely description of his sister 'sighing for her spouse ten times a day'.

The real reason for her sighs, if sighs there were, was in any case the extremely handsome stalwart figure of Charles Brandon, Duke of Suffolk, whom she ultimately married, though not before the extra complication of making a splendid but short-lived alliance with the reprobate King Louis XII of France. Louis was both a divorcee and widower of fifty-four. Mary was all of eighteen summers. Displaying to one of the English diplomats 'the goodliest, richest sight of jewels that ever I saw', Louis merrily announced, 'They are all for her, but not all at once! For I would have many kisses and thanks for them.'

A violent storm raged during Mary's Channel crossing, one of the largest ships of her accompanying fleet being lost with all hands, but the marriage of State achieved at least a lull of peace in the interminable Anglo-French wars. King Louis rode to Abbeville to meet his bride, to find her to his chagrin 'so encased in goldsmith's work' that she could not dismount for his embrace. With this difficulty repaired, Mary made an enthusiastic state entry into Paris with 'her breast full of jewels' and within a week was both wedded and crowned Queen of France. 'I cannot sufficiently express my delight in her,' Louis wrote. This was more than true and three months later, his strength shattered, it caused levity throughout Europe when the heralds announced that King Louis was dead.

In April, Mary Tudor, Queen of France, returned from exile to marry her Duke of Suffolk, bringing with her 'winnings from France' amounting to the then fabulous fortune of £100,000 worth of jewels, and the happy pair were more than content enough to 'depart into the countrie, having spent liberallie on Housekeeping'. (Even in this alliance another chapter of tragic history was in the making, for their first-born daughter Frances, was to become the mother of Lady Jane Grey.) In January, 1533, Mary had enjoyed marriage to Charles Brandon for eighteen happy years when she learned of her brother Henry's marriage to Anne Boleyn. Some say that Anne Boleyn's progress to court and the consequent disgrace of Mary's close friend and sister-in-law, Queen Katherine, greatly distressed her and hastened her end. Anne Boleyn was crowned Queen on the last day of May in Westminster Hall; and only seven weeks later, a Court scribe recorded, 'This year on Midsummer Eve died the French Queen, sister to the King and wife to the Duke of Suffolk.'

## 5　The Tudor Daughters

Few royal 'ladyes' have so thoroughly commanded modern attention as the two Tudor Queens Regnant, yet their earlier lives as
princesses remain as hazy for most of us as the blue wood-smoke
that rose from the graceful new Tudor chimneys of St. James's
Palace and Hampton Court. Henry VIII's two daughters have the
distinction that they were not only born as acknowledged princesses, but moreover were often styled so. Both were born in the
old red-brick palace of Greenwich, with a gulf of seventeen years
between them, and the far wider chasm, afflicting the sisters all their
lives, of the divided loyalties that sprang from the King's ever-
changing affections. After the long and anxious sequence of still-
births and miscarriages, Mary Tudor was the long-awaited first
living child of Henry's first wife, Queen Katherine of Aragon,
while Elizabeth was born to Anne Boleyn as an undesired daughter,
a bitter disappointment when Henry longed with such intensity
for a son.

Both the half-sisters were christened with great pomp and ceremonial, and each was proclaimed 'high and mighty Princess of
England' only to suffer the deprivation of that title when his successive marriages caused each in turn to lose their father's favour.
'Princess for all that!' Mary cried, weeping with indignation, to
the sensation-loving crowds, on learning that she had been dis-
owned and was to yield her title to her new-born sister, Elizabeth.
It was Elizabeth's turn four years later, after the King's marriage
to his third wife, Jane Seymour, when Mary was restored to comparative grace while Anne Boleyn's daughter was eclipsed in regal
status. 'How haps it?' she asked, with a child's directness, 'Yesterday my Lady Princess, and today but my Lady Elizabeth?'

Henry again changed his mind when Jane Seymour succeeded in
giving him his heir, Prince Edward, and the two sisters attended
their half-brother's christening in Hampton Court chapel, Mary
as a godmother and the four-year-old Elizabeth carrying the

baptismal over-robes, though still so small herself that she had to be carried by the Queen's brother, Edward Seymour.

The Tudors are a first approach to the modern aspect of the monarchy, even to royal gossip. As a two-year-old, clad in cloth of gold, Mary had been betrothed by proxy to her cousin, Charles, the Dauphin, and the Venetian ambassador could not resist recording that the child had approached a gaudily-decked French admiral and asked, 'Are you the Dauphin of France? If you are, I wish to kiss you.' Her youthful public popularity, too, presaged the modern phenomenon, as was shown by the Christmas gifts from ordinary people, now a rosemary bush spangled with tinsel, the gift of 'a poor woman of Greenwich', now a basket of apples offered by 'the child of a poor woman', who was none the less pleasantly rewarded with elevenpence.

As heiress presumptive, Mary was early removed from the pestilent risks of the lower Thames and taken higher upstream to a household of her own at Ditton. The gossipy Venetian ambassador has told how he knelt and kissed her hand, 'for that alone is kissed by any noble of the land, nor does anyone see her without kneeling and making obeisance'. Some French gentlemen were offered a repast of cherries, strawberries and wafers and, like any child showing off, the Princess entertained them 'with most goodly countenance playing on the virginals'. Her mother, Queen Katherine, supervised her education, corrected her Latin exercises, guided her needle and taught her French, Spanish and Italian. There were to be no romantic stories, but her reading included 'parts of the Old Testament', the works of Plato, Cicero, Plutarch and 'selected' Horace. Her garments were fastidiously supervised 'so that everything about her be pure, sweet, clean and wholesome'. But years later when Elizabeth was the same age, after Anne Boleyn's execution, the King's displeasure fell heavily on his younger daughter, and her disgrace led to short commons and actual privation.

Her governess, indeed, was driven to write to the Lord Privy Seal 'beseeching you that my Lady may have a mess of meat to her own lodging', begging, too, for clothing, 'for she hath neither gown nor kirtle, nor petticoat, nor no manner of linen . . .' Rejected and disregarded as she was, Elizabeth was never betrothed, although at an early and happier stage the King of Sweden had proposed marriage overtures on behalf of his son. Mary's engagement to the Dauphin equally failed to survive disfavour, and when both sisters were declared illegitimate and removed from the Succession, the manoeuvres of other suitors were seen to wane. Mary's account-books meanwhile tell us of her gifts to her young sister, the pretty boxes and singing-birds, and her own taste for flowers and clocks, greyhounds, and strawberries and cream.

With the advent of their brother, Edward, both girls could be more freely received about the court. Mary was able to buy her sister five yards of yellow satin and to give her 'pocket money for play'. When Edward came to the throne as a boy of nine, Mary emerged from obscurity to a status akin to princess royal, but Elizabeth—then fourteen—was closest in age and sympathy to the young monarch, who not long since had been her boon companion at Hatfield. 'There can be nothing pleasanter than a letter from you,' he wrote, when they were separated. 'It is some comfort that I may hope to visit you soon (if nothing happens to either of us).' And in sending the young King her picture, Elizabeth responded with sisterly wit and encouragement: 'For the face, I grant I may well blush to offer, but the mind I need not be ashamed.'

Her own educational studies, in fact, matched those of Mary. Her tutor, Roger Asham, reported that she read more Greek in a day than many of the clergy in a week. She spent three hours every morning reading history, and for lighter pursuits engaged in riding and in her exquisite needlework. When in her teens, her affections were also pursued by the outrageous Lord Seymour with his playful slaps and tickles and horseplay. He came in nightshirt and slippers to make flirtatious visits at dawn, so that at the sound of his step Elizabeth and her maids trembled and rushed into hiding. The ploy did him no good, and his ambitions ended hideously when he was proved to have plotted against the life of the King and was beheaded in the Tower.

\* \* \*

In 1553 the boy king Edward VI died of consumption. In her thirty-eighth year, Mary Tudor was proclaimed Queen and the two sisters rode into London side by side, deafened by the saluting guns and cheerful church bells and, at Aldgate, touched by the charming sight of a host of kneeling children. When Mary was crowned, Elizabeth stood behind the Queen in crimson velvet robe and golden coronet, whispering to one official that her coronet was too heavy. And so it seemed in bitter truth within the year when Mary wished her sister to embrace the Catholic faith and, in desperate tears, Elizabeth asked if it were her fault if she did not believe. Yet whose fault else? When Thomas Wyatt vainly rose in his wild rebellion against Catholic rule and invaded the streets of London with two thousand men, Elizabeth was arrested and brought to London under suspicion of having been implicated in the Wyatt plot. She was certainly innocent and yet, at twenty, already knew well that innocence might be no defence.

Taken to Whitehall, she had the curtains of her litter pulled back so that all might see her. She was dressed all in white, 'her look proud, lofty, superbly disdainful', as the envoy of Philip of Spain reported. Five weeks after Lady Jane Grey had been beheaded in the Tower, Elizabeth was hurried down-river by night and realized the ghastly prospect when the barge grated against the steps of Traitor's Gate. With proof or not, she feared that for lack of being able to communicate with her sister, she might be put to death.

It was raining and, with a final attempt at resistance she sat stubbornly down on the wet paving. 'Madam, it were best you came in,' said the lieutenant of the Tower, 'for you sit unwholesomely'. 'Better sit here than in a worse place,' she replied.

Her captors tried persuasion. 'I never thought to have come in here,' she said. 'I come in no traitor, but as true a woman to the Queen's Majesty as any is now living.' When force seemed inevitable, the Earl of Sussex remonstrated to the would-be gaolers, 'Let us take heed. She was a King's daughter and is the Queen's sister. Have ye sufficient commission?'

One man broke down and wept, and the princess stood up and berated him for giving way. But then she entered the gateway and was led to the first floor of the Bell Tower, and found herself enduring the worst hour of her life when the doors were locked and barred behind her. Years later she confessed to the French ambassador, de Castelnau, that she fell into such despair that she thought of asking to be beheaded not by the axe but by the sword, as her mother had been.

In reality, the charges against her could not be sustained and, after two months imprisonment, Princess Elizabeth was moved to the less rigorous confinement of Woodstock. It was a year before the sisters met. Under the conviction—a delusion, as it proved—that she was to have a child, Mary was reminded of the custom that the heir presumptive should be present at the birth of the heir apparent, and Elizabeth was summoned. An early historian asserts that Mary urged her husband Philip to watch through a peephole at their meeting and judge between them. In the event, Elizabeth knelt tearfully to the Queen; the sisters were reconciled, and the Princess could presently settle down again to a happier existence 'with nothing spoken or done without the Queen's knowledge'.

Four years later, and two months after her twenty-fifth birthday, the habit of caution had become so ingrained that, though knowing her sister was mortally ill, Elizabeth did not at first trust the news of her death. She was walking in the park at Hatfield when the Lords of the Council came to make obeisance to her as Queen. Playing for time, she had a quotation ready from the 118th psalm, but it remained unspoken until a horse came galloping through the trees and her messenger, Sir Nicholas Throgmorton, dismounted to kneel and offer her Mary's black-and-gold betrothal ring. This could never have left her sister's hand, Elizabeth knew, unless she were dead. 'This is the Lord's doing,' she then said, in Latin. 'and it is marvellous in our eyes.' But tears rose unbidden as, with her nobles, she turned and walked under the lowering November skies back to the house.

# BOOK ONE

## The Bygone Pageant

'. . . present the princess, sweet chuck, with
some delightful ostentation'
—*Love's Labour's Lost*
Act 5, Scene 1.

# 1  In Stuart Times

## I

On a wild March night in 1603 a messenger arrived at Holyrood-house 'blooded with falls and bruises', having ridden four hundred miles to Edinburgh in three days to tell King James VI of Scotland that he was now also King of England. James waited only to be proclaimed at the Mercat Cross before setting out for London, giving instructions that his consort, Anne of Denmark, should presently 'follow softlie' with their children. And south of the border two months later a rapturous welcome surrounded the slight, fair figure of the King's only daughter, who was then six years old.

For forty-five years England had known a famine of princesses. Only the old remembered the youthful Lady Elizabeth who had once ridden through London with her sister, a vision of silver; and throughout her reign as Queen there were no young royalings to add demure grace to State occasions, gazing shyly from processionals or prettily accepting nosegays during royal visitations. And now, at last, another princess—and an Elizabeth at that—blossomed in the parched soil of loyalty.

As 'sole godmother', the Queen of England had sent a message, but no christening gift, to her namesake's baptism in the grey Chapel Royal of Holyroodhouse, in those days so remote from England. (Her proxy, as connoisseurs of traditional continuity might care to note, was none other than Robert Bowes, who figures in the family tree of our present-day Queen Elizabeth the Queen Mother.) The Lyon Herald had proclaimed the child as 'Lady Elizabeth, first daughter of Scotland'. But the enthusiasm as she travelled south clearly marked her as the first daughter of England, too.

For fear of over-excitement the little princess, blonde, bright-eyed and agreeable, made a separate journey intended to avoid the lavish receptions and entertainment that awaited her elder brother, Prince Henry, who travelled with the Queen. Her younger brother, the three-year-old Duke Charles (the future Charles I) was so frail and delicate that he could not yet be moved from his nurse's care in Dunfermline Palace. But the princess's progress was by no means secretive or sheltered, with her thirty horsemen and her trumpeters, her comptroller and clerks, her maids and mistress-nurse and her two governesses, the senior travelling in the litter with her, and the younger riding horseback alongside. The trumpeters announced the princess at every town and at the gates of every hospitable estate; the people rushed to see her pass and the crowds grew thicker and more demonstrative as the news ran ahead.

At York the citizens presented a purse of 'twenty angells of gold', at Leicester the mayor and aldermen came to her lodgings in solemn procession with gifts of wine and sugar. In her new costume of red-brown satin, the child accepted the offerings and watched the attendant revels with composure. Reaching Coventry, in due course, she banqueted alone in a gilded chair of state, enthroned on a dais, before riding with equal dignity through streets lined with spectators. Pageants were hastily prepared for her; sermons given for her delectation in crowded churches and the 'respectful festivity' increased the more the regal cavalcade neared Windsor. With this early impetus of welcome to the Stuarts, the child's popularity struck so deep that it has never yet been erased. Who has not heard of the princess under her romantic name as Queen of Hearts or her married title as Queen of Bohemia, the Winter Queen?*

Three years after this inaugural royal progress, Guy Fawkes confessed that it had been an element of the Gunpowder Plot to have seized the person of 'the Lady Elizabeth, the King's daughter' and proclaim her Queen. The news was carried to the country house at Combe where she was quietly brought up in rural seclusion, and her outraged response showed that her young head had not been turned by the fevered public adulations. 'What a Queen should I have been by this means?' she cried indignantly to her comptroller, Lord Harrington. 'I had rather been blown up with my

* The miniature likeness by Nicholas Hilliard has always been styled 'The Pearl of Britain' and some historians have also referred to her as Princess Royal, taking the title as belonging of right to the elder daughter of the king. But no contemporary evidence has come to light for this and the Act of Settlement of 1701 refers to the eldest daughter of James VI and I only as 'the most excellent Princess Elizabeth, late Queen of Bohemia'.

royal father in the Parliament House than wear his crown on such condition!'

The Harrington account-books and letters disclose that the educational routine of a King's daughter had moved away from the classical learning of the first Elizabeth towards a less stern curriculum. 'To make women learned and foxes tame,' wrote King James, 'has the same effect, to make them more cunning', and the young new Elizabeth studied Italian and French, music and dancing, writing and composition, but these were no longer exceptional subjects for ladies of high birth. Her day was still rigorous, with early rising, family prayers and then a full hour's holy reading. Yet there were lighter diversions, and at an early age, the records tell us, she set aside her baby dolls, her 'twa babeis' in favour of 'a rough dog' and the luxury of parrots and a monkey.

Above all, this Stuart Elizabeth strikes a chord for our own time in her affectionate correspondence with her brother Henry in which she fondly tells him of her favourite riding lessons: no fewer than twenty horses were kept in the stables for her use. On Twelfth Night at Hampton Court she presented the prizes at a tournament and her brother, Lord Harrington noted, was 'calling often for her Grace to ride abroad with him'. At thirteen she began moving more in the world of the court, and went down to Woolwich one day to inspect a warship named after her brother *The Prince Royal*. Not only was this the largest man-of-war yet built, but the name must give us pause. Although contemporary documents style Henry 'the most high and mighty Prince', the naming of the vessel affords us proof that the traditional title of the eldest Scottish princes had survived on men's lips, if not in writing. Not that the choice of name of the great ship takes us much farther in our quest for the founding of the style of Princess Royal. At the end of the month Henry received the more certain and resounding title of Prince of Wales, and Elizabeth had the satisfaction of watching his investiture in Westminster Hall and appearing in a masque in the evening to the joy of her young brother, Charles.

The launching of *The Prince Royal* was, in fact, less pleasurable. The Royal Family gathered for the spectacle, but at the dock watergates the ship stuck fast, nor could she be budged until the following day when, in spite of a furious storm, she 'went away without any straining'. Was it a portent? Men were amused, at all events, to know that Henry had gone down to Woolwich again, ready to wet the ship with wine the minute she floated, and that he drank a can of the ship's beer for good measure. Similar stories were told of the King's daughter, who enjoyed watching processions from the Palace windows, flinging flowers at the mummers and, legend has it, charmed Shakespeare into writing *Twelfth Night*. In public popularity there was little to choose between Elizabeth and Henry. They made a pair, their success as substantial as that of Prince Charles and Princess Anne today. Henry was handsome and intelligent, with a witty and original cast of mind, his letters to his sister full of drollery. 'Women are sociable creatures,' he once apologized for his absence, 'but you know that those who love each other best cannot always be glued together.'

He fully shared his sister's love of both good music and good horses and competed with her at times in writing verse; he was good at games, a good shot and a good sailor. Our own Prince of Wales studied the science and magic of kingship during his course in anthropology at Cambridge; and Henry similarly studied manuals written by his own father to instruct him in kingly principles. Even the redoubtable Ben Jonson, who flattered few, forecast that he would grow into a hero equal in stature to the Black Prince, but the prophecy was doomed never to be tested. At the age of eighteen Henry fell ill after unwarily swimming in the Thames in the heart of London and died, some say of typhoid. Had this brilliant prince lived, history would probably have been different and a king might not have lost his head. Henry's last words were the whisper, 'Where is my dear sister?'

She had been refused admission to his sick-room for fear of infection, and wildly attempted to disguise herself and bribed servants and guards in a pathetic attempt to reach his bedside. Six months later, she left England as a foreigner's bride and, despite the misgivings of her elders, insisted on sailing in the great ship named after her brother *The Prince Royal*.*

* Despite the feminine gender of ships, the ship's architect, Phineas Pette, mentions in his autobiography that it was called *The Prince Royal*. No vessel was given an equivalent name until the British warship *Princess* was renamed *Princess Royal* in 1728. According to Manning and Walker, thirteen other ships subsequently bore the name *Princess Royal*, the last as recently as in the Battle of Jutland in the First World War.

## II

After the centuries of child alliances of state, Elizabeth Stuart's marriage to the Prince Frederick, Elector Palatine of the Rhine, was perhaps the first romance of the poetic kind that grips modern attention. They were married in the old royal chapel of Whitehall on St. Valentine's day with bride and bridesmaids all in cloth of silver and great crowds massed to see them go to church. The young couple were both sixteen, Elizabeth's darkly handsome bridegroom the elder indeed by only four days; and years later, when they seemed a staid family couple, their correspondence whenever apart was still one of love.

'My soul's star', wrote Frederick and, because he was dark and brown-eyed she tenderly responded with 'mon petit black babie'. He would end a letter, 'Love me, I beg, for ever' and Elizabeth was to confide that she knew contentment only in his company. Known as it was throughout Europe, their 'verie true love' heightened their seductive public image. One contemporary visitor reported them 'so deeply loving that it was a joy to all that behold them'.

Frederick's realm extended through southern Germany to the borders of Bohemia, now Czechoslovakia, and their home, Heidelberg Castle, has seemed steeped in at atmosphere of sentimental charm to this day. The prince laid out gardens, grottos and fountains for his princess; their apartments glowed with colour, and they celebrated their sixth wedding anniversary in a new palace ballroom built for her delight. With their children around them, their domestic happiness seemed complete. And then came a terrible dilemma and a fatal decision.

The King of Bohemia, a Catholic, was deposed on account of his religion, and the Bohemians offered Frederick the crown. He accepted, with as much calm assurance and certainty as if answering a summons of destiny. Two months later, the youthful King and Queen—they were still aged only twenty-three—entered Prague amid scenes of fantastic triumph. In Protestant London, joybells rang and Cockneys danced around their bonfires. Then Elizabeth began learning Czech and discovered that some of her subjects were calling her the Winter Queen. The phrase conjures up visions of sledges decked with softly luxurious furs and of a beautiful consort riding through snowflakes, the wind warming her cheeks. The true facts were more sinister. The Jesuits had invented the nickname to imply that the new monarchy would not last until spring and would vanish with the melting snows. They were, in fact, six months premature in their chilling calculations. But central Europe was already falling into the interminable religious battles of the Thirty Years War. Powerful Spanish and Austrian forces were soon at the gates of Prague, and before the winter came again the defence of the city collapsed.

While Frederick strove to rally his army, the Winter Queen had sent her children to safety and now had to follow them into exile. Even the sanctuary of Heidelberg itself was to be denied her, for this had early fallen to the enemy among the spoils of war. She was never to see it again. King James would not lift a finger to help his daughter, and only Frederick's uncle, the ruling Prince of Orange, came to the rescue by offering them a refuge at the Hague.

The Netherlanders found their guest a woman of many friendships, so steeped in acts of kindness and consideration that they affectionately dubbed her the Queen of Hearts. Her housekeeping bills, always impractical, grew heavier as she strove to support every Bohemian or Palatine fugitive who came to her door. The tradesmen were patient and lenient. Then, in 1625, news arrived that her young brother, whom she had last seen as a stammering boy, had become King Charles I of Great Britain. For five years, until the birth of her nephew, the future Charles II, Elizabeth was heiress presumptive to the British throne, and brother Charles placed her on a pension, his generosity and sense of duty to her so urgent that on one occasion he pawned some of the Tower of London guns rather than delay dispatching her remittance.

Although some experts in these matters have maintained that, as the King's sister and eldest daughter of a king, Elizabeth ranked at this time as Princess Royal, no announcement was made of this disposition and no documentary evidence has come to light. It was as the Electress Palatine, Queen of Bohemia, that she remained at the Hague, within reach of her ardent Frederick whenever he could return from his campaigns. Frederick was godfather by proxy to the infant Charles II and, in the following year, Elizabeth similarly sponsored her 'best neece', the Princess Mary, who was born at St. James's Palace on November 29th, 1631. Here, again, we fall in peril of false trails; for that prodigious Victorian biographer of royalty, Agnes Strickland, boldly assured her readers that Mary, 'eldest daughter of King Charles I and his consort, Henrietta Maria of France, was the first Princess Royal of Great Britain who inherited that title at birth'. Yet one fears that the decisive Miss Strickland was mistaken, and ten years at least elapsed before the prospect of improvising such a titled lodged wistfully in any man's mind.

### III

Certainly no contemporary State records described the new-born daughter of Charles I as a Princess Royal. Versed in etiquette as he was, the Swedish ambassador merely reported 'the birth of a young princess and her prompt baptism with the name of Mary for fear lest she might not live'. But all went well and, in Whitehall Palace within the month, the King's treasurer was concerned with being charged for 'the diet of the Lady Mary's house, which is twelve dishes for Lady Roxburgh, the governess, and seven for the rockers' and, he added fretfully, 'This will preclude any saving . . .'* Two years later, his clerk was still urging economies 'for the Prince and Lady Mary'. The upholsterer, he complained, was putting fine down at three shillings a pound into chairs, stools and bolsters, where the best feathers at 14 pence a pound would serve. And when cloth of gold at £2 per yard was in order for covers, extravagant cloth of tissue at £8 a yard was being used. Attempting to jump on the royal band-wagon, the Marquis of Hamilton suggested that he could furnish the King and Queen 'with all provisions for their stables, including those of the Prince and the Princess Mary in return for £7,000 yearly'. His offer was ignored, for the stables were in fact costing only £6,000 a year.

Yet royal state was undeniably increasing. The total establishment of the royal children included, beside governess and nurse, a lady of the bedchamber, a gentleman usher, the watchers or rockers, two pages, four footmen, five kitchen servants, a coachman and groom, a seamstress and laundress and an occasional French apothecary who found it very difficult to extract payment for his 'medicaments, perfumes, sweet powders and odoriferous waters'. In the summer, the nursery group removed to Richmond, and

* State Papers, Charles I, Dom. 5. 206.

Princess Mary's first childish scrawls were to figure in the correspondence of her Aunt Elizabeth, late of Bohemia.

In 1632, when the intense grief of widowhood came to the
Queen of Hearts, Charles I prepared for his sister to return to
England and had Eltham Palace refurnished for her use; but home
was with her own children—and she had no fewer than thirteen,
most of them surviving to grow up in the continental milieu they
had always known. 'I must prefer the welfare of my poor children
to my own satisfaction,' she wrote. 'The last request their father
made me was to do all that I could for them, which I wish to do,
loving them better because they are his.' Now within sight of her
forties, she had a new mixed role to play, as mother, dowager,
aunt and royal counsellor. So thorough was her supervision, so
astute her match-making, that her descendants were to be found
in every ruling monarchy in Europe as the years went by. Her
youngest daughter, Sophia, by no means least, is remembered for
example as the stout-hearted Electress Sophia of Hanover, ancestress of the four Georges of the House of Hanover, of Queen
Victoria and the House of Windsor.

Elizabeth's English nieces and nephews, the five children of
Charles I, are familiar to us from the Van Dyck painting—Charles
and Mary, James, Duke of York, her namesake Elizabeth, and
Anne. With no little perturbation the Queen of Bohemia secretly
learned that the Prince and Princess of Orange were proposing the
marriage of their young son, William, to one of the King's daughters, 'unripe of age' as they all were. Her own son considered it
'a great sauciness that they should demand the breeding of so great
a King's daughter' and Elizabeth of Bohemia could not but agree.
'They seek to get my eldest niece,' she reported indignantly, 'but
that I hope will not be granted; it is too low for her.'

She perceived, indeed, what might have been called 'a situation'.
The Prince of Orange had faced snubs for marrying a mere lady-
in-waiting—'one of my women', as Elizabeth wrote, with less than
her usual good nature. His Excellency's cheeks had burned and he
was resolved that his son should never incur such shame. One of his
first manoeuvres was to apply to Cardinal Richelieu for agreement
that he should be styled 'Altesse' (Highness), a small fee to exact for
alliance with France against Spain. The right was accorded and on
December 14th, 1636, Louis XIII gave his assent. Some three weeks

later the French ambassador at the Hague read the King's letter aloud to the assembly of the States General.* The concession closely effects our quest, for it had long been the usage of the French Court to give the eldest daughter of the King the style of 'Madame Royale'. The stout Princess of Orange, née Amalia of Solms, fully shared her husband's soaring social ambitions. The new Highnesses were not to be put off by the King of England's hint of prospects with his second, rather sickly daughter, and their aim for young William was soon nothing less than Princess Mary's hand, at no matter what expense.

The Queen of Bohemia dashed off one of her impetuous letters —'I cannot see what the King can gain by precipitating this marriage'—but in reality the Prince of Orange put forward extremely attractive financial proposals which the King could scarcely resist. The bride was to be guaranteed an annual income of £11,500 for life. This made good reading to Charles I, still struggling to pay off £250,000 of his father's debts. At a nod, he would be free of further expense for his daughter and he rose irresistibly to the bait.

The marriage contract recites fourteen terms for the marriage of 'Prince William, son of Frederick Henry Prince of Orange and the Princess Mary of Great Britain . . . eldest daughter of His Majesty of Great Britain', but nowhere makes use of the title of Princess Royal, a distinction on which the snobbish Frederick Henry would certainly have insisted if it could have been accurately applied. Visiting the House of Lords to acquaint parliament with his intentions, the King similarly expressed the matter only as 'the marriage of the Lady Mary and the Prince of Orange'. Mary, then aged nine, first met her fourteen-year-old bridegroom in the garden of St. James's Palace while she was suffering from a heavy cold, snuffling and sneezing, her face swollen. William, however, saw a child with wide brown eyes and auburn hair, and diplomatically wrote home that she was 'more beautiful than her portrait'.

Twelve days later, Princess Mary took part in the wedding ceremony as if playing a game, and the public bedding afterwards was treated by the Court more as an amusing diversion. Having disrobed in private into her night things, the child was formally lifted into the huge state bed, a grandeur of blue velvet and white plumes.

* L. Aitzema, *Saken van staet. en oorlogh, 1635-40,* IV, 's-Gravenhage 1659, pp. 471-5.

Large flambeaux of white wax, we are told, 'diffused a bright and glorious light'. In this stage setting, the King and his sons ushered in the bridegroom, clad in nuptial grandeur in embroidered blue *robe du nuit* and slippers, and William clambered into bed 'though at a respectful distance'.

'After I had been some time in the bed, I left and was led to another chamber where I slept', the young Prince informed his father. He did not mention that the proceedings grew more frolicsome when he lost a slipper, which the Queen's dwarf, Geoffrey Hudson, retrieved 'from somewhere near the Princess' after burrowing under the bed-hangings. Amid the general mirth, perhaps the eighteen-inch dwarf discovered, too, that the hem of the bride's nightdress had been sewn around her ankles for protection.

## IV

The marriage contract stipulated that Princess Mary should not be 'transported to the Low Countries' until the age of twelve, but Henry Frederick of Orange could not resist displaying his daughter-in-law in triumph to his subjects, and when Prince William returned to Holland, he was followed only a year later by his bride. Escorted by a squadron of fifteen ships, the Princess Mary and her mother, Queen Henrietta Maria, crossed the North Sea during the storms of March, an ill-chosen time for sailing that cost them a baggage ship which sank off Rotterdam, not only with the coffers containing the Queen's sacramental plate but also with the chests with all the court gowns and spare clothing of her ladies.

The Queen of Bohemia rode to meet her niece and Queen Henrietta, a sister-in-law whom till then she had never seen, and both the royal ladies undoubtedly approved the regulations for Mary's new home at the Hague: 'No one shall be qualified to enter the bedchamber of the Princess unless qualified to do so: above all, no men . . . When her Royal Highness eats in private, she is to be served by her bedchamber women . . . When she goes out in her coach, there shall be care that no men are to be put therein . . .'

These precautions were no more than prudent, for Mary's marriage was not to be solemnized under Dutch Reformed ritual until her twelfth birthday, and a revised family agreement ensured that the young husband and wife should not be domiciled together until she had reached the age of fifteen. While the Princess placidly continued her education under her governess, Lady Stanhope, at one end of the palace, her husband completed a more permissive private tuition with a luscious young companion named Jenny d'Alonne at the other.

When Queen Henrietta Maria sailed home to England after spending nearly a year in Holland, Mary however began to appear at the more formal Court functions in her own right—and indeed as the only princess enjoying royal precedence—and a more difficult domestic situation developed. Her father-in-law, a snob to his fingertips, always swept off his hat in her presence, a notable gesture with the feathered broad-brimmed cavalier hats then in vogue, and then he pointedly remained bare-headed before her indoors or out. If his wife Amalia demurred that she herself did not receive such courtesies, surely rightfully to be enjoyed by a Princess of Orange, Frederick Henry pompously explained that the rulers of Orange enjoyed the title only of Highness and not Royal Highness. Amalia could not stomach such nonsense, and perhaps Frederick Henry at first considered it tactful to conceal from his wife or at all events soft-pedal the distinction for their daughter-in-law that so obsessed his imagination. In March, 1642, the Dutch envoy, Heenvliet, who escorted Princess Mary from England, is careful to use the title 'la Princesse Royale', in correspondence with Frederick Henry, although he does not seem to have used it officially during any of the marriage negotiations. The title is found also in the rules for the reception of Princess Mary written in French and drawn up by Frederick Henry. But unfortunately for our curiosity, the document is not dated and the last page is missing as if to obliterate any signature.

Once Princess Mary was in Holland, it is evident that Frederick Henry lost no time in announcing that she should always be addressed as 'Princesse Royale'. After her marriage, her brothers, who should have known best, addressed her as Princess of Orange but never apparently as Princess Royal on the necessarily formal covers of their letters. It may seem conclusive that the distinction thus originated in 1642 as a courtesy title improvised by a Dutchman, perhaps with some authority from Paris. The seeker of closer documentation faces the chill reminder of an editor of the calendar of Charles I's State Papers that many were carried about by the government ministers themselves during the Civil War 'from place to place, till they finally perished' and the archives of the Royal House of the Netherlands take us no further on this exacting point.

In the year 1660 the diarist John Evelyn occupied himself in making a fair copy of the earlier pages of his journal and transcribed one passage thus: 'On the 27th April, 1641, came over out of Holland the young Prince of Orange with a splendid equipage, to make love to His Majesties eldest daughter, the now Princess Royall'. The original page was then destroyed, but the final tag implies that Mary was not Princess Royal in 1641 although the title had indeed become hers in the 'now' of 1660. Closer still, a letter from Mary's husband dated February 24th, 1649, now in the archives of the Royal Dutch House,* advises Amalia's nephew, the Governor of Orange, that he should follow 'les ordres que la Princesse Royale'. A year earlier, a Puritan newspaper writer in the *Moderate Intelligencer* rumoured that the Princess Royal was 'receiving the superstitious Sacrament', a false report which at least shows us that the distinction had passed into the common usage of the printed word.

And certainly the 'style and title' was in orthodox use in November, 1646, when Prince William and Princess Mary set up in their joint domicile, and from England, as if to return a compliment, William was appointed to the Order of the Garter. Early the following year the Princess had set out through the Flanders mud to visit her mama in Paris. Queen Henrietta had sought refuge at the French court from the Commonwealth turmoil in England, though not without risk from unfriendly ships in the Channel, and not without penning a charming letter to her husband: 'I am giving you the strongest proof of love that I can give . . . hazarding my life that I may not incommode your affairs . . . Adieu, my dear heart!'

Princess Mary left the Hague with a procession of only three coaches 'and but one maid of honour' with no need, as she clearly considered, to impress her young cousin, Louis of France. Sir John Conyers watched her effect on the boy monarch with amusement. 'The Princess Royal has been very well received. The King says he never saw a more handsome Princess.'† Aged eight, Louis XIV

* Koninklijk House Archives, The Hague, G. Huygens Sr. 7.1.

† S.P. Charles I, Dom. 19, 1645–7, p. 525.

already understood that a King should speak in compliments. The date was February 25th, 1647, and for the first time we may note that the Princess Royal was mentioned by this title in British dispatches.

As for hat-doffing, Prince Frederick Henry of Orange snatched off his night-cap on his death-bed when the Princess returned home: even *in extremis*, precedent came before tenderness. In her father-in-law's last days, in any event, the physicians feared for his reason, and the news that the Princess Royal might soon be having a baby, thus making him a grandfather of royalty, brought on 'a sudden shock' which caused his death.

The prospect on which the old prince so disastrously pinned his hopes ended in fact in a miscarriage. On Mary's part, the frantic anxiety of events in England may well have hastened this disappointment, for after five years of civil war she faced the desperate certainty that Cromwell had seized London, and she learned that her father, the King, was a prisoner at Carisbrooke Castle.

## V

Princess Mary and her Aunt Elizabeth were the best of friends and closest of neighbours at the Hague. On a wet day, the Queen of Bohemia ordered her coach to pay a birthday visit to her niece, 'not by land but by water', as she wrote, 'for it rains is if it were mad'. Scarcely a week passed when they did not exchange family news in a companionship quickened by increasing anxiety. They each hurried to share every message from England, where Elizabeth's two sons, Rupert and Maurice, had both fought for the King, from the raising of the Royal Standard at Nottingham until after the crushing defeat at Naseby. Mary's younger brother, fifteen-year-old James, was taken prisoner and then escaped disguised as a woman and reached safety in Holland. When the Princess heard that he had landed she could not suppress her excitement and ran down to the street gates of the palace, flying across the cobbles, to fling her arms about him.

But then came the hideous shock of her father's execution. The groan that went up in Whitehall as the axe fell upon the neck of Charles I was echoed throughout Europe. The Queen of Bohemia wept—and then fiercely told her household that if any English ambassadors, Cromwell's men, should call on her, they were to be thrown downstairs and kicked into the street. Mary shed her tears, but as wife of the ruling Prince of Orange, she was upon more delicate diplomatic ground. Her brother, Charles, was now Charles II, unproclaimed and unrecognized, and it gave her neither satisfaction nor ease in her grief to hear that a mob had surrounded the home of a Cromwellian British agent, breaking his windows and shouting 'Long live King Charles and the Princess Royal!'

Though young James was safe, the fate of Charles indeed remained uncertain. Just turned twenty, he had briefly visited his sister in Holland and his mother in Paris and then cheerfully put to sea to head an army in Scotland. His optimism appeared justified when, like all the Scottish kings, he was actually crowned at Scone.

Meanwhile, Princess Mary was confidently expecting a baby, whom she hoped—after the early disappointments—might indeed be 'a lusty true child'. As she and her young husband awaited the happy event, Prince William spent the time riding and hunting and playing spirited tennis, with so little regard to the November weather that he caught a chill from sweating too freely. On the afternoon of her niece's nineteenth birthday, the Queen of Bohemia received an urgent message to attend the Princess. She broke off a letter, 'Whether it be labour or not, I know not, but I must go to her . . .' At the palace she heard that the Prince was suffering from an infection and was kept in quarantine in his own apartments. Her niece was happy but lethargic—'deadly lazy', as her aunt put it—and not for the first time she urged her to exercise.

And then suddenly the palace was stricken with terror, with murmurings and whisperings. Throughout the night and the next day the doctors went soft-footed up and downstairs, until the Princess had to be told of the dreadful certainty that her husband was dying. She had the presence of mind to go to her room before she broke into tears, and presently her aunt had to be summoned to the Palace yet again, this time to help to break the final irrevocable news of widowhood.

All the women and nurses attendant on the Princess donned full mourning, and the rooms where she awaited her lying-in were all hung with black draperies. The men who pinned up these ghastly trappings had scarcely put away their ladders before the baby was born: a new Prince of Orange. In a church decked with sable black two months later, when the baby was christened, the people of the Netherlands were not slow to note that the Princess Royal had caused the baptismal robe to be trimmed with ermine, a touch of royal grandeur never before seen in Holland. It was a token, of course, of the infant Prince William's share of royal blood, and yet a portent, too, of future events. In Whitehall Palace, thirty-eight years later, he jointly accepted the crown of England with his wife and cousin, another Mary, the Princess Royal's niece, and so inaugurated the prosperous reign of William and Mary.

## VI

As we have noted, the specific duties of a Princess Royal have never been defined and probably there are none. Since the title implies that the holder is the first and most royal of royal daughters, holding rank above all others, a modern bearer might be expected to carry out the foremost and most important of the feminine regal tasks other than those of the Queen. In Victorian days, the Queen's eldest daughter was thus valued by receiving a Civil List annuity 25 per cent higher than her sisters, a sum still faithfully remitted to Berlin after her marriage when she had been living in Germany for twenty-five years. In the financial assessment of the revised 1972 Civil List, the Queen's eldest daughter will receive no more, after marriage, than her aunt, Princess Margaret, and advocates of women's lib may note that as a married princess her rating will be £15,000 less than her younger married brothers. Their widows, too, will receive a £20,000 annuity, but there is no provision for a princess's widower. In the earlier civil lists of this century, Edward VII's three daughters ranked as a group, enjoying £6,000 apiece with no financial distinction, and George V's only daughter, Princess Mary, received less than a quarter the sum accorded her younger brothers. Nor was this recognition increased (except by £300) when her brother, George VI, came to the throne.

These reflections would be out of place if they did not bring us back to that other Princess Mary, of Stuart, when she found herself no longer the wife of the ruling Prince of Orange. As his widow, she found herself styled Princess Royal as of right and fought furious battles for her precedence, but was often denied it. As a wife, she had sat at table with her exiled brothers while her husband dined apart with lesser men, his Government ministers, who could not be permitted to sit at table with the sons of a king. In her dark weeds and cap as the widow of a Prince of Orange, Mary however found herself relegated as one of the two dowager princesses of that little Dutch state. Her mother-in-law, decidedly her senior in age and experience, claimed the guardianship of the new infant Prince, with the right to name nurses and tutors. Apart from youthful motherhood, Mary had only her claim to royal precedence to help in the battle for care of her child, although this was perhaps sufficient to erode and quell the self-confidence of the one time Amalia Solma. After verbal battles, Mary emerged like a leading shareholder in a company, with a 50 per cent vote in making decisions in regard to her son, against the 25 per cent vote of her mother-in-law and the 25 per cent vote accorded her brother-in-law, the Elector of Brandenburg.

More than any other element of prestige, Mary had always defended her royal first-footing, even to refusing to attend a wedding if there appeared a risk that a well-born German bride might take precedence over herself. After the Battle of Worcester, when her brother Charles II hid in hedgerows and oak-trees before making his perilous way out of England, the Princess Royal was above all the first to uphold the family honour of the Stuart Royalists in the Netherlands and elsewhere. Holland was full of penniless exiles and fugitives, and the Princess Royal was the only Stuart to enjoy an assured income, from her annual dower of 100,000 florins (£11,500). Nearly three times as much as Princess Amalia received, this sum was bolstered too by gifts and bounties that had come from the rich commerce of Amsterdam in her husband's time.

In contrast, her mother, Queen Henrietta Maria, while housed in the magnificence of the Louvre, was but the impoverished guest of Anne of Austria and had at times to stay in bed to keep warm. When they could not dine at court, the Princess's brothers in Paris were reduced to eating decidedly humble pie in cheap taverns. To regain her health and strength after the birth of her baby, Mary sawed wood for exercise and gave the logs away to help warm her brother's followers. 'My dear niece begins to mend in her looks and health,' wrote the Queen of Bohemia, 'since she saws billets every morning.' And this dear Aunt Elizabeth in turn, though now a practised royal exile, also had stringent financial problems.

With an ever-growing horde of refugees who looked to her for subsistence, and with her own English allowances cut off, the former Queen of Bohemia sold her horses, her pictures and much of her jewellery. 'We had nothing to eat but diamonds and pearls,' wrote her daughter, and the saddest moment of bargaining came when she secretly pawned her wedding-ring. Princess Mary helped her aunt through these desperate straits when they came to her ears, but the older woman proudly kept her difficulties to herself. Fortunately the Dutch tradesmen equably regarded the Princess Royal as a surety for the mounting debts, but even the rich House of Orange was forced to recoup its royalist charities by selling land. A Dutchman once said that the Princess Royal's English relatives and their friends 'scented food like scavenging rats'. The daughter of one of the emigrés, pretty Anne Hyde, was given a post as maid-in-waiting to the Princess, a kindness of great historical consequence when Mary's younger brother, James, fell in love with Anne Hyde and secretly married her. Sir Edward Hyde, who served Charles so faithfully in exile, totted up the household accounts one summer and found everything 'entirely owed for', the meat and drink, the firing and the candles.

Yet youthful hunger was accompanied by youthful merriment. There still exists a spirited and delightful letter written by Charles to his aunt while freely enjoying the Princess Royal's hospitality: 'I am just now beginning this letter in my sister's chamber, where there is such a noise that I never hope to end it. We are thinking of dancing, in which we find two difficulties, the one for want of fiddlers, the other somebody to teach the new dances . . .' Certainly Aunt Elizabeth liked to see the young people happy and was sure that affairs would mend. The death of Cromwell aroused her hopes but seemed at first to make no difference. Then suddenly there was a flurry of messengers back and forth across the North Sea. And one day Charles urgently sent for his sister and his aunt to see a trunk that had been brought to him that day by a deputation of fourteen citizens from London. He flung open the lid with the air of a conjuror and revealed £50,000 of gold coin. The King had been invited to return home at last, and this was a liberal payment of advance expenses.

## VII

In all the long British story, there has never been more rejoicing than when the Monarchy was restored after the eleven years of dour republicanism under the Cromwells. On May Day in London, bells rang, bonfires blazed and people went on their knees in the street to drink the health of the coming King; and in Parliament men wept for joy as they carried the vote for the new Constitution. All this had an intense emotional effect on Princess Mary, at a distance from the joyous tumult in England and yet at the heart of the Royal Family. In her palace at the Hague, Charles received visitors hour by hour and, at the wish of the government of the States of Holland, the Royal Family dined in public each day: watched, that is, by everyone of sufficient rank to secure the entrée. A band played through the endless courses, toasts were drunk 'with tears of joy', and from time to time old friends knelt to the King for the accolade of knighthood.

By night Mary could scarcely sleep for excitement, and through the crowded days her little son was constantly at her side, watching the processions, now a pageant of decorated tableaux staged in one city, now a great military parade held in another, that made the boy shout with excitement. Young William was now also recognized in the English Succession; and among those who crowded into see the Princess Royal and kiss her hand was Samuel Pepys, counting himself glad and fortunate to be among those commanded to escort the King safely home to England.

The emotion grew insupportable. Long before dawn, on the day Charles was to sail, fifty thousand people lined the dykes to watch the royal departure. Riding out to the ship with her nephew, sharing the unbelievable dream, the Queen of Bohemia heard a great shout when he went on board. 'All the jolly English tars cried out, "We have him! We have him! God bless King Charles!"' she noted jubilantly. Before sailing, all the Royal Family dined together, which Pepys thought 'a blessed sight to see'. The Princess Royal was to visit England as soon as possible, yet, at their leave-taking, under the pressure of such intense emotion, brother and sister wept.

The Princess indeed delayed her journey for four months and so did not witness the indescribable scene when Charles rode into London, a slim dark young man, riding bareheaded through the clamouring thousands, while girls threw flowers from balconies and windows, and the roar of the crowds drowned the tumultuous bells and the thunder of the saluting guns. In her garden at the Mauritshouse, Mary watched her son playing tennis, unable to rid herself of a premonition that if she, too, went to England she would never see him again. Her aunt vainly tried to reassure her that no harm could befall such a strong, healthy lad. By September the intricate arrangements for the Princess Royal's visit were complete. The admiral's ship awaited her with an escort of seven warships, and she could procrastinate no more.

A 'great concourse of persons', officials of all kinds, came to see her off. She had hardly stepped on board than a man ran up the gangway, and the Princess knew from the looks of consternation that he was clearly the bearer of bad tidings. Her heart must have stood still, but her son was safe. The news had to be broken that her youngest brother, Henry, had died in England of smallpox.

It seemed in keeping with this gloomy leave-taking that the voyage was hazardous, her ship running onto the Goodwin sands no less than six times, with such crashing and creaking that all on board feared for their lives. The King and his brother, James, Duke of York, set out down river from London in the State barge to meet the Princess, but her convoy was so late in reaching Margate that the king had a mind to return to London . . . and then, at last, her little fleet was sighted. It was eighteen years since Princess Mary had last seen England, and she landed 'with a company of a hundred persons' but feeling alien and alone. The spectacle a day later when the gilded barges were rowed upstream, the guns of the Tower booming in salute, all the bells ringing, was intended to echo the King's own homecoming. Hundreds of small craft sailed out in welcome. But the 'assembled multitudes' saw very little of the Princess Royal. Pepys was unimpressed, the following Sunday, on seeing her in Whitehall chapel. It seemed more urgent to note that the King had laughed at the ill-sung anthem.

In Holland, as Princess Royal, Mary had nobly upheld the dignity and honour of the Monarchy, but in the brilliance of the Restoration she seemed bewildered and out of her depth, with none of the dazzling charm, 'civility' and commonsense tact that endowed her brother with such instant distinction. Parliament had voted her £10,000 a year, and for that she hid behind the curtains of her coach. Perhaps she could not fling off her fears for her son, so implicit in her depressing mood of foreboding. The King took her to the Cockpit playhouse and evidently she looked so bored at some British music, as Pepys observed, that the King 'bade them stop and make French music'.

The public were agog to see the King's sister, but she dined in public within the precincts of Whitehall Palace only once. The common people indeed saw her but once in eight weeks, when she left the Palace one morning to revisit the scenes of her childhood at Hampton Court. A boat prepared for her on the river was hung and cushioned curiously with black, and her horse-trappings were similarly of melancholy black velvet and silver lace. The King could be laughing and gay, and the Princess's appearance dourly rebuked him for not mourning more for their youngest brother. When the November fog swirled around Whitehall she completely withdrew to her own suite of apartments, an eccentricity so in contrast to the gaiety of the court that the town was filled with surmise and gossip. On December 21st, Pepys recorded two rumours, one that the Princess Royal had married a young equerry named Henry Jermyn, Master of the Horse to the Duke of York, and the other that she was dangerously ill.

Only the latter story was correct. Mary indeed never saw her son again, for the physicians diagnosed smallpox (which may well have been measles) and bled her too much and too often. She died on Christmas Eve. In the registers of Westminster Abbey for December 29th, 1660, is an entry of the burial of 'The Princess Royal Mary, the King's eldest sister, mother to the Prince of Orange'. And only two months later, in writing to the Queen of Bohemia, the Earl of Craven had to confide what was no more than the bitter truth: 'The Princess Royal is as much forgotten here, as if she had never been.'

It was left only to Aunt Elizabeth to visit London in the summer of 1661, the Coronation being 'well passed with great gallantry', as she wrote in a characteristic letter. As if designed by providence to tell us of these events, Samuel Pepys saw her at the Opera. 'We stayed a very great while for the King, and the Queen of Bohemia,' he says, and she very literally brought the house down, so many people crowding to see the almost legendary Queen of Hearts that part of the balcony collapsed, showering the ladies and gentlemen below with dust 'which made good sport', as Pepys wrote in high spirits. In her new gowns, she sparkled in company, making every attempt to see and be seen, and writing to her daughters for news of the latest fashions with which she might contribute to the brightness of London. After the Princess Royal's dismal and unimpressive appearance on the public scene, the cold truth glimmered, even amid the lustre of the Restoration, that a dismal royalty added nothing to the strength or popularity of the Throne. But Queen Elizabeth of Bohemia had precisely the magical charm and gift of winning affection that we recognize today in Queen Elizabeth the Queen Mother. As the Genoese Ambassador reported of her, in the days of radiant popularity that crowned her life, 'She is restored to some authority, and thus is heightened the lustre of that affable manner with which she wonderfully conciliates the esteem and love of the court.'

## ENTRACTE

*For more than sixty years the style of Princess Royal lapsed from usage and was all but lost in oblivion. King Charles II left no legitimate descendants, though he dearly loved his daughter by Lady Castlemaine. 'My dear Charlotte, be assured that I love you with all my heart, being your kind father,' he would write. She married the Earl of Lichfield, 'most beautiful bride and most constant wife', as her monument testifies, and would have made a model princess. From Charles the throne passed to his brother, James II, and so to James' two daughters by Anne Hyde, whom he had wedded in a secret but valid midnight ceremony in Whitehall Chapel.*

*Mary was married to Prince William of Orange, that self-same prince, the son of Mary Princess Royal, whom we have seen wrapped in royal ermine for his christening. (In royal alliances the Oranges were as persistent as present-day Mountbattens.) Unassuming and warm-hearted, Mary was Princess of Orange for seven years before her father ascended the throne at Westminster, and the possibility that she might also be dubbed Princess Royal was never considered. Her husband desired his pages to kneel to her, but the only occasion when Mary had insisted on her right of precedence had been a mischievous youthful escapade at the*

Hague, when she ordered her coach to drive against the stream of traffic on the fashionable Voorhout, as was strictly her prerogative. The flamboyant carriage of the wife of the Danish ambassador refused to give way and was crushed in a full-tilt collision, a victory over florid ostentation that endeared the Princess all the more to her unpretentious people.

If her father had shown a fraction of her warmth and humour, he might have held his throne. Instead, when James had fled, Parliament invited William and Mary to reign over Britain in joint partnership and, taking his wife's hand, Prince William accepted for them both.

The couple were however childless. Thirteen years later, Mary's sister, Anne, next became monarch. Of all her seventeen children, only one survived infancy and he, poor frail prince, did not live to see her crowned. The Protestant Succession then passed to George I, Elector of Hanover, grandson—through her youngest daughter, Sophia—of the Queen Elizabeth of Bohemia who had understood the duties and difficulties of royalty so well. Born, appropriately, in the year of the Restoration which so delighted and dazzled his grandmother, he was one quarter of Stuart blood, but German otherwise by birth and nature. It would have over-stressed the Germanic atmosphere of his court of St. James if his eldest daughter, Queen of Prussia by marriage, had also become Princess Royal of England and the title was not then revived.

George I reigned for thirteen years and, in June, 1727, his son succeeded to the throne as George II, schooled in his royal responsibilities and prerogatives by Sir Robert Walpole. The second George appreciated the quirks of the British character, moreover, becoming almost English by adoption himself after years of living in London. He also had five daughters by his wife, Caroline of Anspach, and considered it a clear asset to the monarchy to have a string of cultivated princesses at St. James.

His father's coronation had been unadorned by pretty girls, but George II desired his own crowning not to lack such a pleasing and decorative feature. And ten weeks after his accession, he scrawled his signature across a Royal Warrant, dated August 30th, 1727, conferring armorial bearings upon 'our eldest daughter the Princess Royal Anne'. Thus we can see the distinction officially established for the first time, a notable addition to the pomp and panoply around the Crown.

## 2 The Princess Royal Anne

That other Princess Anne, the first Princess Royal of warranted record, was born in the baroque palace of Hanover on October 22nd, 1709. The influences of music and art surrounded her cradle, for the court of Hanover was counted the best in Germany 'for civility and decorum' and the elegant little opera house of Celle still stands in the vicinity to illustrate its taste and its diversions. Anne of Hanover was so royally born that her cousins included Frederick the Great and his sisters, the future Queen Ulrica of Sweden and Duchess Philippine of Brunswick, and her grandfather, then still the Elector George of Hanover, widened this regal cosmopolitan ambience by writing to Her Britannic Majesty Queen Anne to request permission to name the child after her and to solicit the pleasure of her favour as god-mother. A sick woman with only five years of her life still to run, Queen Anne acquiesced and complaisantly sent the gift of a diamond necklet to her goddaughter.

It had proved equally sensible to endow the baby Anne's two-year-old brother with the name of Frederick: King Frederick of Prussia had a magnificent royal habit of giving gold-plate for his christening gifts. Less fuss however was made over Princess Anne's younger sisters, Emily and Caroline. No compliments needed to be paid indeed with the youngest and she was given her mother's name.

Caroline of Anspach and George of Hanover had married in their early twenties, a young couple 'casting sheep's eyes at one another', deeply enjoying not only their own company but also the court balls and comedies staged for their wedding. George had first seen his bride when pretending to be merely 'travelling or pleasure as a Hanoverian nobleman' and, having surveyed the lady, he then sent an envoy to discover whether she were free and could be approached with a proposal. This Cinderella touch added popularity to the gossip woven around their romance. Yet they were already a married couple of nine years standing, with four children, when Prince George's father was summoned to the English throne.

Princess Anne was a plump and attractive child, despite the blunt-spoken British agent who unkindly termed her 'podgy, ill-fashioned' in his dispatches home to London. The German princes all followed the mode of the court of France, and Anne chattered in French as her nursery language almost before she began to learn German. Her great-grandmama, the Electress Sophia—the Queen of Bohemia's daughter—supervised her education at an early age when modern children have scarcely entered kindergarten. One sighs for a Gainsborough who might have seen the children playing among the fountains and mosaic paths in the gardens of Herren-hausen. On June 14th, 1714, the Electress was strolling there arm-in-arm with her daughter, with young Anne and Fred skipping about them, when the old lady felt faint in the oppression of an approaching thunder-storm. The mystified children were hurried away as she was taken to a summerhouse, and she sat quietly on a chair and died. In London, only two months later, Queen Anne also died in Kensington Palace, and suddenly her little namesake was royal in a closer sense as grand-child of the newly proclaimed King.

Her grandfather and father hastened to London together, the one to be styled King George I, the other George to ride at his side as his son and heir and future Prince of Wales. The Prince having fondly embraced his wife, Caroline, it was agreed that she should follow with the two elder girls after a month, and that seven-year-old Frederick should remain at his studies in Hanover. The baby Caroline was also left behind, her health judged too delicate to travel before the spring. Anne perhaps saw no more than the glint of her mother's tears when they bade her brother goodbye.

Their equerry, Mr. James Craggs, had first come to Hanover to inform the family of the great change in their fortunes, and Anne and her sister, Emily, began the overland journey to the Dutch coast in his charge, travelling three days ahead of their mother. The long journey of nearly a week must have been enlivened for the little girls by their first lessons—from Mr. Craggs—in English. As outriders, they also had the two dark and fiercely protective Turks who had been with their grandfather for thirty years and were to be henceforth their most trusted sentinels. At the Hague a yacht with attendant men-of-war was waiting, and as soon as their mother had joined them, they set off on the autumnal two-day crossing of the North Sea.

Their father drove to Margate to meet them; the new King had created his son Prince of Wales at his first Privy Council, and later that week Londoners were delighted at the sight of the Prince and Princess of Wales driving together over London Bridge, with the two little princesses 'lovely and sprightly' peeping out from a coach behind them. There were friendly crowds to cheer them as they were set down at St. James's Palace and, that evening, the children stayed up late to gaze wide-eyed at the bonfires and illuminations. Walking hand in hand the two little girls also lent an unaccustomed domestic note to the Coronation, 'the sight of the royal children not known for several hundred years', as one loyal preacher asserted, with pleasant if inaccurate enthusiasm. Two days later, Londoners were also charmed by the procession of posies for Princess Anne's birthday and the child herself made a good impression, to judge by the praise of the Lord Chancellor's wife, Lady Cowper, 'Princess Anne, five years old, speaks, reads and writes both French and German to perfection,' she noted in her journal. 'She knows a great deal of history and geography, speaks English very prettily and dances very well.'

In the following week, all the Royal Family occupied a window to watch the unfamiliar pageantry of the Lord Mayor's Show. Then next day, awakened by pealing bells, the Princess Anne discovered it was her papa's birthday, and perhaps she saw something of the guests arriving at St. James's in magnificent new clothes for the first court ball.

## II

Fortunately, in contrast to the excitements of their first reception, the children soon went to live in the pastoral calm of Kensington Palace, then in the green fields beyond London. Every hour of Anne's day was regulated as carefully as a Hanover clock. It was directed that she should rise at seven, pray, 'coiffe' and breakfast, walk from eight till nine, read and then commence lessons, dining at one and then playing shuttlecock, but first walking or talking 'of sensible things'. At an early age, moreover, she was taught to play on the clavichord and music soon became her great passion.

When only eight or nine years old, she clearly merited a skilled music master, and none other than Handel was appointed at a salary rising to £200 a year. If this stipend appeared handsome in those days, it was but a fraction of the £19,000 provided for the princesses' joint establishment and no more than the £200 annually allowed to the office of laundress, a sum additional to the £100 paid through the linen-room to 'a German who does the work'. It compares with the £60 expended for a lace-trimmed suit of bibs, apron, cap and ruffles for Anne's small sister and such petty expenses of the nursery occupants as 'tuning the harpsichord' and 'food for their birds'. Handel nevertheless enjoyed his own small perquisites, and from the lessons improvised for Princess Anne he concocted the *Suite of Pieces for the Clavichord*, which figured in 1720 as his first purely instrumental album to be published. It is pleasant to visualize the thirty-five-year-old Master of Musick at Kensington, in ruffles and bulky velvet, on his way to the five o'clock session with his young pupil, strolling through the arcade walk of the Palace quadrangle still to this day called Princesses Court.

Whenever their parents proposed to spend time at Kensington, however, the children were hurried to St. James's, to be brought back only when the Prince and Princess of Wales had returned to their establishments at Richmond Lodge or Leicester House. On the stubborn issue of the custody of his grand-children, the King adopted an attitude so harsh, unreal and obstinate that the natural parents were not permitted to spend a day with their daughters. The King's judges were called to decide the issue of guardianship and, though some resigned, the majority asserted in the King's favour that a grandfather was indeed the appropriate protector. This victory secured, with his point won, the King appeared lenient and Caroline was allowed to visit the girls once a week provided there was no fuss. Princess Anne would wait at a window for first sight of the sedan chair, carried without guards or retinue, which the Princess of Wales was ordinarily reduced to using for conveyance. The bereft mother poured out the anguish of these occasions in a spate of letters to her cousin in Paris, the Duchess of Orleans, often scribbling letters of twenty-five pages—and one week as many as forty-three. The harassed Duchess could scarcely cope with the flood. 'It takes me all my time, you may imagine,' she told a less emotional correspondent.

Inevitably the King's strictness led to subterfuges and pretences and young Anne could not help but be embroiled in deception. In the summer of 1718, after not seeing her father for six months, she secretly sent him a basket of cherries which her sisters had helped her to pick in the Kensington garden. The prince broke down and wept when he found hidden in the fruit a message that 'their heart and soul and thoughts were always with dear Papa'. Shortly afterwards Princess Anne herself fell ill with the dreaded symptoms of smallpox, and her mother rushed to Kensington Palace only to find, according to Lady Cowper, that the two Turks, Mohammed and Mustapha, sternly barred the way.

In desperation, Caroline sought an audience with the King, merely to be rebuffed with a message that he had himself appointed a physician. In her agitation she wrote an 'utterly submissive letter' and it was only then that the King consented, 'she might go, provided she took neither doctor nor physic'. Eventually Caroline was permitted to nurse her daughter back to health and, taking heart from her success, Prince George also wrote submissively to his parent. Father and son duly met. The Prince could make little of his father's angry mutterings except the words, 'Your conduct! Your conduct!' Yet the breach was healed, the quarrel patched up.

Princess Anne recovered, disfigured 'not too much', and there was a notable sequel. Princess Caroline chanced to hear from the author, Lady Mary Wortley Montagu, of the success of the surgeons of Constantinople in practising inoculation and, being restored to favour, she persuaded the King to reprieve five criminals from the scaffold provided they submitted to the needle as a test. The experiment was successful. The Princess had her younger daughters, Emily and Caroline, inoculated; and the scourge of smallpox, which had carried off so many of the princess heroines of our tale, flinched in defeat at last.

### III

Princess Anne was seventeen when George I flew into his last rage and had a stroke in his coach at Osnabruck, and the news reached Kensington that her parents were at last King and Queen.

In the next month or two, Handel must have enlivened her music hours by placing before her the dazzling anthems and marches which he composed for the coronation, almost as fast as they flowed from his pen. Not long before, Handel had given a recital at the newly enlarged organ in St. Paul's Cathedral for the Princess and her mother, clearly demonstrating that there was no more accomplished organist in England, if not in all Europe. Now the great anthem, *Zadok the Priest* (since played at every coronation, from George II to Elizabeth II) was first rehearsed before the new Princess Royal Anne. After the ceremony in Westminster Abbey, that arch witness, Mrs. Delaney, enthused over the enchantment of the Princess Royal and her two younger sisters walking beneath the royal canopy carrying the Queen's diamond-spangled train. 'They were dressed in stiff-bodied gowns of silver tissue, embroidered with silver trimming, with diadems on their heads, purple mantles edged with ermine and vast long trains. They were very prettily dressed and looked very well.'

It was useless for Lord Hervey to sneer that the glitter had been borrowed from the jeweller. Anne celebrated her eighteenth birthday the following week, and at the feasts, fêtes, masquerades, court balls and drawing-rooms that marked the new reign she found herself a centre of attention. It was hardly surprising if it all went a little to her head after the cloistered years in Kensington. Although she now had a younger brother, aged six, as well as five sisters, she had always found herself senior in precedence of the junior set. Now she realized, all too well, that the heir to the throne, to the flattery and richness and prestige, was her elder brother Fred in Germany, whom she could scarcely remember. 'I would gladly die tomorrow,' she said impulsively, 'if I could be Queen today,' and the phrase never ceased to be repeated and maliciously distorted.

Far from being too deeply envious of her brother, the Princess could hardly wait to see him, puzzled because his arrival from Hanover was so long delayed. The new King was in fact as distrustful of his heir as his own father had been. Royal Anne was prevailed on to pass the time by taking the waters at Tunbridge Wells, enjoying the shops and the morning crush on the Pantiles, though the press of people was far from crushing when gentlemen with white wands preceded her to ward off the over-inquisitive. 'Her Highness charms everybody by her affable and courteous behaviour,' gushed Dr. Arbuthnot. 'She is the strongest person in the place, if walking every day be a sign of strength. I tell her Highness she does more good than the waters; for she keeps some ladies in exercise and breath that want it.'

The following month Anne warded off her puppy fat still more vigorously by hunting, riding to hounds so violently that she quite frightened her sister. 'P.S.—we are just come back from hunting —in good health!' Emily thankfully concluded a letter to her governess, Lady Portland. But their long-lost and long-awaited brother arrived in December, a prodigy of amiable sensibility who delighted Anne by showing that he fully shared her love of music, and at once pleased Mr. Handel by organizing the sisters into a juvenile court orchestra. Frederick played the cello to Anne's harpsichord, and a charming old painting shows them scraping away: Frederick with his cello; Anne at the keyboard; Emily with her lute.

'Fred' added a manly and youthful note of gaiety to the Court. Mrs. Delaney particularly enjoyed a ball for Queen Caroline's birthday, 'the squeezing and crowding, being buffeted about and crushed . . . The clock struck twelve, the French dances were just over and every man took the woman he liked best to dance country-dances. The Prince set the example by choosing the Duchess of Bedford.' Mrs. Delaney scarcely noticed the man with whom Anne danced, so eagerly was she noting her toilette. 'Princess Royal had white embroidered with gold and a few colours intermixed . . .' On another occasion, the Prince 'surprised the Queen and all his dear sisters with a very pretty entertainment at Richmond'. The highlight of the evening was a play acted for their delight upon the lawn.

On Princess Anne's twenty-first birthday Fred similarly engaged John Rich, the impresario of Gay's *Beggar's Opera*, to produce a masque in the Dutch garden of the little palace at Kew. Over a thousand lamps 'disposed in an elegant manner' may have warded off some of the late October chill. The entertainment concluded with fireworks, cascading to cries of family delight and, as the *Universal Spectator* remarked, 'Their Royal Highnesses were pleased to express their satisfaction'.

These were the good days when it seemed nothing could ever mar the happy reunion of brother and sister, but their fervent emotions rapidly cooled. The Prince was quickly at odds with his father over debts and money, and with his mother, too, during one of the King's visits to Germany, when the Queen was appointed Regent instead of himself. Princess Anne found that she preferred to take her parents' part during the family rows; disenchantment set in and the atmosphere soured noticeably. Youthful rivalry also sparked off differences between the new Princess Royal and the new Prince of Wales, and everyone took sides when their squabbles blazed into the public eye—and ears—in the absurd vendetta that became known as the opera war.

The King enjoyed the majestic and measured music of Handel. The Prince preferred the lighter, less calculable airs of the new Italian opera. It was the old, perennial story of entrenched authority and rebellious youth, of established taste and decided innovation. The Princess Royal attempted to encourage her music master into novel experiment within his own established field. She heard with enthusiasm of his presentation of a biblical concert story of Esther in an hospitable tavern, the Crown and Anchor, complete with the choir of the Chapel Royal, and suggested staging it with costumes and scenery at the new King's theatre in the Haymarket. If Anne seemed weak in what might today be called social conscience, her musical conscience was sturdy indeed, and with her help Handel's *Esther* was produced as the first public performance of oratorio in England. A month or two later the King and Queen and Princess Royal attended the first night of *Deborah*, 'an oratorio or sacred drama', but the Prince of Wales was pointedly absent.

The feud deepened when Fred instituted a new opera company of his own at the theatre in Lincoln's Inn Fields, financed by the Duke of Marlborough and other allies, and his producer slyly stole Handel's singers one by one. While Princess Anne and her parents sometimes sat in the draughty Theatre Royal surrounded by empty seats, the crowds jostled wildly on the steps of Lincoln's Inn. The operas became the rallying grounds of the King's or Prince's factions, those who were for the King and his ministers versus those who supported the Prince in his opposition tactics. 'The delight of everybody's heart seems to be set upon the King's sitting by himself,' wrote Lady Germaine to the Duke of Dorset. 'The Prince was as eager and pressed me as earnestly to go to Lincoln's Inn Fields opera as if it had been a thing of great moment to the nation.' With far heavier sarcasm, the Princess Royal said that she 'expected in a little while to see half the House of Lords playing in the Prince's theatre in their robes and coronets'.

Yet the bitter intensity of the quarrel all but ruined Handel, and especially the dire loss of his principal singers. The rivalry came to an end only with the comparatively unexpected appearance of a suitor for Princess Anne's hand. The Princess was then twenty-five and had begun to wonder whether she would ever marry or remain feuding for the rest of her life. For the Court gossips, the surprise factor about her prospective husband was not that he was yet another Prince William of Orange but that he was so very ugly. Grand-nephew of that William of Orange who had ruled Britain jointly with Mary some forty years earlier, his appearance dashed any romantic anticipations, for the would-be bridegroom was swarthy, short, ill-shaped in features and undeniably a hunchback.

'A miserable match', shrieked Lord Hervey, while another chronicler found the aspirant so malformed 'as to seem from behind that he had no head and from the front as if he had no legs'. The Queen herself almost washed her hands of the affair, intimating that it was solely her daughter's choice; 'I never said the least word to encourage her or to dissuade her.' But the crowds loyally cheered the Dutchman's coach, even on its way to the wrong opera-house. Parliament voted the Princess a jointure of £80,000, but even with this relief to his purse the King had second thoughts on contrasting the dream and the reality, the beauty and the beast, and kindly told Anne that the betrothal need not go forward if she wished to change her mind. Anne responded firmly, 'I would marry him if he were a monkey'. The King drily replied that there was monkey enough.

Happily, the quarrel between brother and sister was outwardly healed when Frederick good-naturedly took William about to show him the sights of London. Whatever his exterior, the Prince of Orange had great charm of manner and a heart of gold, and even the cynical Hervey had to agree that a wife would grow accustomed to the *figure* of her husband. While the marriage arrangements were going forward, it also happened that Prince Fred fell ill, and the world had an opportunity of true insight into the Princess Anne's affections. She had formerly shunned her brother, as she said, to show her disapproval of 'setting oneself at the head of a faction of fiddlers'. Now she visited his sickbed nearly every day, displaying a depth of affection that curiously made the King downcast and jealous.

Meanwhile Handel of course composed a wedding anthem, and the wedding eve was notable for a gala performance at the Haymarket of an operetta notably attended not only by the intending bride and groom and the King and Queen but also by the convalescent Prince of Wales. Next day the gorgeous extravagance of the wedding showed that George II had spared no expense. The Chapel Royal of St. James's, we are told, 'was fitted up with an extreme good taste, and as much finery as velvets, gold and silver tissue, galleons, fringes, tassels, gilt lustres and sconces could give'. The bride with her eight trainbearers, dressed alike in white and silver, with great quantities of jewels, is claimed by some authorities to have inaugurated the lasting fashion of having bridesmaids. The reception afterwards was all that Mrs. Delaney, for one, could have hoped. 'Such crowding, such finery I never saw.' The custom was still observed of guests being invited to see the bride and bridegroom sitting up in bed; and once again history is obliged to Lord Hervey, who considered that the Princess Royal had 'a lively clean look and a fine complexion' and thought that the Prince of Orange looked 'less shocking and ridiculous than one could have expected'.

## IV

And so for the third time within a century a Princess of Britain, a Princess Royal, sailed the North Sea to become the chatelaine of the House of Orange and the faithful wife of the Stateholder. Her father, it was waspishly said, gave her a thousand kisses on departure but not one guinea; her mother never ceased crying for three days, and her brother deliberately took no leave of her, as he explained to the Prince of Orange, for fear of upsetting her too much. From the moment of the wedding until they sailed from Gravesend, moreover, it was noticed that Princess Anne always behaved to her husband 'as if he had been an Adonis', turning towards him whenever he spoke, hanging on his words and applauding everything he said to anyone else. People found it 'most extraordinary' that she 'made prodigious court to him'. The pattern of history also repeated itself, for the Princess Royal outlived her husband, after providing an heir, as the first Princess Mary of Orange had done. (The Princess Royal Anne was also the direct ancestress of Queen Juliana.)

Her marriage, though it lasted only the span of seventeen years, was an exceptionally happy one. Her genuine fondness for her husband became proverbial, and their only public tiffs arose from her extreme jealousy of other women, a jealousy invariably without cause. Her brother, 'poor Fred', affected mock annoyance because she had married before him, but he married the seventeen-year-old Princess Augusta of Saxe-Gotha two years later with a wedding that his sister might have planned to the last organ note, complete to a Handel anthem. Anne continued to use her influence to help the composer in any difficulty, and they probably met again in 1737 when, too ill to compose a tribute in honour of her tenth year as Princess Royal, he journeyed to Aix-la-Chapelle to take the waters.

Music, his old pupil found, mixed well with marriage and maternity. She formed her own small chamber orchestra at the Hague, which she directed from the harpsichord in frequent palace concerts. Singers from London were invited to Holland, including Handel's celebrated favourite soprano, Maria Strada. Eager to oblige the Princess of Orange with the latest news and gossip, as the *Daily Post* announced, Maria set out for Breda just a month after the Princess of Wales had given birth to the boy who was to be King George III. Probably she was able to tell Princess Anne that the proud young father's own love of music at this time led to the making of a double keyboard harpsichord, the wonderful instrument that is still at Windsor Castle, and she may have hinted that the temper of his father, the King, remained as uncertain as ever.

Anne herself had two children, a son and a daughter, both with such difficulty that it became touch-and-go whether the doctors could save her life. Alarmed at the prospect of having her first child among strangers, she had returned to England for the first lying-in but found the King in one of the moods that Anne called 'the devil to everybody that comes near him'. Indeed, he inhospitably proposed that she had better not stay. Often his household could find no reason for his ill-humour, though Anne was always more understanding. 'My God,' she said to Hervey one day, 'I am ashamed for you, who have been so long about Papa, that you know so little of him. In his worst humours, it is always because one of his pages has powdered his periwig ill or a housemaid has set a chair where it doesn't use to stand.' But George soon began snapping so angrily at every mention of her name that she thought it best to leave, if only for the sake of domestic peace. During the subsequent stormy sea-crossing, sheer fright brought on false labour pains and the ship returned to Harwich, but the King remained gruffly adamant and she again set out, this time to be met safely by her husband and to give birth in Holland to a son.

When her husband, Prince William of Orange, duly succeeded his father as ruler of the Netherlands, it was rumoured before long that Anne was the power behind the regal chair. Certainly she could draw on a fund of commonsense and expertise in the problems of the worthy Dutch burghers. She had learned statecraft at her mother's side when Queen Caroline acted as Regent during George II's annual visits to Hanover, and it was no coincidence that Prince William's ten-year rule in Holland turned out to be an era of untroubled prosperity.

Prince William died in 1751 only a month before Frederick, Prince of Wales, perished of a chill and, at a double stroke of fate, Anne lost both her husband and her brother. Her people in Holland none the less elected her without hesitation to the position of 'Gouvernante' or Regent for the seven-year-old heir. Thus Anne's adolescent dream of ruling a country and being Queen in a sense came true. Now when she heard of her father's worst tantrums, she could snub his ambassador, and the King in retaliation never paid her a visit during his journeys to Hanover. Frederick the Great of Prussia had to spare her some attention to ensure that the English forces fighting the French were not loaned troops from Holland, and evidently Frederick found personal grounds for admiring her knowledge and her character when she helped to guide him around the art galleries of various rich Dutchmen, during his visit to Holland in 1756.

In her last illness her doctors could not but admire the strength with which she read and signed the marriage contract for her daughter's union to the Prince of Nassau-Walberg and the letter to the States General requesting their consent to the match. The Princess Royal Anne died on January 12th, 1759. In London, Handel heard with sadness the last tidings of his fond pupil and, old and fat, weary and blind, he followed her to the grave three months later.

## ENTRACTE

*For thirty years more, in the mid-eighteenth century, there was no Princess Royal under warrant. From Anne in 1759 until Charlotte Augusta in 1789, the distinction lay unawarded, though not in fact disused. In 1760 a fair and good-looking bachelor of twenty-two was proclaimed King. This was George II's grandson, George III—son of the demised Frederick, Prince of Wales. He was destined to reign, though not always to rule, for longer than any other king in English history. Seven of his sons survived infancy and he had six daughters, all but one of whom lived into the last century, a plethora of great-aunts for the young Queen Victoria.*

*For George III was not long a bachelor, and he deferred his coronation until a Queen could be crowned at his side. The seventeen-year-old Princess Charlotte of Mecklenburgh-Strelitz was betrothed to him by proxy within six months of his accession. She had never travelled much farther than her father's garden in Strelitz, but arrived in London on September 7th, 1761, and was wedded that same evening.*

*The Coronation of George III and his Queen Charlotte took place two weeks later. Their first child, the future George IV, was born eleven months later and created Prince of Wales within the week. Then came another son, and another, and it was not until five years of marriage that their fourth child proved to be a daughter. She was named Charlotte Augusta Matilda after her mother, and grandmother, but it was not until more than twenty years later, that George III officially gave his eldest daughter the title of Princess Royal.*

# 3   The Princess Royal Charlotte

## I

'Sept. 24th, 1766. Going to visit my grey mare when a servant told me that Her Majesty had been brought to bed in the morning of a Princess Royal.' So wrote Lady Mary Coke in her diary, with her lively sense of occasion, and by every highway in the kingdom the news spread that after the sequence of three healthy sons the young Queen Charlotte at last had a daughter. Loyal toasts were drunk and bonfires blazed in celebration. The little princess was the first to be born in the new royal residence of Buckingham House— the Queen's House, as it was known—and those admitted to St. James's Palace as usual to drink the Queen's caudle especially prided themselves on seeing 'that first in quality of female infants, a Princess Royal'.

Were they mistaken? The King's son and heir, born a mere prince, had been created Prince of Wales when only five days old, by Letters Patent under the Great Seal, and further: 'Prince of Great Britain, Electoral Prince of Brunswick Luneburg, Duke of Cornwall and Rothesay, Lord of the Isles and Great Steward of Scotland'. But the establishment evidently took for granted the precise status of the first girl. The *Annual Register* was to record that on October 27th, 'H.R.H. The Princess Royal was christened by the Archbishop of Canterbury'. George II's eldest daughter, the Princess Royal Anne, had been gone only seven years; her style and title remained fresh in the memory and so George III's first daughter was given equal rank by habit and repute, one might say, by the instant verdict of public opinion, as well as the King's vigorous pleasure. His Majesty's subjects enjoyed the marzipan of titles; the old style was taken for granted, without the slightest disputation and the caudle-drinkers indulgently feasted their eyes on the child without any tiresome legal quibbles in mind.

It was a long-established custom for young mothers and convalescents to share their caudle with visitors. This was a hot recuperative drink of fine oatmeal or crushed biscuits, beaten with egg yolks and mixed with spiced and sweetened wine, and the Court ceremoniously offered caudle rather than seem to fail in hospitality. Ladies who had been presented knew that the mulled refreshment included the privilege of seeing the baby; forty guests were admitted to St. James's each day between the hours of twelve and three, and the custom was observed until the birth of the last of Queen Charlotte's fifteen children. In the Queen's guard-chamber the ladies found a buffet spread with little cakes and the steaming urns and lidded caudle-cups, and perhaps for the Princess Royal the royal caudle set of Chelsea porcelain of 'fine blue celeste enamelled in Cupids' or the Derby set 'in fine gold chainwork' were prominent.

The royal kitchens prepared seventy-two quarts of caudle fresh each day, more than enough to give every visitor a rosy view of the proceedings. In small groups, the viewers were ushered into the drawing-room to find the infant Princess displayed beyond a gilt railing, in a carved and gilded cradle upon a dais beneath a canopy of state. Lined with white satin, the cradle was spread with crimson and gold lace, edged with a sheet of Brussels' lace, and nearby sat the nurse, a velvet cushion on her lap to support the baby when out of the cradle. These royal shows were highly popular, so much so that one year when there was no new baby the King incautiously announced that the royal children would hold a levee instead. The outraged nobility found themselves expected to bow or curtsey to three pudgy infants; the seven-year-old Prince of Wales, wearing the Order of the Garter, the future Duke of York, adorned with the Order of the Bath, and the three-year-old Princess Royal Charlotte Augusta Matilda, seated on a sofa between her younger brothers.

The caricaturists, including the malignant Gilray, had a field-day, but nothing diminished the King and Queen's belief that their family should be seen by the people, high-born or low. As the children grew older, the public were admitted on Thursdays to the grounds of Kew Palace where the boys were sometimes to be seen playing cricket or working in the fields of their model farm. To this day, showcases at Kew display some of the children's toys and possessions, the Princess Royal's silver rattle and their alphabetical blocks: with 'Q' for quince, one notices, rather than Queen.

Once a week, in summer, the Royal Family walked across to Richmond Gardens, the youngsters two by two in precedence followed by their parents, first the Prince of Wales and his senior sister, then the next two boys and the two younger girls, all paired in crocodile formation, with the youngest children and their nurse-maids shepherded by the King and Queen. The Prince of Wales revelled in the admiration of the crowds. The Princess Royal as a young girl hated these promenades, loathed being one of the first to face the curious gaze of the onlookers and quailed as she met their searching eyes. 'Princess Royal has excessive sensibility, a great sense of injury, a great sense of her own situation, much timidity,' sympathetically wrote her friend, Mrs. Harcourt. 'The extreme quickness of her feelings show in perpetual blushes.' Others around the Princess thought her shy, even clumsy, despite a good figure, 'never elegant in exhibition'.

At the core of her shyness was her rank, the strange special distinction of being Princess Royal, setting her apart. Her own mother spoke of her and addressed her as Princess Royal, never Charlotte. To her brothers and sisters near her own age she was always Princess Royal, though the younger children called her 'Royal', probably the utmost that baby lips could frame. Her governesses, the household and the doctors all addressed her as Princess Royal as if that were her name. Her nearest sister, Princess Augusta, two years her junior, was in clear contrast given the affectionate diminutive of 'Puss'. When her second brother, Frederick, the Duke of York, made his first journey abroad and sent gifts from Hanover, he added explicit instructions that the first package was 'for Princess-Royal and the other for Puss. The other two little things are for Mary and Sophia . . .'

The gift was perhaps a sketch-book of a new kind, for drawing had become a favourite preoccupation. Unlike her predecessor, the Princess Royal Anne, with her ardent admiration of Handel, Charlotte 'heard music almost with pain'. Before attending a concert, she once wrote to her younger brother, Augustus, that she hoped she could stay awake. Incapable of perceiving rhythm, her first ball was an agony of humiliation, when she lost her shoe and had to cling to her gallant elder brother. 'Her Highness hopped, The Musicians stopped, Not knowing what to do,' wrote the rhymesters. It hardly improved matters that the accident occurred under the reproving eyes of her mother. 'She was always under restraint with the Queen,' wrote the observant Mrs. Papendiek years later. 'Timidity always brought her forward as ill at ease, while out of the Queen's presence she was a different being.'

From another angle, indeed Charlotte* showed good judgment and a sweet temper. Fanny Burney noticed how freely she allowed the young children to pull her about, never complaining. As one of the Queen's ladies, Miss Burney had an intimate and perceptive view, but others at court also noticed the Princess's sweet and forebearing nature. 'Pray give me your love, for I wish for your love so much that I think you must give it me,' she once wrote in a delightful letter to her governess, Miss Goldsworthy. When painting his series of Windsor family portraits, Gainsborough avowed to his artist friend, Angelo, that 'the sweetest, the most lovely of that youthful group always appeared to me to be that of the Princess Royal'. She was also one of her father's favourites, and he alone called her by her intimate christian name, Matilda, and noted the tender care and affection she showered on her younger sisters. In the royal library at Windsor there remains a book that he once gave her as a New Year gift, tenderly inscribed to 'my Ever Dearest Daughter, Matilda, Governess to her Three Younger Sisters'.

And it was with his eldest daughter that the ailing King chose to go out for a drive on the terrible November day in 1788 when he first seemed to take leave of his senses, giving so many orders to the postillions and climbing in and out of the carriage so often that, as Fanny Burney put it, the 'fear of a great fever hanging over him became more and more powerful'.

The King was in fact suffering from an inherited family illness with symptoms far more akin to physical sickness than the insanity feared at the time. Three weeks later, when the doctors moved him to the seclusion of Kew, he begged that the Princess Royal should accompany him, though this small comfort was refused lest she should be in danger. Telling of this years later, the Princess could not restrain her tears. The Queen was terrified, and all the records show that it was 'Royal' who proved a tower of strength to the distracted family.

In the new year it seemed that the King might never rule again.

* An unwary reader should not confuse her with the later Princess Charlotte (1796–1817) d. of George, Prince of Wales (later George IV).

Plans for a Regency were put in hand, though not without ensuing problems. Clearly the Prince of Wales and the Queen could help to govern the country but, in the event of their illness, who then followed? Five of George III's other children were then of age and, on examining their merits, the dismaying discovery of a long-standing oversight was made. By formal legal definition the eldest daughter had never formally been given the title of Princess Royal and in reality she held no higher form of rank than any of her sisters. The unaccountable error had to be made good as swiftly as possible.

Fortunately the King recovered. Early in April 'Royal' herself organized a gala at Windsor at which the King made his first public appearance since his illness, and on April 23rd the Royal Family drove in state to St. Paul's to the official thanksgiving service for his recovery. Precisely two months later, on June 22nd, 1789, the title of Princess Royal was conferred officially on Charlotte Augusta Matilda. Three months later, her twenty-third birthday was celebrated with special distinction. All the glories of a court ball were revived at Windsor, but to the disappointment of the birthday girl no new or eligible young men were present.

## II

Only three years older than the Princess Royal, the Duke of York wrote sympathetically from his army billet that he knew 'what a dreadful life she must lead'. After the King's return to Windsor the atmosphere became stifling. Although George III was to enjoy good health for the next twelve years, his family never again knew complete peace of mind. The Queen could never free herself from the haunting thought that the nightmare distress of the breakdown might recur. 'I want you all to be happy,' she told her children. But there was the insistent fear for her husband and the constant worry of her eldest son's wanton extravagances, with the lies and deceit of his secret marriage to Mrs. Fitzherbert. Anxieties no less deep lay over the alliances of her other sons, and with every fresh family distress a nervous storm broke around the head of the luckless 'Royal'.

The Princess now acted as her mother's secretary and reader, which usually entailed being the Queen's constant companion, with little if any private time to herself. Royal enjoyed no financial independence and the Queen scrupulously controlled her wardrobe allowance, a restriction not improving her haphazard dress sense. The wilder the princes became in that permissive Georgian society, the deeper the Queen's determination to protect her daughters. Newspapers were vetoed save with the Queen's express approval, even the innocuous books of Fanny Burney. The Princess Royal said that it was like living 'in a cloister not a kingdom'.

Coming as it did after a carefree childhood, such restraint led inevitably to a sense of grievance. When the Queen sought to lessen ill effects by banning correspondence between her sons abroad and her daughters at home, the practice developed of 'shewables', meaning messages which could meet the Queen's restrictive eye, as distinct from more intimate and truthful letters secretly carried by intermediaries. These subterfuges scarcely improved matters between Queen Charlotte and Royal, more adult than the other girls and yet treated more as a child.

One day, when the Prince of Wales had called to see his mother and the Princess and bantered good humouredly with them both, his sister slipped out afterwards and begged to speak to him for two minutes in private. 'She then told me how much obliged she should be if I would never joke with her respecting the smallest trifle in the presence of her mother,' George reported the incident to his brother, 'as I did not know how she suffered for it afterwards, how she was treated . . .' Brother Frederick sympathetically responded, 'I will tell you fairly that nobody pities her situation more than I do or wishes to see her married sooner.' Not surprisingly, the Princess was becoming ultra-sensitive. Because she had been born near Michaelmas, her mother had the fond habit of calling her a goose. Yet the term rapidly appeared one of opprobrium and even insult that became insupportable.

In this repressive atmosphere, an unquestioned family convention had grown up that the King should never be approached on family matters and, in particular, he showed a rooted reluctance to discussing his daughters' marriage hopes. The eldest Princess was only fifteen when Lord Chandos raised the possibility of a state marriage to the Emperor of Austria, but nothing emerged beyond diplomatic talk. Later on, a Prince of Orange inevitably appeared as a suitor, only to encounter the King's invincible hostility to the thought of losing any daughter in a continental alliance. The royal brothers not infrequently made furtive reports to one another on possible bridegrooms. Frederick the Great's grandson was mentioned, and the Duke of York dolefully commented, 'I cannot think that she can expect to marry the Prince Royal here, because she is now four and twenty and he is but 21.'*

Peter of Oldenburg, heir to the dukedom of that name, presented himself to the enquiring brothers: a widower for ten years and father of several children. Hardly eligible as a husband for the Princess Royal of England, although she viewed the prospect radiantly; her 'cheek turned to damask rose', as her sister Elizabeth reported, whenever his name was mentioned. 'If it could be brought about,' wrote Royal hopefully, 'it would be the properest situation.' But the King fumed and fussed and the opportunity slid by.

Not for the first time, the Princess fell into such low spirits that the doctors wondered if she had not a touch of her father's ailment and ceased to talk of the patient with their customary discretion. 'Convinced that she now has no chance of ever altering her condition, she is fallen into a kind of quiet desperate state, what is commonly called broken-hearted,' noted James Burges, the physician. Another eminent medico, Sir Lucas Pepys, bluntly told his colleagues that since he saw no chance of her being able to marry, he feared for her life or her understanding.

This was putting it strongly. Yet Royal saw no alternative to the tepid routine of the terrace walks at Windsor or the sluggish annual visit to Weymouth where, as she complained in exasperation to the Prince of Wales one wet summer, 'If we had not the resources of the Playhouse, I don't know what would become of us.' Clearly this was long before royal princesses were ever-occupied with their insatiable routines of official duty. Yet we read that the Princess Royal accompanied her mother in schemes of benevolence and philanthropy and one year the elder sisters took part in a visit to the University of Oxford, during vacation time, 'going in and out of the colleges'. Another year, the Royal Family paid a visit of inspection to Whitbread's brewery, amid heartfelt cheers, and a West Country tour took them further afield, to the

* The phrase of 'Prince Royal' as a definition for the heir apparent of Prussia is of interest, although the usage appears to have scant historical evidence in Europe before the eighteenth century.

naval base at Plymouth and to a ladies' boarding-school at Sherborne, where the pupils all loyally wore the inscription 'God Save the King' across their white uniform.

One can see the shape of distant things to come, even if these functions were mere pencil sketches to the glowing royal canvas of the busy future. One is led to the interesting reflection that the endless duties of today's supporting cast of the monarchy may have originated as an antidote to boredom. The Prince of Wales saw all too clearly the cause of his elder sister's pale looks and intense depression: 'the constant restraint, the tiresome and confined life . . . but what was worse than all, the violence and caprice of her mother's temper, which hourly grows worse, to which she is obliged to be absolutely a slave . . .'

And then, when the Princess Royal was in her thirtieth year and her prospects seemed blackest, there came an envoy to the King asking that the Hereditary Prince Frederick William of Wurttemberg might seek his eldest daughter's hand. The unrelenting monarch kept the representative waiting for four months. The would-be bridegroom was a widower with three young children, the brother indeed of Peter of Oldenburg's dead wife. In the background lingered an unpleasant rumour that Frederick William's wife had run away with a Russian and was perhaps still alive. The King brooded and hesitated while the weeks went by until the Princess grew feverish with waiting. When, after some months, her father finally gave her freedom of choice, she accepted her suitor much in the spirit of a blind date, for she still did not know what he looked like and had but a vague idea of his age.

A miniature of the Prince arrived, showing him to be rotund of feature but firm-chinned and soldierly, and another three months passed before her father permitted her to send a portrait of herself in return. When Royal proposed to send a small trinket as a betrothal gift, the King sternly forbade her, and would permit nothing. Her future husband was to come to England, and it is small wonder that the nervous bride succumbed to jaundice as the time drew near. 'She is ten times yellower than yesterday,' Princess Elizabeth reported to the Prince of Wales.

Frederick William had still expected that some small engagement token would arrive, if only to create a good impression among his people but the King remained enigmatic and unwelcoming. 'Not a ring to show!' cried the Prince, ruefully extending his fingers to his ally, Lady Harcourt. 'Not a ring to show!'

## III

George III's unwillingness to yield his daughter to the hazards of a continental marriage was the logical outcome of the terror spread through the courts of Europe by the French Revolution and the rapid rise of Napoleon. At one time the King even pleaded the inclement weather to cause the Hereditary Prince of Wurttemberg to postpone his arrival and so gained a purposeful respite of six months. When, irretrievably, the patient bridegroom landed at Harwich in April, 1797, the King intimated that nothing was ready and said he had better remain incognito. An absurd situation developed. The newcomer obliged by pretending not to be there at all and he visited friends, while the Princess ignored his presence and worked herself into a frantic state of nerves.

When they eventually met, after a month's delay, she was 'almost dead with terror' and tongue-tied at the sight of the corpulent middle-aged man who took her hand. 'The Queen was obliged to speak her answers,' says Fanny Burney. 'The Prince said he hoped this would be the last disturbance he would ever occasion her. She then tried to recover', and with an effort indeed she succeeded in joining in the general conversation.

Only two weeks later, they were married at the Chapel Royal. The bridegroom was in fact better looking than most people had expected. The bride was supposed to have made her own trousseau stitch by stitch—there had been ample time for it—but her sister Augusta wrote more truthfully, 'It was Mama. You know what a figure (Royal) made of herself with her odd manner of dressing. Mama said "Now, really, Princess Royal, this one time is the last. I cannot suffer you to make such a sight of yourself, so I really will have you dressed properly." '

In 'a nuptial habit of white satin', with a train of fur-trimmed crimson velvet, the Princess went to the altar of the Chapel Royal as indeed a final credit to her family. In a uniform silk shot with gold and silver, richly embroidered, with many decorations, the plump bridegroom looked his best, but could not outshine her. As the wedding reception drew to an end, the finery was sprinkled with tears. The bride's five sisters surrounded her, sobbing wildly. The bride in turn clung weeping to her father, who could not speak, while tears flowed down his cheeks. Only the Queen, shrewd and sensible, made sure that the Princess took with her lengths of silk and other rich materials to be made up in 'the fashion prevalent in her new country'. The happy pair left in the King's travelling post-chaise for a honeymoon at Windsor, and were intended to embark on their journey to Wurttemberg five days later. But, character-istic of the prevailing absurdity, the frigate assigned to them was involved in the mutiny of the Fleet at the Nore and another delay ensued before a substitute ship could be found.

Lady Charlotte Bruce was to accompany the couple part way and at the last moment a royal messenger rushed up the ship's gang-plank waving a letter for her. It was from the bride's youngest sister, the fourteen-year-old Princess Amelia (whom incidentally the Princess Margaret of our own day so closely resembles in looks). 'My heart is so full with parting from my dear Sister that I cannot write. Pray say everything that is kind to dear Royal—tell her how sincerely I love her.'

## IV

Royal had married not merely to escape the bondage of Bucking-ham House and St. James's and Windsor, not only because she found traits to admire in her husband or thought it high time to have one, but also because she passionately longed to have children of her own. Packed into her luggage were two complete layettes of baby clothes, one for a boy, one for a girl. Her eldest brother had become the father of a girl—Princess Charlotte—only the previous year, and in writing to her brother of 'dear little Char-lotte' she confided, 'I look forward with great anxiety to the moment when I shall be equally blessed'.

Now she travelled to her goal along roads rutted by Napoleon's armies and felt an extra savour of reality to her dream when she first met her young step-daughter. Princess Catherine of Wurttem-berg was just in her teens, 'a very handsome girl, the image of her father', as Royal wrote home. Her elder stepson was away at school, but the younger boy was no less pleasing. She was soon calling him 'my little Paul . . . a very comical boy . . . The Duke' she added, 'accuses me of spoiling him!' It was as well that she adopted these children and took them to her heart so affectionately, for she was to be denied her fond hopes and, in the following year, her own baby was still-born. Her husband's tragic letter with this news speaks with its own pathos; among her letters lodged in the Royal Archives: 'Our dearest hopes of the summer are suddenly destroyed.' And to her father the Princess presently wrote in a shaky hand, 'I trust that I submit with resignation to the will of the Almighty . . . the loss of the little thing I had built such happiness on.'

Shortly after their marriage, Frederick William succeeded as Duke of Wurttemberg on the death of his father, and his wife was thus Princess Royal, Duchess of Wurttemberg. Within five years Napoleon elevated him to the rank of Elector, his wife thus Electress. A strange link of marriage then occurred, for Royal's good-looking step-daughter, Catherine, married none other than Napoleon's brother, Jerome, and so the eldest daughter of the King of England became unintentionally step-mother-in-law to the brother of her country's worst enemy. In some token of this relationship, Napoleon sponsored Wurttemberg as a kingdom. This was at the time of the short-lived Peace of Amiens, and the new Queen of Wurttemberg, Princess Royal of Great Britain, could not resist writing to her mother with a touch of the style by which Queens may formally address one another, 'My very dear Mother and Sister'. Queen Charlotte's indignation was intense.

The new Queen was never to see her parents again. Her husband, however, was so affectionate, considerate and endearing that he made up for much. When she had first arrived in Wurttemberg as a bride, he had hung a portrait of her father in her room, copied from the original painting at Windsor, and other thoughtful and sympathetic gestures continued to deck her married life. As a wildly absurd whim, she asserted on one occasion that she would like a couple of kangaroos; and her husband not only ultimately provided a pair but built a graceful little house for their shelter. During the brief Peace of 1805, Royal and her husband had some English visitors and one of them, Lady Brownlow, has left her impressions of, in effect, two domesticated little dumplings, the King playing whist at a table cut out to fit snugly around his immense middle the Queen 'shapeless, with a pleasant good-humoured face, her hair frizzed and powdered'.

Then, alas, the wars began again and for nine anxious years the plump Queen was practically cut off from her family. It is Napoleon, in visiting her capital, who next tells of his appreciation. Royal found herself expected to entertain him, and she evidently played all the right cards. 'It was of course very painful to me to receive him with civility,' she observed, in defending this meeting years later, 'but the least failure on my part might have deprived my husband of this kingdom.' Royal, indeed, treated her visitor with flattering respect. When he admired some Lyons embroideries she grandly assured him they were her own handiwork, and the Emperor went away correspondingly impressed.

Her tactful connivings fended off many French inroads on her people and her Wurttembergers at home knew little of the hardships that so desperately oppressed Coburg farther east. Her feminine diplomacy was laid out with every delicacy, still later, when writing her brother—who had since become Regent—a careful but slightly whitewashed account of the course of events in her husband's little dominion during the Napoleonic interlude. For nine years, as she said, she had been 'cut off from all confidential correspondence with the best and dearest of relations'. These were years when she developed her own interests: her 'charities unbounded', her model farm 'quite in the English style', the art of painting on porcelain—some of her pieces are still preserved at Windsor. As time went by, she happily watched the progress of the courtship and marriages of her step-sons. But what happiness it was, after Napoleon's defeat, to receive a special emissary from London, to be able to talk over the illness of her father and to have the first real news of all her sisters. 'How much it soothes my mind to be acquainted with every circumstance,' sighed the rotund little Queen.

The Prince Regent proposed a visit to England, but now it was her husband's turn to put his foot down, taking umbrage because the invitation was addressed to the Queen of Wurttemberg rather than to its King. Royal pretended to be not sufficiently well to make the journey, and a cynical ambassador was amused to note her cough 'in a very painful and violent manner', with one eye on her husband, in farcical proof of the apology. Though her husband grew irascible in his last years, she handled him lightly. 'You must take no notice of him,' she sometimes warned her friends—and he died in 1816. Henceforth she always wore black and kept a widow's cap in her pocket which she donned for visitors or official events. When the Prince Regent unwisely hinted that husband and wife had not always seen eye to eye, she took up her pen indignantly. 'Believe me, never could I have been as happy with him as I was had not our minds been congenial.'

With her step-son now King of Wurttemberg, she discovered a new serenity in her role as Dowager Queen and found that the affairs of her adopted land involved her so deeply that she felt no real wish to visit England. Two of her younger brothers, Kent and Cambridge, paid her visits instead, to be followed in 1819 and 1821 by two of her sisters. Princess Elizabeth, having recently married the Prince of Hesse-Homburg, was now within a two-day coach journey but found her 'greatly changed'. So must it often be in families after long separation. The following year Princess Augusta confessed, 'Had I not seen the picture I should not have recognized her. What strikes most is that from not wearing the least corset her hips are something quite extraordinary.' Even the attraction of her brother's coronation as George IV was not sufficient to draw Royal home to England, and nearly seven years elapsed before she at last made the journey.

She was now sixty-two and wrote to prepare her brother beforehand, announcing in the style of the day that she was 'an old woman whose strength does not allow her doing many things'. For boarding the yacht indeed she requested 'that there may be a chair to draw me up in, with my shortness of breath'. Despite these warnings, the King was determined to entertain her royally. We have this final glimpse of the visit in 1827 when the Dowager Queen drove to Royal Lodge and, as Princess Augusta noted, the King was 'enchanted with her company'. A dinner party had been arranged on the banks of Virginia Water and 'after coffee we took a delightful row until after nine o'clock by moonlight, my sister and the dear King as happy as it is possible to be'. And no doubt the company earlier in the day had included the eight-year-old Princess Victoria—the future Queen—whom Royal had looked forward to seeing. 'I long to see Vicky,' she had written, 'and hope she will take a fancy to me.'

The Princess Royal died the following year. On the previous evening her English maid read to her, as she did most evenings, and the Princess as usual listened attentively. Then she said, as her maid closed the book, 'There, my dear, you have done, and I thank you. You will never read me another.'

## ENTRACTE

*King George IV's only daughter, the Princess Charlotte, passed from the scene before he came to the Throne. Born in 1796, and named after both her aunt, the Princess Royal, and her grandmother, Queen Charlotte, she died in childbirth in 1817, a year after her marriage to Prince Leopold of Coburg. He subsequently became King of Belgium and has gained a more lasting renown as Queen Victoria's celebrated 'Uncle Leopold'. With the passing of the Princess Royal Charlotte, Queen of Wurttemberg, in 1828, the distinction lapsed for the third time and remained vacant for twelve years.*

# 4 Princess Royal, Empress of Prussia

## I

At two o'clock in the morning of November 21st, 1840, Buckingham Palace was flung into a ferment by the imminent arrival of Queen Victoria's first baby. Servants were roused from their beds, candles newly lit, fires freshly stoked and a frantic procession of housemaids carried cans of hot water along the endless mirrored corridors to the Queen's bedroom. At the chill break of dawn, messengers rode horseback to gather in the Prime Minister, the Archbishop of Canterbury, the Home Secretary and other yawning Ministers and personages innumerable.

'Nothing ready!' the young Queen scribbled, during some respite later that day, in her private journal. In the same volume, on February 11th, Queen Victoria had written of the rapture of being with Prince Albert on their honeymoon. The baby expected shortly before Christmas was more punctual than foreseen. All those about the Queen confidently expected a male heir to the Throne, the first occasion—as they reminded one another—of such an event for more than eighty years. Albert sat at his wife's side as the morning hours passed, swallowing a hasty breakfast and foregoing his lunch. Then, shortly before two p.m., those waiting in the ante-room heard the cry of a child and the voice of Dr. Lacock came to them through the open door, 'Oh, Ma'am, it is a Princess.'

'Never mind,' said the young Queen, cheerfully. 'It will be a Prince next time.'

'A fine healthy princess,' Dr. Lacock now reassured her.

Prince Albert then hurried off to give the news to a Privy Council meeting, 'a princess', we may note, and not a Princess Royal. 'Albert, father of a daughter,' the jubilant husband next wrote to his brother, 'You will laugh at me!' And a footman crossed the cobbled forecourt of the Palace to secure a written notice to the railings: 'This afternoon at ten minutes before two o'clock the Queen was happily delivered of a Princess . . . Her

Majesty and the young Princess are, God be praised, both doing well.'

*The Times* lost no time nevertheless in styling the baby 'Princess Royal', and we soon find Queen Victoria incautiously using the phrase as she writes to her Uncle Leopold that the Princess Royal, not yet four weeks old 'gains daily in health, strength and, I may add, beauty'.

But the Queen saw her infant daughter only twice a day at this stage, and much of the credit for the baby's improvement was due to Mrs. Packer, the wet nurse, who had 'studied with a view to becoming a public singer' and from whose operatic bosom the Princess extracted her first nourishment. (The diet was subsequently discouragingly varied with ass's milk.) Victoria, indeed, at first remained aloof from the duties and pleasures of maternity in a way that might dismay us today. It was Albert who dandled the baby in his arms and carefully carried her on his lap during the Christmas journey to Windsor. It was Albert who warned the coachman to be on his guard for ice or pot-holes, and who no doubt supervised the baby's travel dose of dill-water. Over the holiday, the Queen watched the baby being bathed, which was only the second time she had joined this domestic ceremony. And undoubtedly it was Albert, with the secretarial aid of the invaluable Stockmar, who ensured that the child truly received her 'style and distinction' when fifty-nine days old, with the Royal Warrant of January 19th, 1841 conferring arms on 'Our most dear daughter the Princess Royal'. If the proud young papa did not actually carry the baby to her baptism three weeks later, he composed a solemn chorale for the occasion and was prime stage manager at the christening at the golden font in the Palace throne-room when the child was named Victoria Adelaide Mary Louise.

To the Queen for a time she became 'Pussy' . . . 'quite a little toy for us'. Instead of bathing the baby, the Queen painted her—in water-colours, to be exact—and found 'the Child' an irresistible study when at play with a dog and, later on, during Landseer's drawing and etching lessons. Yet when the Prince of Wales was born—on November 9th, 1841—Pussy was found to be 'terrified and not at all pleased with her brother'. She was in fact no longer the plump infant whom the Queen found too heavy to carry, but a pale, thin little waif whose sickly looks led to one of the rare quarrels between husband and wife. Albert stormed that the nursery women had mismanaged the child and poisoned her with calomel. 'And you have starved her!' he flung at his wife. The Queen wailed that he wanted to drive her out of the nursery; she was miserable and wished she had never married him.

The storm quickly subsided, of course. The nursery was re-formed. The Queen was soon giving thanks on knowing 'what *real* happiness means', writing her journal while holding Pussy on her lap. Albert liked to play the organ dandling his son on one knee and dancing his daughter on the other. One of the Queen's charming sketches in her picture-album shows Pussy, more sturdy and rounded now, trying to clamber into a bath-tub. Soon she was 'all graceful and prettiness, very fat and active'. As Princess Royal she was taken out driving every day in the carriage so that the crowds could see her, and was received with so many smiles that her governess considered she would soon have seen 'every pair of teeth in the kingdom'.

At the age of four or five she came down regularly to family luncheon. Returning to Osborne years later, she remembered all the fond summers of her childhood and found her little wheelbarrow and garden tools, marked with her initials, still in the thatched garden-shed, and her toy cooking implements still polished and bright in the playhouse of the rustic Swiss Cottage.

## II

'Pussy' could do no wrong. When she outgrew the nickname and graduated to 'Vicky' she remained her Papa's favourite more firmly and fondly. In contrast to the harsh tutorial discipline and stinging disapproval meted out to her younger brother, Bertie, the Prince of Wales, the Queen found Vicky 'very clever . . . far above her age'. She appeared the perfect examplar indeed of the early Froebel methods of learning by play, which her governess, Lady Lyttleton, practised with quiet tact and commonsense. While Bertie suffered under a tutor aptly named Birch, Vicky spiritedly refused to ask forgiveness for her minor misdemeanours, 'for I mean to be just as naughty another time'. While Bertie was 'stubborn', any obstinacy on Vicky's part appeared to her parents simply to demonstrate force of character. Her wilfulness funished material for indulgent family anecdotes, and she got away with it, 'the sly little rogue'.

Stepping into her early teens, it was Vicky however who brought the status of Princess Royal a new prestige and tangible public reality unknown during earlier reigns. The sources of her youthful early popularity sprang deep from the mainstream of Victorian family sentiment. As the first-born in the romance of the young Queen and the handsome and manly Prince Albert, she was never to be usurped in public affection by her younger brothers and sisters. When Landseer painted her in a family group, the ringlets and smiles were duplicated in best-selling tens of thousands by the popular engravers. The Queen approved the widespread sale, and considered that such portraits 'would do good'. The art of public relations had not yet tinged the vocabulary and Landseer's sugared child was a fixed public image, growing continually more remote from the real personality. Yet the more cultivated elements of public opinion would have been attracted, too, could they have known, that as time went by the Princess was studying Latin declensions before breakfast and reading a carefully edited version of Gibbon's *Decline and Fall*.

Prince Albert was also his daughter's chief tutor, encouraging her to read English history and to study Shakespeare, as well as to share his own painting lessons. Father and child sat side by side, when she was barely ten, as he took her into his own intellectual world, couching the political news of the day for simple juvenile digestion, and taking her more closely into his confidence as he gravely explained his plans for the great 1851 Exhibition. As the shimmering miracle of the Crystal Palace rose in Hyde Park, he took Vicky along to share his sense of wonder and achievement. The workmen paused in astonishment at the sight of the little girl wandering among the scaffolding, and marvelled that she asked sensible questions.

On the great opening day, the ten-year-old child was entrusted with the responsibility of guiding the twenty-year-old Prince Frederick William of Prussia, and she showed him round faultlessly, answering his questions in effortless German, her knowledge of the exhibits never failing. Prince Albert meanwhile watched their companionship with close approval, seething with plans that his plump and pretty eldest girl and the tall, slim, fair German prince should one day be joined in marriage and link Prussia and

England in a partnership to ensure the lasting peace of Europe. The Prince Consort lived to see the marriage and the first-born son and daughter of the marriage, though spared the knowledge that his dream of peace would collapse in hideous war.

Not five years after the Exhibition, the young Prince 'Fritz' visited Balmoral and met, not the child who had shown him around a crystal wonderland, but the same Vicky grown into a thoughtful and attractive girl of fourteen. She had travelled a little since their last meeting, visiting Paris with her parents, catching a happy glimpse of herself while waltzing in the Gallery of Mirrors at Versailles and deciding that perhaps, after all, she was pretty. The coquette was dawning in the blue eyes of the teenager. Driving out with Mama one day, she is said to have dropped her handkerchief for the satisfying fun of seeing the equerries race to retrieve it, and the Queen, wisely, stopped the carriage and ordered her to fetch it herself. But trudging through the Balmoral heather with the impressionable Fritz, Vicky knew what was expected. She gave his hand a perceptible squeeze, and the young man spent a sleepless night and next day asked her parents if he could 'belong to the family?' The possibility was agreed and the plot thickened. Out riding with the Princess a few days later Fritz seized his opportunity. They had moved a little away from the others and he dismounted to pluck her a sprig of white heather. On returning to the Castle, she rushed to her mother's room and broke into tears declaring she had never been so happy in her life, for Fritz had kissed her. And then came the change from tears to joy, as the Queen noted in her journal, 'with an indescribably happy look'.

The betrothed innocent was not yet fifteen and Prince Fritz, of course, agreed to await his bride for at least two years. Yet the secret betrothal was already widely known before he revisited Osborne in May, 1857, just six months before Vicky's seventeenth birthday, a visit timed with Prussian precision. His uncle, the King of Prussia, blandly assumed the wedding would be in Germany, an idea Queen Victoria crushed out of hand. 'The assumption of its being too much for a Prince Royal of Prussia to come over to marry the Princess Royal of Great Britain in England is too absurd . . . Whatever may be the usual practice of Prussian Princes, it is not every day that one marries the eldest daughter of the Queen of England. . .' And so Fritz came and saw and was reconquered by a new Vicky, the more womanly princess whom Winterhalter painted just then with her wide eyes and full red lips and charming bouffant coiffure.

The marriage was to prove extremely happy, although destined to be steeped in tragic circumstances. By a mischance the official engagement announcement was timed when the court was in mourning for the last of the sisters of that earlier Princess Royal who had become Queen of Wurttemberg, but it was becoming increasingly difficult to find occasions when the courts of Europe were entirely free of formal gloom in the ever-changing galaxy of royal relatives. More decisively to be judged a portent was an incident at Windsor when Vicky had just replied to one of her first letters of congratulation and the taper of the sealing-wax accidentally set fire to her dress. Her arm was burned and painful for some time; and historians have seldom failed to note that her eldest son was to be the hated Kaiser Wilhelm who set the world in flames.

Victoria and Albert had been married on a rainy February day at the Chapel Royal, St. James's. Vicky and Fritz were espoused in the same setting on a day of January mist and walked down the aisle to Mendelssohn's Wedding March, a piece which has retained its popularity ever since, thanks to the inaugural performance for the royal bride. For the first time also the young couple appeared on the Buckingham Palace balcony to acknowledge the tremendous crowd and so instituted a tradition long to be observed for royal weddings. Then, at Windsor, Vicky found herself alone with her bridegroom and felt miserably tongue-tied.

Although she was to spend the next thirty years with Fritz, she had hitherto matched companionship with him for no more than thirty days. She was to face lifelong exile, too, with a host of cold-featured Prussian relatives, few of whom she had met until her wedding reception and a honeymoon dinner-party at Windsor, and only when she clung to her mother in farewell did all the consequences—the enormity—of accepting Fritz sweep her in a tide of emotion. On her wedding-eve, she had told her mother. 'I hope to be worthy to be your child', and the Queen saw that it was like 'taking a poor lamb to be sacrificed'. From the royal yacht that carried the newly-weds on the first stage of their journey 'home'—to Germany—the bride wrote to her father, 'I thought my heart was going to break when you shut the cabin door . . . I felt weighed down by grief . . . I miss you so dreadfully.' Yet she was now a Princess of Prussia, and she had never been more of a Princess Royal than when, stepping ashore at the Scheldt, she set her own feelings aside and gaily smiled and waved to the waiting crowd.

## III

There is a story that one of her new in-laws welcomed the little bride that wintry February in Berlin and enquired, 'Are you not frozen?' Vicky responded with her brightest smile and answered, 'I have only one warm place—and that is my heart'. And it was true that she shivered despite the rapturous welcome from the packed roadsides: Germany was far colder in every way, more alien and much more terrifying than she had expected, The comparative warmth and domestic cosiness of Buckingham Palace, Osborne and Windsor had ill-prepared her for the dreary pomp and chill Berlin Schloss, nor could she have ever imagined beginning her married life in a horrifying suite of second-floor rooms which had been unoccupied for eighteen years, ever since a former king had died there. Fritz never appeared to notice the tattered brocades, the cobwebs that blackened the curtains, the dust that lay grey on the threadbare carpeting. The wind whistled down the large chimneys, mysteriously blowing doors open of their own accord until young Vicky half-believed the eerie stories of haunting by the Hohenzollern White Lady, as one of the Princess Royal's maids-of-honour has told.

There was no bathroom, no wardrobes for her pretty dresses and nothing better to read by than candlelight. But what was worse, her boudoir adjoined the dark death chamber of the former king, where nothing was ever changed except the wreaths on the counterpane. Vicky discovered that the servants distrusted her as a newcomer: she resolved to make the best of things and 'keep out of scrapes' but found that a hint of complaint, no matter how tactful, angered everyone and often Fritz himself. She had besides to acquaint herself with the rules of court etiquette far more stiff and unbending than any she had ever known in England. When she accidentally sneezed during a court reception, the old Queen—her aunt-in-law—haughtily cautioned her that a sneeze was not permitted in the presence of the Sovereign. Vicky said with irresistible laughter, 'We do not have such customs at home' and then ruefully perceived that she had said very much the wrong thing.

'We are young and inexperienced in a difficult position,' she wrote to her mother. 'I must confess that I cried bitterly last night at the thought of your going to dear Osborne, and without me. My pretty rooms that I loved so much . . .' Were there tears as she grasped her pen? On the other hand, a new home was in preparation in the fresh air of Potsdam—or rather, an old palace was put into repair—the ancient so-called Neue Palais that had mouldered since the days of Frederick the Great. Perhaps Vicky was exaggerating years later when she told her daughter, Sophie, that she had found thousands of dead bats in the rooms, and beds so full of insect life that they were fit only for burning. But the walls glowed golden in the sunlight; in the gardens Vicky saw flowering shrubs struggling beneath the knee-high weeds, and she and Fritz instinctively felt that they could be happy there.

Yet the struggle of renovation was long and tedious. The young couple's plans seemed constantly hindered by the procrastination of Fritz's uncle, the King. Without his autocratic permission, the builders could not provide piped water to replace the one pump in the courtyard, and he insisted on being consulted at every turn. It was a wonder, Vicky would hint good-humouredly, that she could have a child without an official mandate. Queen Victoria thought so, too, and insisted that her Scottish specialist, Dr. Martin, should be on hand in Berlin 'just in case'. The baby's arrival seemed imminent on the night of the Princess's first wedding anniversary, and a son was born two days later, though with such difficulty and danger that the German doctors abandoned hope. Only an urgent summons to the resourceful Dr. Martin saved both mother and child.

The year of absence had diminished none of the Princess Royal's popularity in the land of her birth. 'People here are all in ecstasies,' wrote Queen Victoria. 'Such pleasure, such delight—as if it were their own Prince and so it is too!' Only the irony of distant future events undermined her words. Then forty-two quarrelsome sponsors had to be invited to the christening. 'Most alarming!' said Queen Victoria, when she heard of this large gathering of godparents. For some months Vicky could not bring herself to tell her mother that her baby's left arm had been injured at birth. The little boy was all the more precious to the young parents, unaware as they were that the disability would be permanent.

Vicky had hoped to bring the baby to England for his grandmama to see him when he was five months old, but this was forbidden by the King's doctors and she came alone. It was wonderful to see her family again, to be greated jubilantly by her brothers and sisters, to find herself in the familiar rooms at Windsor. And yet in so many ways she felt a different person; the girl, with all her illusions, and the young wife and mother were no longer the same. She found herself eagerly writing to Fritz, 'In this room I experienced the happiest moment in my life when you took me in your arms as your wife and pressed me to your heart.'

## IV

When Vicky reached her twenty-first birthday, she thought it 'a most uninteresting age . . . I wish it was my eighteenth', although the two anniversaries were spanned by three years of astonishing event. She was married and doubly a mother: her daughter, Charlotte, was born when she was still only nineteen. Early in 1861 the old King of Prussia died, bringing Fritz a step closer to the throne and Vicky to her new role as Crown Princess. At her father-in-law's coronation, she found the ceremony one of 'magic tinges . . . wonderful beyond description', unaware that she herself seemed an enchanted figure to the hundreds in Konigsberg Cathedral and the thousands in the cobbled streets.

Yet the new reign was to intensify the rigid controls around Fritz and his wife and deepen the incessant demands of court etiquette until Vicky felt, as she said, 'a sort of slave'. In particular, her mother-in-law, the new Queen, insisted on her presence through a ceaseless round of court functions and thought nothing of arous-ing her from bed late at night if she felt a need of companionship. The Princess Royal had been trained to give philanthropic help to schools and hospitals, and was shocked to discover how ill such insitutions were run in her new country. As Crown Princess she felt an obligation to give a lead to a better state of affairs, but found that she dared not say a word on any improvement, since this would imply criticism of shortcomings at court. The only well-kept, buildings, she once said indignantly, were the barracks. But she had to submit to 'busy idleness', as she wrote to her mother, 'active waste of time'. She must avoid contention, ignore whole spheres of useful influence and could safely only dabble in painting and music to express her personality. Three weeks after her twenty-first birthday, the Princess heard from Windsor that the Prince Consort was ill but getting on favourably. Two days later she was, in fact, at the piano when Fritz came to her with a telegram in his hand and from his tragic look she knew that her father was dead.

Her first thought was to go to her mother at once. 'To be separated from you at this moment is a torture,' she wrote. But besides the anguish of grief there were early symptoms of pregnancy, and the doctors again officially forbade the journey. Fritz explained as best he could that the physicians meant well and merely desired care to be exercised for a child-to-be who might strengthen the line to the throne. To endure denial on such grounds, as if she were no more than a machine for maternity, could not have angered Vicky more deeply. She mastered her sense of humiliation if only to help keep the peace, for Fritz's sake—anything to quieten the constant troubles between Fritz and the King. Diplomacy soothed both sides and the Princess safely travelled to Osborne in early summer and returned in good time for her second son, Henry, to be born in Berlin.

Ultimately, Vicky had eight children, the youngest of whom, Princess Margaret of Hesse, endured the hardships of the Nazi war and lived to see the coronation of Elizabeth II, an old lady with memories of the reigns of two Queens Regnant and the lives of three Princesses Royal. One of this Princess Margaret's twin sons, indeed, married Princess Sophie of Greece, youngest sister of none other than our own Prince Philip, Duke of Edinburgh, thus completing a remarkable royal link with modern times.

Vicky herself died in the present century, in the same year as her mother. Yet this, too, rounded off a strange pattern of coincidence, for Fritz died in the same year as his father. Historians distinguish Vicky today as the Princess Royal, Empress of Prussia. But apart from her girlhood and early years of marriage, she spent twenty-seven years as Crown Princess of Prussia and was Empress for only ninety-nine days before spending thirteen years in semi-retirement as Dowager Empress and widow. After the three centuries in our cavalcade of princesses royal, she was the last to be, in any sense, victim of a marriage of state or convenience. Among princesses innumerable, she was moreover the only one to hold the valid distinction of Princess Royal almost from the cradle to the grave.

The status was never an easy one. Bismark rose to power in Prussia, the prototype of Hitler, wielding his baleful influence over the King, her father-in-law, convinced that the Princess could never 'leave the English-woman at home and become a Prussian'. Her own Fritz was in the Army, called to service whenever the mailed fist hardened into military action. 'They reprove me here for being too English,' she sadly wrote to her husband, during the frontier hostilities with Denmark. 'At home I am too Prussian. I can do nothing right.' When the Prussian army invaded Danish territory, the family rift became almost unbridgeable, for Vicky's closest brother, the Prince of Wales, was of course married to Princess Alexandra of Denmark, who saw all her family engulfed in the unprovoked war. Yet to her mother, behind these differences, Vicky could write privately of her love of England, 'my country which I shall love to my dying day, and be too proud to have belonged to ever to let myself forget'.

Tiny but obvious clues, a broken lock, a letter misplaced, soon warned the Princess that Bismark had planted spies within her household. The smell of tobacco as she lifted a desk-lid, papers disarranged when they had been tidy, enlarged suspicion to certainty. Torn between the land of her birth and the country of her married life, her worst crisis was during the Franco-Prussian war of 1870, a war which Vicky had thought Britain could prevent. Convinced that Fritz would be killed, she flung all her energies into a hospital which would tend wounded French and German troops alike, with nurses from a training school which she had inaugurated four years earlier. Because she disapproved of the bombardment of Paris, high circles in Germany considered her to be pro-French and at times almost an enemy agent. 'The order of the day is to vilify my wife,' Fritz despairingly mentioned in his journal.

When the war was won, however, the German principalities and petty kingdoms were for the first time a united realm, and Fritz's father was proclaimed German Emperor. (The reflection that her daughter would one day be an Empress made Queen Victoria wonder why she had herself not officially assumed the title of

Empress of India, and preparations for a Royal Titles Bill to make this possible were put in hand in London two years later.) Yet Vicky cherished no illusions of imperial grandeur. Her fears were for her son, Wilhelm, already—in his teens—riding at the head of victorious troops in his white uniform, boasting that he would one day make the German army the greatest in the world.

'You need not fear he will be brought up in a way to make him proud and stuck up,' Vicky reassured her mother. 'I hope to instil all that is most Christian, therefore most liberal, into his mind.' Like his pathetic crippled arm, these ideals were doomed to wither. On March 9th, 1888, when Fritz at last became German Emperor in succession to his own father, he took his wife, his Empress, in his arms and then sent a message to the new Crown Prince bidding him to be 'an example to all of fidelity'. But at this moment of the great change of destiny in their lives Vicky and her husband both knew their son could be no solace. Fritz was himself a sick and stricken man. Among the many messages of his accession, he could only thank his doctors for 'making me live long enough to reward the valiant courage of my wife'.

For Vicky, tragically, there could be no reward. The details of her husband's illness, amid the quarrelling doctors, are too painful to relate; and he had reigned as Emperor for ninety-nine days when he breathed his last. In her dazed state during her first shocked hours as a widow, Vicky did not realize why officers of Wilhelm's Hussars were searching her home, looking for papers that Fritz had already placed for safe keeping in England. All was in turmoil and, unable to withstand this callous invasion, she left the palace that night by a side-door with two of her ladies and sought refuge in a farmstead where she and her husband had often spent happier days.

The Empress was still only forty-eight when she returned to Windsor a few weeks later to seek the rest and recuperation of which she was so much in need. Her later portraits show a woman who had known great sadness, and steadfastness too. She could not however resist the urge to return to Germany and to settle in Fritz's native land, among the scenes and friends they both had known. 'One must never be frightened,' she once told a child. 'You may meet many things in life which seem terrifying and insurmountable, but if you face them with courage, you will find that somehow you are able to bear them.'

# ENTRACTE

The Princess Royal, Empress of Prussia, held the distinction of her initial style and title for more than sixty years and for longer than any princess before her. When she died in August, 1901, her younger brother was already King of England, reigning as Edward VII. Now the King and his beautiful consort, Queen Alexandra, had a son, later George V, and three daughters, the eldest of whom, Princess Louise, Duchess of Fife, was accorded the style and title of Princess Royal in the King's birthday honours of November 9th, 1905:

'The King has been graciously pleased to declare that His Majesty's eldest daughter, Her Royal Highness Princess Louise Victoria Alexandra Dagmar (Duchess of Fife), shall henceforth bear the style and title of Princess Royal. His Majesty has also directed that the daughters of Her Royal Highness shall bear the style of Princess prefixed to their respective Christian names, and that they shall have precedence and rank immediately after all members of the Royal Family enjoying the style of Royal Highness.'

# 5 The Princess Royal, Duchess of Fife

## I

Destiny dealt the Monarchy a poorish hand in princesses towards the closing years, or rather decades, of the last century. They stare from the old photographs of family groups at Abergeldie or house-parties at Sandringham, looking wan and snuffly; and one can readily believe Queen Victoria's dictum to her own eldest daughter, the Empress Frederick, that 'the health of those girls is not enough looked after'. Perhaps the unsmiling, apathetic effect was due to the time exposure, or else to a different matter of timing, for it can be argued that they were born too soon, too rapidly, one after the other—Princess Louise of Wales in 1867, Princess Victoria of Wales in 1868, Princess Maud of Wales in 1869. The sequence is all the more debatable when one remembers that their two elder brothers, Prince Albert Victor (Duke of Clarence) and Prince George (later George V) were born respectively in 1864 and 1865. The children were seldom more than eighteen months apart, usually less, a tribute to the maternal vitality of the young Princess Alexandra, Princess of Wales.

The first-comer, as is well-known, made his imminent arrival evident during a skating party at Windsor and was born, a three pound twelve ounce baby boy, two months premature, that same evening. Only a Windsor town doctor attended the unforeseen event, the infant's layette was in London, and so the child was hastily wrapped in a flannel petticoat, and when the royal doctors arrived and fussed around the young mother she laughed in their faces. The birth of her first daughter was to be more difficult.

She, too, was a winter baby. The young parents, not then married four years, had spent Christmas at Sandringham Hall. Despite the bright log fires, the old house struck cold and damp. In the New Year the snow was slow to melt and the Princess returned to London complaining of a raging throat and agonizing pain, especially in her knee. The doctors, in fact, diagnosed rheumatic fever and the surgeon, Sir James Paget, cautiously affirmed that Sandringham Hall might be damp and that dampness might be a contributory factor.

The Prince of Wales declared they would never spend another night there again. Nor did they, until the new Sandringham House was ready for occupation nearly four years later, a marvel of modernity complete with 'piped heating' and a light tramway in the cellar to help carry coals to every room. Five days after the onset of her illness, the Princess gave birth to a daughter, in desperate pain, 'wishing for choloroform very much' as her husband wrote pathetically, though the doctors thought it best it should be denied her. The child who entered the world thus unpropitiously was a future Princess Royal.

'The child ought to be called Victoria,' the Queen wrote forcefully, meaning as a first name. But the young mother wished her to be called Louise, after her favourite sister-in-law. She wished, too, to compliment her own sister, Dagmar, who had just married the heir to the throne of all the Russias, and she had her way. There were also many friends and relatives, both English and Danish, who had not yet acted as sponsors to her children, 'such hosts of sponsors', as Queen Victoria grumbled. On May 10th, when the baby was three months old, Alexandra had to be wheeled in a chair into the christening ceremony in the Marlborough House chapel. She was indeed to be lame for life, as a result of her illness, and walked with stick or parasol ever after.

'Louise Victoria Alexandra Dagmar' . . . they were pretty names for an unpretty child. When her two sisters were born within the next two years, first Victoria and then Maud, Queen Victoria still considered them 'puny and pale . . . poor frail little fairies'. Others however thought almost the opposite, and saw them as 'rampaging little girls', thoroughly spoiled, half-smothered in mother love, and almost beyond the control of their nurse, Nanny Blackburn. The Duke of Devonshire lent his suburban house, Chiswick Park, to the Wales's for several summers, and the children were driven out from Marlborough House to play in the grounds on summer afternoons, clambering over the ornamental sphinxes and obelisks so riotously that the scars remain to this day. A protesting gardener was kicked savagely on the shins; an unwary tutor who taught the boys to shoot with bows and arrows soon found himself pressed into the target role of a running deer. It seems appropriate that Chiswick House became a lunatic asylum a few years later.

Royal cousins, Tecks and Battenbergs, thought the Wales's a harum-scarum lot, though often amusing, and country house romps —riding a pony up the staircase to the bedrooms, sliding hilariously down the staircase on a tea tray—were long remembered. All the service-bells in the house were rung one morning, bringing out the staff in pandemonium. Princess Alexandra, who was deaf, missed most of the uproar. 'They *are* dreadfully wild, but I was just as bad,' she fondly apologized to a guest. Admitting that the boys were 'a handful', the Prince of Wales allowed the servants to administer chastisement, and the boys and girls alike soon grew inured to smacks and cuffs. The young 'Wales's' were in fact an early instance of the indulgent creed of not repressing youthful high spirits. The Duchess of Teck thought the girls 'a dear little trio' when she watched them riding their ponies to hounds for the first time, at an age when most children were unseen and not heard in the nursery. 'Wild as hawks' was Queen Victoria's more descriptive phrase. 'Such ill-bred, ill-trained children! I can't fancy them at all.'

Bringing up her own family with kindness but strictness, she could never have agreed that rollicking self-expression might create a lively, self-confident and pioneering new generation of royalty. For bets of a penny each, Papa—the Prince of Wales—would sit in one of his opulent armchairs and allow his small fry to race slices of buttered toast down his outstretched trousered leg, the smoother the butter the faster the slide, contests that never reached the Queen's ears. In her role as 'Motherdear', Alexandra took pains to have them all taught music and loved to take the girls home to her parents in Denmark. One of her few differences with Queen Victoria occurred, indeed, when the Queen refused permission for little Louise to undertake the journey.

The Prince of Wales wrote in no uncertain terms to his mother. 'Alix has made herself nearly quite ill with the worry. You can imagine how hurt and pained she has been . . . her whole life is wrapped up in her children'—and the Queen changed her mind. The children themselves eagerly looked forward to these excursions, the opportunities for enjoyment with Greek and Danish cousins of their own age, when the grown-ups would be too busy to notice their even wilder uninhibited freedom. Holiday visits to their grand-mama at Balmoral, on the other hand, resulted in 'outbursts'. While her elder sisters broke into floods of tears, the youngest, Maud, was known to stamp her feet and scream, 'I won't, WON'T go!'

Princess Louise could be mollified only when travelling trunks were seen to be stuffed with 'battered toys and rickety old dolls'. All the childhood affections of the group centred on these old favourites rather than the stream of new and novel playthings. One of the Chiswick footmen took pity on the boys in this respect and spent all his spare time carving them wooden boats. The parents seemed undisturbed when the girls' governess, Miss Brown, re-ported that they could hardly be 'bothered with books'. In their later teens their playmate and distant cousin, Princess May of Teck (who became Queen Mary) discovered with surprise that their education was languishing behind her own. Her mother, the Duchess of Teck, included May in her own philanthropic activities, teaching her always to think of others less fortunate than herself, taking her to a home for infirm widows to hand out packets of sugar and tea, and encouraging her to take a dinner to a destitute family.

May was no prig but on one occasion when vigorously describ-ing one of these expeditions, she found that Louise hardly knew what she was talking about. Princess Alexandra—Motherdear—also scarcely realized that her children were growing up. 'A *children's party* for Louise's *nineteenth* birthday,' Princess May wrote to one of her aunts in disgust. 'Does that not seem too ridiculous?'

## II

The fact is that the Wales sisters were never encouraged to emerge from family life. In those warm, cluttered rooms where they sur-rounded themselves with an accumulation of small objects—china animals, sea-shells, tiny vases—they lived in a warm juvenile world where they were Looloo, Toria and Maudie, while always their brothers were adored as 'Eddy' and 'Georgie'. As the Princesses Louise, Victoria and Maud, they stiffly prided themselves on being thoroughly royal and, in the course of this assertion, became too shy to utter a word.

And so the Wales daughters gaze lugubriously from the photographs, unsmiling even for Motherdear's amateur camera. Their lively cousin, Queen Marie of Roumania, never forgot the melancholy that seemed to creep into their every sentence: 'It gave a special quality to all talks with them, as though life would have been very wonderful and everything very beautiful if it had not been so sad.' The Baroness de Stoeckl similarly amusingly noted the characteristic conversation of one of the three sisters, Princess Victoria, while visiting an old folks' home in Harrogate. 'Poor dear, how long have you been here?' the Princess questioned one inmate. 'Twenty years? You must miss your home, you must be so lonely. My heart breaks for you.' The old lady attempted to reassure her that this had long been home and that all the other patients were her friends. 'Poor, poor dear,' murmured the royal visitor. 'You think you are so happy, but you are not.' By the time such enlivening remarks had been repeated in every ward, the entire old folks' home was in tears. 'It is wonderful to do some good, cheering up these poor old souls,' said the Princess, as a parting shot.

Princess Louise was no better equipped, driving at her mother's side in the park, watching the hats politely doffed, or else 'graciously attending' a floral church service to benefit a children's hospital. Her mother occasionally toured her through the Great Ormond Street Children's Hospital, but the only fruit of these visits was that Looloo's future husband ultimately became president. Seldom encouraged to share the popularity of the Prince and Princess of Wales, the Wales girls were also over-shadowed by the more lively prestige of Queen Victoria's younger daughters. One can imagine the zestful captions of modern times if we had a Princess Lulu or even a Princess Loo. But for Princess Louise of Wales there was the especial lifelong handicap of confusion with her aunt, Princess Louise, who in fact outlived her. The light of biography shines with comparative brightness on the elder Princess Louise (later Marchioness of Lorne, Duchess of Argyll) and but dimly on Princess Louise, Duchess of Fife (and eventually Princess Royal). In the long account, both temperament and training unfitted her to the latter distinction. As *The Times* was ultimately at pains to sum up, 'The public appearances entailed by her rank were few and this accorded well with her own inclination.'

In her twenty-first summer, Looloo seemed particularly low and depressed, and lively Princess May felt called on to mount a rescue operation. This was readily done by including her in a family holiday to Switzerland and the Italian lakes. The future Queen Mary eagerly looked forward to the jaunt, 'as we are great friends and so fond of each other', but Looloo's spirits were as dismal as the rainclouds that concealed the Alps. From St. Moritz she was eager to move on to Como, from Como to Bellagio, always 'anxious to see a place to say she had been there' but quickly bored if she could not move to the next. The Duchess of Teck decided she had 'the same inert, apathetic nature' as her brother, Prince Eddy, but in fairness she may have misjudged the true cause of Louise's alternating moping and restlessness. In reality, the Princess was worrying about a man with whom she found herself falling in love and wondering, too, with her utter lack of self-confidence, whether he or anyone else would ever be willing to marry her.

She had doubtless heard something of the difficulties years earlier when her Aunt Louise had fallen impetuously in love not with a foreign prince but with the young Scottish Marquess of Lorne. The marriage had not turned out happily, and within seven years Aunt Louise's aversion to her husband grew so overwhelming that, when he served his second stint as Governor-General in Canada, she refused to accompany him and risked a public scandal.

Would family history repeat itself? The shy young Louise had intimate cause to ponder the question, for the man on whom she had set her heart was also a Scotsman, whom everyone called Macduff, one of her father's friends, tall and rugged in looks but with the drawback of being eighteen years older than herself. The public romantically imagined that she had first seen him from a distance while watching the guns at Sandringham. The family picture was that he was one of the few closer friends of the Prince of Wales of whom the Queen approved, a Scotsman of irreproachable lineage, of vast ancestral acres and banking wealth. Through one family line, he was a great-grandson of William IV and Mrs. Jordan, which was respectable enough, and he was in fact a Balmoral neighbour and had served as Member of Parliament for the adjacent constituency of Elgin and Nairnshire. Shortly after he had succeeded his father as sixth Earl of Fife, the Queen had entrusted him with a mission to Germany to invest the King of Saxony with the Garter, which was favour indeed. In Looloo's earliest memories, however, he had been a cheerful victim of April Fool jokes and apple-pie beds. Her brother George's early letters are full of references to shooting days with 'Papa and Eddy and Lord Fife'. The fishing at Gordon Castle with Macduff was so good one year that Looloo and Maudie got one each, while in the deer-stalking season, George reported that 'Macduff managed to get five and seven each day, sometimes before breakfast'.

Despite the measure of his public career, Macduff was also abnormally shy. At Princess Beatrice's wedding, when eighteen-year-old Louise was a bridesmaid, it was said that he and Louise naturally sought each other's company as the two shyest people there. On account of this, his first intended meeting with the Prince and Princess of Wales, as a very young man had been a non-starter. He was supposed to have been at the head of the Mar clan to meet the royal couple but nothing would induce him to go, and the Earl of Sandwich had to head the march through the snow instead.

If strategy is necessary in wooing a princess, Macduff did his best by leasing Castle Rising, near to Sandringham. Princess Looloo, in fact, got her man and in July, 1889, the Queen approved their engagement with outward 'gracious pleasure' and deep inward satisfaction. 'It is a very brilliant marriage in a worldy point of view,' she frankly summed up for her daughter Vicky in Germany, 'as he is immensely rich'. Writing to Macduff himself she struck a more kindly note: 'That my beloved grandchild should have her home in dear Scotland and in the dear Highlands is an additional satisfaction.' Looloo's closest friend, Princess May, however, viewed the match with some reservations. 'For a future Princess Royal to marry a subject seems rather strange,' she wrote to her Aunt Augusta. 'Don't you think so?'

It also deeply interested the Tecks to learn that Lord Fife had taken East Sheen Lodge, close to their own home, White Lodge, in Richmond Park, so that the newly-weds would soon be their neighbours.

III

Once announced, the wedding plans went forward with astonishing —though innocent—celerity. To 'get things over quickly' might alleviate the bride's dreadful nervousness of public ceremonial, even for her own wedding in the comparative privacy of the Chapel Royal, Buckingham Palace. Princess Alexandra's lifelong companion, Charlotte Knollys, none the less said that there had never been anyone more in love, and thought it appropriate that the wedding anthem 'O Perfect Love' was to be sung for the first time. Princess May was one of the eight bridesmaids, 'in pink *faille* and crepe de chine' with pink rosebuds in her hair. Amid the white roses and huge palms in the Palace chapel, everyone could forget that the July weather was as 'gloomy as November', though Queen Victoria considered the bride 'very pale . . . too plainly dressed' and noticed that she 'had her veil over her face which *no Princess* ever has and which I think unbecoming and not right . . .'

To one of the younger wedding guests, Miss Marie Adeane, nevertheless, 'Princess Louise was lovely'; and the bridegroom, too, she thought, looked 'a nice man, his manner to the Queen being particularly good'. This same mordant spectator found the Duchess of Teck 'rather like a large purple plush pincushion' and the Queen 'not too mournful in black and silver brocade'. Then the bridegroom lost his way, she noticed, in the 'have and to hold' sentence, so that the Archbishop had to repeat it, and 'there was also a good deal of fumbling with the ring'.

At the wedding breakfast, the Queen unexpectedly made a brief speech and announced her intention of creating the bridegroom Duke of Fife and Marquess of Macduff. Then our useful witness, Miss Adeane, found that everything ended beautifully. The groom 'provided a splendid coach with gorgeous footmen in green and silver livery and carried off his bride in great style. I went down to the door and saw the very last of them, the cheering so tremendous . . .'

The Shah of Persia had offered his palace at Teheran for the honeymoon, having met the couple in London, but they declined these exotic delights, preferring the charm and retirement of Sheen. The more immediate effect of the marriage was the surprise blossoming of Looloo, who soon seemed quite a different person. 'She looked so pretty, almost as pretty as her mother,' one Richmond guest was to write that autumn. 'Pretty blue eyes. . . looking so mischievous and happy.' Even to the searching gaze of the Duchess of Teck, Louise was soon 'in particularly good looks, and both seemed very flourishing . . . so thoroughly happy and contented that it does one's heart good to see them'. In the exclusive self-contained world of friends and relatives, indeed, the Fifes could forget their shyness and seek their pleasures as they pleased. We find them spinning off to Brighton as guests of the Arthur Sassoons, and soon taking a house there with a magnificent sea view above Madeira Walk. They sped through the quieter lanes behind the South Downs enjoying the new fun of bicycling, and one hears of Louise at the opera or at first nights or playing the organ in Sandringham Church or entertaining the Comte and Comtesse de Paris and their beautiful daughter Helene at Mar Lodge, where the Fifes hospitably filled the house for the salmon-fishing. But of public affairs and royal duty there is scarcely a word.

It was in private life, and private lives, that the Princess excelled. One gains the impression from her few surviving family letters that if a marriage bureau with a royal warrant had been possible in her day, the Princess Louise, Duchess of Fife, could have capably managed it. Brother Eddy, for example, had lightly fallen in and out of love a dozen times, but when he fluttered his languid eyes at the lovely Helene, his married sister did everything possible to open a path to the altar. As a Roman Catholic and daughter of the pretender to the French throne, Helene may have been wildly unsuitable. Yet the difficulties heightened Looloo's enthusiasm and she arranged a string of meetings for the two at Sheen and Mar Lodge until in August, 1890, they became privately engaged.

Even the Queen approved, after Louise had campaigned indefatigably for her brother. Not until it became clear that the Comte de Paris would never agree to his daughter's change of religion did the Queen sadly mention that it should be 'let alone for the present'. Eddy, after all, was next but one to the Throne. The Princess Helene went to Rome that autumn to make a personal plea to the Pope, only to find no hope of gaining approval. But since one possible bride was unsuitable, Louise was already casting around for another, and we need not be surprised to find Princess May soon visiting Mar Lodge for the first time. 'A funny looking place', she found it, 'with scattered houses with verandahs.' For rustic effect, the verandahs were supported by three trunks, creosoted black, and when Mar Lodge caught fire four or five years later the timbers formed spontaneous tinder and the buildings blazed to the skies.

For other 'lover's meetings' there was also the town house in Portman Square, which the Fifes had furnished by degrees and done up 'in very good taste', as the Duchess of Teck saw with approving but perhaps envious eyes. 'The walls are for the most part silk, the decorations being in white stucco, with fine old mahogany doors. *Très chic*.' Among other adjuncts was a nursery, and the first occupant in May, 1891, was a daughter, Alix (later Princess Arthur of Connaught). The Princess of Wales rushed to see the baby. 'I was a happy grandmother and held my little naked grandchild in my arms. It squeaked like a little sucking pig.' A few months later, Looloo had the pleasure of recording that Eddy and May were engaged.

They had celebrated their betrothal by going to see *Cavalleria Rusticana*, with its music then bewitching London. Looloo speedily set about organizing a Boxing Day dance at Sheen for the couple, and made sure that the Viennese band played the 'Cav' melodies again and again. 'It was most charming and we all thoroughly enjoyed ourselves,' ardently wrote Princess May.

And then Looloo's youngest sister, Maudie, caught influenza at Sandringham, and, a week later, Eddy realized that he, too, had flu. Within a week the family gathered in horror in his little room and in London the great bell of Westminster Abbey began to toll. The newsboys ran shouting through the streets and thus Britain learned the shattering news that the heir presumptive to the Throne was no more.

## IV

With the pertinacity that she rarely displayed in public, Princess Louise began to help repair all their lives. Towards the end of that sad year of 1892 she learned that she was to have another baby, and while in retirement she made a point of inviting Princess May to Sheen and writing to her brother George about it. This encouraged Georgie in turn to pursue a diffident but affectionate correspondence. 'I am glad that you often go and see Louise at Sheen . . . you have often been in my thoughts lately,' he would write to May.

Louise's second daughter, Maud (later Countess of Southesk), was born in April, 1893, and was four weeks old when George returned from visits to Athens and Rome and stayed with his sister at Sheen. May came to tea, and all three trooped up to the nursery to see the new baby. Like an arch conspirator, Louise then said, jokingly, 'Now, Georgie, don't you think you ought to take May into the garden to look at the frogs in the pond?' If she soon peeped from the windows to see what was happening, her eyes met a rewarding scene. 'We walked together in the garden,' May recorded in her diary. 'He proposed to me and I accepted him. Louise and Macduff were delighted.' Such was the betrothal of the future Queen Mary and King George V.

Another visitor at East Sheen Lodge that summer was the Princess Royal, the Empress Frederick, who praised the 'charming house' so much that Queen Victoria came over to see for herself. At this moment of time, before George and Mary married and raised their family, the Queen must have been aware of the frail links of the succession. Not many months earlier, George had also been seriously ill with typhoid fever. Had he been taken, as well as Eddy, Princess Louise would have been heiress-presumptive. Instead, Looloo's two younger sisters were bridesmaids at Princess May's wedding in the Chapel Royal and —somewhat to May's chagrin—Looloo herself helped George choose wallpapers and carpets for the newlyweds' home at York Cottage, Sandringham.

The following year, May was on a brief holiday in Switzerland, recuperating from the birth of her first baby (the future Edward VIII, the late Duke of Windsor) when she chanced to see a fire in an Alpine village. 'The fire-engines were so slow,' she wrote, 'that five small wooden chalets were burned to the ground. It was horrid to see.' By coincidence, it was just a year later that Mar Lodge with its little chalets was destroyed in the same way. The Fifes accepted this domestic disaster philosophically and Princess Louise, undismayed, promptly pencilled a rough sketch for a new Mar Lodge, chiefly distinguished by two wings of guest-rooms: the elaborate red-roofed building, with deep eaves faced with mock black timbering that still dominates the upper Dee (and is suitably now an hotel). There were in fact no fewer than one hundred and twenty rooms as Looloo's modest idea of a home. And why not when Macduff was president of the British South Africa Company, with its royal charter—granted shortly after his marriage—and its vested interest in the Transvaal and Rhodesia, in diamonds and gold?

Queen Victoria humoured Louise by laying the foundation-stone of the new house, grandly driving over in a carriage with four greys and two out-riders on greys. The bagpipes skirled, and the Fife men 'with spears and kilts looked well', as Lady Lytton noted. 'The little ladies Fife came down muffled in shawls (the daughters Alexandra and Maud, aged four and two), delicate but such little dears. The *many* dishes were well prepared.' This was the Mar Lodge of infinite hospitality and Scottish entertainment which figures so often in Edwardian reminiscences. Macduff had been saddened to lose his great collection of stags' heads in the fire but resumed his enthusiasm until three thousand skulls 'decorated' the arched pine rafters of the enormous new ballroom. After a day of deer-stalking the finest carcases formed the grisly centrepiece of triumphant Scottish reels, wildly danced by torchlight. (The Mar fire, one must mention, had been caused less dramatically by a plumber who forgot a lighted candle.)

While the new mansion slowly rose, Princess Louise also dedicated herself to a more delicate fabric in the skilful architecture of yet another marriage. Her two sisters were now in their late twenties and even the tactful Empress Frederick cast discreet hints that it would not be wise to leave them in marital vagueness much longer. 'Toria' was beyond helping. She first lost her heart to one of Macduff's friends, a member of the Baring banking family but unfortunately a commoner and thus judged ineligible; and later she fell in love with her father's equerry, Sir Arthur Davidson, a match equally decreed impossible by her parents. Like so many unmarried daughters of the time, Princess Victoria became, as the Grand Duchess Olga said, 'just a glorified maid to her mother'. But Maudie—or 'Harry' as she was now nicknamed—was more amenable, very pretty just then, as the Empress Frederick noticed, 'like a little rose, with her bright eyes'.

Since no one more likely seemed in view, Looloo's judicious glance fell on her bachelor cousin, Prince Charles of Denmark, second son of the King, unconsidered hitherto since he was three years Maud's junior and very much looked it. 'A very nice young fellow, brave and modest', Lord Esher thought him. This youthful potential husband was in the Danish Navy and chanced to have a shore leave in London, whereupon Louise made sure that he partnered Maudie to dances and first nights and was constantly thrown into her company at Portman Square and Sheen. The engagement came in the nick of time, only days before he was posted on a five-months cruise of the West Indies. A year later, the Czar Nicholas was a percipient visitor at Mar Lodge when the couple were concluding their honeymoon there and wrote that he found it 'rather strange for them to be husband and wife'. Indeed, the first child of the marriage, the present King Olav of Norway, was not born until seven years later. Though Princess Maud had to make her home in Copenhagen, she lamented that her husband was always at sea, and suffered rebukes from Motherdear that she must on no account forget she had married 'a *naval* man'. There were no other children.

For Princess Louise a more personal sequel to her match-making awaited her in 1905, when the Norwegian people decided that their country should become a kingdom and invited Prince Charles to the throne as Haakon VII. Looloo was delighted that Maudie would become a Queen, although it was not a role she would ever have desired for herself. She had found her father's coronation as Edward VII, three years earlier, a hideous ordeal with its processions and publicity and only the need of taking her children to see the King in his robes beforehand had persuaded her to play any supporting part at all. The King could see for himself that Looloo was not the stuff of which Princesses Royal are made. With his youngest daughter about to become a Queen, however, the need for enhanced distinction for his eldest girl gained fresh urgency. Haakon was to be proclaimed on November 18th, and on November 9th Edward VII's Birthday Honours began with the announcement, 'The King has been graciously pleased to declare that His Majesty's eldest daughter, Her Royal Highness Princess Louise Victoria Alexandra Dagmar (Duchess of Fife) shall henceforth bear the style and title of Princess Royal . . .'

There is no sign that Louise welcomed her new style and dignity. On the contrary, she stayed away from her father's Balmoral weekends more than ever, keeping even her children secluded from near relatives. Her happiest hours were still spent alone, salmon-fishing her favourite and well-tried pools in the reaches of the Dee, and her landing of seven large salmon in a day remained the record for a lady's rod for several years. The new status of 'Royal Highness' for her daughters was nevertheless welcome, and before her brother's coronation as George V in June, 1911, she battled for their right to wear the robes of royal princesses, which was doubtful by paternity, professing herself 'hurt' when she met refusal. Since her eldest girl, Princess Alix, was short-sighted and insisted on wearing academic-looking spectacles, the ensemble would not have been conducive to royal glamour.

## V

In the winter of 1911 the newly-crowned King George and Queen Mary were looking forward to the great adventure of their coronation reception in India, while the Princess Royal and her husband planned to winter in the warm climate of Egypt, as they had for three or four years past. The evening before 'George and May' sailed, the Fifes attended the private dinner-party at the Palace, and then early in December set out themselves, with their two daughters —then aged twenty and eighteen—on the liner *Delhi*. 'We were so peaceful and contented,' wrote young Princess Alix. They knew a few of the other passengers and now could relax as if incognito, which of course they always decidedly preferred.

Louise had rarely felt so close to her husband as when alone with him aboard ship on these winter journeys. They encountered rough seas in the Bay of Biscay but in dear Macduff's company, the Princess said, she always felt secure. The night of December 13th was particularly black and stormy: no one could sleep, but the captain's bulletins had reminded them they were off the coast of Morocco and would soon reach the calm seas beyond Gibraltar. At two a.m. Macduff estimated reassuringly that they were under the lee of Cape Spartel. Then there was a splitting and grinding crash and the shouts of men: the liner had run aground.

The Fifes began throwing on their clothes unaware of the extent of the disaster. Macduff was still in nightshirt and dressing-gown, helping his wife, and their daughters had already come to the cabin when an officer asked them to don their lifebelts and go to the deck saloon without further ado. It seemed incredible to learn that the crew were ordered to man the boats and to hear the calm request for passengers 'please to stand firm' until their boats were ready. An officer asked the Princess to come to one of the first boats, but royal behaviour patterns are not erased so readily; the girls were transferred, yet the Princess Royal and her husband firmly refused to leave the ship until all other passengers had done so. They did not know until later that many of the lifeboats were smashed on the rocks by the heavy waves and, though many struggled safely ashore, some passengers and sailors were drowned.

The lifeboats of H.M.S. *Edinburgh* also came on the scene and it was only behind the last cluster of passengers that the Princess at length descended the long steep ladder and jumped into the out-stretched arms of the crew. 'Waves were huge,' she wrote after-wards. 'They swept down on us and filled the boat, we baled but not any good, water came up to our knees and she sank, flinging us all out! We floated in our belts, waves like iron walls tore over us, knocked us under. Admiral Cradock gripped my shoulder and *saved* me! Thank God my Macduff and children both on beach but had been under too.'

'Breathless and shivery', as she termed it, the party then had to walk through the gale and lashing rain four miles along the shore, trying to wring out their clothes, guided only by the distant light of Cape Spartel. Macduff gave his own soaked dressing-gown to a woman and had only his nightshirt. The lighthousemen did their best to warm and dry them out—and lent Fife a pair of trousers—but then they next had to set out on mules to ride ten miles through the storm in order to reach the safety of the British Legation in Tangier. By way of period atmosphere, *The Times* asserted that, 'The Princess Royal conversed with great vivacity on little incidents'.

'By God, sir, she was splendid,' a seaman told *The Times* corre-spondent, as if in Drury Lane melodrama. But it was not until much later, after writing exciting letters to all her relations, that the Princess Royal remembered publicly to thank the officers and crew. The Fife's donation to the fund for the families of seamen who had drowned had to wait on the subscription from the King and when he gave £120 protocol required them to give £100.

Despite the shipwreck, 'an extraordinary nightmare', as the Princess called it, they soon continued their journey aboard the *Hampshire* to Port Said, and then to Cairo and Khartoum. Yet the hours of exposure had drained off their strength more than they imagined. At Assuan the Duke of Fife caught a chill and in Princess Alix's words, 'a great tragedy was suddenly cast upon us. In ten days he died of pneumonia'.

The Duke of Fife was brought home in state aboard H.M.S.

*Powerful* and buried in the private chapel of Mar Lodge where, nearly twenty years later, he was followed by his widow. Princess Alix married Prince Arthur of Connaught in 1913, and Princess Maud (mother of the present Duke of Fife) married the eleventh Earl of Southesk in 1923. Between these events, the Princess Royal was all but obliterated from public memory, save to the local tenantry who made much of her patronage of the Braemar Games. When she died in 1931, though aged only sixty-three, she seemed an unfamiliar figure of the distant Edwardian past to a new and younger generation.

Today Mar Lodge is an hotel, where helicopters fly in the sportsmen who come for the salmon fishing and grouse-shooting or who answer the lure of the unrivalled herds of red deer. There are modernities and yet much of the furnishing is still unchanged. Royal portraits still adorn the walls, and in Macduff's snuggery cigar smoke still wreathes around the deep red Turkish ottomans while the conversation at times is still of gold and diamonds and world commerce. Unique among hotel facilities, there is the oddity that guests may ask the receptionist for the keys of the private chapel. There the tombs of the Duke of Fife and the Princess Royal lie side by side, and the hotel visitors may pay their respects, a subtle eccentricity of royal hospitality that might have appealed to the publicly shy but privately ever-sociable Looloo.

## ENTRACTE

*King George V and Queen Mary, the earlier 'Georgie' and 'May' of family life, reigned from 1910 until January 20th, 1936. With the passing of the Princess Royal, Dowager Duchess of Fife, at her home in Portman Square, on January 5th, 1931, the 'title and distinction' was again in vacancy. Nearly a year later, Princess Mary, Countess of Harewood, only daughter of the King and Queen, was declared Princess Royal in the New Year Honours List.*

## 6   Princess Mary, Countess of Harewood

### I

As the Victorian era faded into the reign of King Edward VII, at the turn of the century, one of the small bedrooms of York Cottage, overlooking the lake in Sandringham Park, was shared by three small children and a nursemaid. The two small boys were each to be proclaimed King, the eldest (born in 1894) as Edward VIII, the Duke of Windsor of modern times, and the second (born in 1895) as George VI. The third child, their sister, Mary, was born in 1897, the year of Queen Victoria's Diamond Jubilee, and narrowly escaped being named Diamond. She was in fact christened in Sandringham Church as Victoria Alexandra Alice Mary, and first gained public mention as Princess Victoria of York. It was only during the revision of royal names and titles upon her grandfather becoming King that she became known as Princess Mary. She has of course stepped into history as the only daughter of King George V and Queen Mary, but her more personal lustre lies in having brought true significance to the distinction of Princess Royal, for she it was who created the role, under her mother's inspiration, in the double texture of duty and dignity as we think of it today.

At the age of nine, she was taken abroad for the first time to see her uncle and aunt crowned King and Queen of Norway, and the dignified processions and solemn ceremonial proved unforgettable to the impressionable child. 'She behaved quite beautifully through the long service,' wrote the future Queen Mary, who had maintained a commentary of whispers in Trondheim Cathedral, explaining the significance of the ritual, step by step. More impetuously she mentioned in a letter a few days later, 'Little Olav has fallen in love with my Mary, who is rather shy and blushes at his advances'. One catches an unguarded hint of match-making, not to say maternal absurdity, for Prince Olav was only four.

In family upbringing, however, Queen Mary failed for years to distinguish between her string of boisterous sons and her only daughter. Princess Mary was no different in mischief or daring and, as her eldest brother has recalled, 'her yellow curls concealed a fearlessness that commanded our respect'. More than ever, when younger brothers came on the scene, between the years 1900 and 1905, the elder children formed an adventurous threesome, racing wildly down the long hill to Wolferton on their bicycles, roughly playing football, hazardously climbing to their own secret eyrie in the trees, and galloping their ponies down the Sandringham lanes. 'Mary was our close companion . . . loving horses, she rode better than Bertie or I,' said the Duke of Windsor, years later, when he remembered with nostalgia the pleasures of the Sandringham countryside where 'we could roam to the limits of our physical capacity'.

Then there was the exclusive London thrill of watching the ceremony of the Changing of the Guard from the garden wall of Marlborough House, where all three solemnly learned to salute the Colour as it was carried past. So keen was their enthusiasm that a Scottish footman named Cameron organized the trio into a squad. 'Armed with wooden guns, we paraded every morning with Cameron in the role of a drill sergeant. Forsyth (the King's piper) marched ahead playing his pipes. It was great fun . . . especially at Sandringham when the King walked down sometimes to inspect us.'

In contrast, the three also shared dancing lessons and more feminine preoccupations, learning to crochet and make woollen comforters—as the scarves were called—for one of their mother's numerous charities. When Mr. Hansell, the tutor, arrived, the trio at first shared early lessons on dark winter mornings, in the chill York Cottage schoolroom, though this mixed class was not a success. 'I must keep Princess Mary apart,' the harassed Mr. Hansell reported. 'Her disposition is mercurial. One can enforce discipline and order of a sort, but as long as she is in the room her brothers cannot concentrate.' And so Mary at last gained a French governess, a Mlle. Dussau, who made French a compulsory language for all the children at mealtimes and presently organized a class of small girls to give her pupil the companionship she felt she needed. With such staunt future friends as the Duchess of Devonshire, Lady de Trafford and Lady Hillingdon as fellow pupils, this established the precedent of the private class formed at Buckingham Palace fifty years later for Prince Charles and Princess Anne.

Cecil Sharp, who taught Princess Mary singing, was the first to discover her special musical aptitude, later to be so marked in her sons. Her father could not bear her to play her scales within earshot and she often went to practice on a regal gilt piano at Sandringham House, where, since her grandmother was increasingly deaf, she disturbed no one. In her teens, Mary's mezzo-soprano voice was so good that Melba said she could have become a professional, a fairly safe form of flattery. Her private education was, in fact, better than usual for princesses in those days and, under her mother's tutelage, her early training in both the voluntary duties and firmer responsibilities of royalty was unexcelled.

Watching from a window at Marlborough House to see her husband proclaimed as King George V, one of Queen Mary's first regrets on suddenly finding herself Queen was that her children were so little prepared. Princess Mary had celebrated her thirteenth birthday only two weeks earlier, and yet in fact her attainments were already considerable. As she rode to the coronation of 1911 in a state carriage with her brothers, her coronet, being slightly oversize, threatened to be dislodged, but she sat erect and was seen to reprove the younger boys for misbehaviour, 'truly giving them a wigging'. Looking down from a balcony in Piccadilly, another girl of thirteen—who was keeping her own brothers in order—noticed this particularly and remembered being 'deeply impressed by her lovely fair hair and skin'.

Amid the overwhelming splendour of the Abbey, in her robe of state, Princess Mary played her own small part perfectly. With moving dignity, she curtsied deeply to her brother, the new Prince of Wales, before moving to her appointed place. Next day, the Princess accompanied her parents on the State Drive through cheering London: there were few events of State in which she was now not to have a share. The following day she embarked with the King and Queen for the coronation naval review of the warships at Spithead. And so the fantastic stream of events continued throughout the month, culminating in an event pleasantly fitting to a girl of her age, a visit to 100,000 children who were the King's guests at Crystal Palace.

From that maelstrom of shrill noise, 'a vast spectacle of her own generation', Princess Mary emerged with an emotional sense of dedication deeper than any that touched her eldest brother, 'fainting with heat and nervousness', at his investiture as Prince of Wales at Caernarvon a week or two later. When her parents left on their long Durbar visit to India, she returned to the schoolroom with the extra task of writing to them every other week, a series of letters that mix family incidents and national events with conscientious fervour. Another occurrence that helped mould her budding personality was a visit at fifteen to her oldest living relative, her great-aunt Augusta of Strelitz, a grand-daughter of George III.

'Most delightful is your proposal to bring Mary,' wrote this old lady, then in her ninetieth year, and Queen Mary noted her daughter's reaction with intense interest: 'Mary delighted . . . awfully interested . . . and very observant.' This was Princess Mary's first visit to Germany, only two years before the curtains of the 1914 war closed. The young princess returned to London with her mind aglow with motoring expeditions and evenings that had been spent looking at old photograph albums and with hours of family talk, learning of family history past and present and all that it might entail.

## II

'Mary is dying to hunt and has no one to go out with', wrote King George early in 1913, with concern that, as so often with princesses, companionable boys of her own age were scarce. A girl could not ride to hounds alone and Mary was forced for a while to practise her venturesome fences and hedges in the private reaches of Windsor Great Park. Neither of her elder brothers shared her enthusiasm. Although he later became addicted to the thrills of polo and steeple-chasing, the Prince of Wales considered riding lessons 'a dull chore'. 'Bertie'—the future George VI—was then away at sea aboard H.M.S. *Cumberland*, and the Princess picked up what expertise she could from grooms and occasional visits to riding friends. In those days, her father was perhaps her principal riding teacher, and London-ers often saw Princess Mary with the King, enjoying the early morning riding in the Row. Gruffly severe as he was with his sons, King George never had a harsh word with his daughter, and in-deed the Princess's relationship with each of her parents was one of 'understanding sympathy that needed no expression in words'. Thus on the August day in 1914 when Britain went to war, she shared the acute burden of their responsibilities and anxieties and was anxious to evolve new duties of her own.

The scheme of Princess Mary's gift-boxes has a naïve air today, but it was a plan that she organized and launched herself with a seventeen-year-old's impetuosity, which put to good purpose the eager patriotism of friends and followers of her own generation. 'I want you all,' she said in her first public appeal, 'to help me to send a Christmas present from the whole nation to every sailor afloat and every soldier at the front'. The money poured in and hundreds of thousands of servicemen received tin boxes packed with tobacco, cigarettes or chocolate, with Princess Mary's portrait on the lid, and a message from Princess Mary and 'friends at home' wishing the recipient 'A Happy Christmas and a Victorious New Year'.

The boxes permanently established the Princess as a responsible and popular royal figure. The point of contact seemed so close and genuine that many soldiers and sailors kept their tins and years later, when she toured Canada, brought them out to show her with touching affection. But the young Princess Mary's attitude was one of total involvement: when not visiting hospitals or munition plants with her mother, serving at soup kitchens or packing parcels with Girl Guides, she knitted endlessly. When wool became scarce, relatives visiting the Palace would often find her fingers still busy unravelling outworn old woollen garments. In her journal for 1915, Queen Mary mentioned the shocking war casualties encountered on the hospital visits with her daughter and the sadness of seeing badly wounded men 'without arms, legs, eyes'. It was a rare occasion if the Princess was steered aside to tour less distressing wards with one of the younger nurses, and such instances were apt to become all the more imprinted on her mind. Years after being escorted round the military hospital at Netley in this way, the Princess was taken round again by the same nurse, promoted to matron, and remembered her so well that she took up the conversation where they had left off twenty-seven years earlier.

More regularly, through the air-raid era of 1916-18, she walked across the Green Park from Buckingham Palace to Devonshire House where she worked for a Voluntary Aid Detachment. People grew used to seeing her and saluting her, just as local Londoners had grown accustomed to her as a child when she walked across from Marlborough House with her governess every

Friday to put half her pocket money in her savings account at the post-office opposite St. James's Palace. To be royal entailed setting an example and, when needful, to be seen doing so. Princess Mary had been so thoroughly grounded in the precept by her mother that it became second nature. A Princess Royal, Victoria's daughter, had been sure that royal duty ran, like ripples in a pool, far beyond the throne; the subsequent Princess Royal, the Duchess of Fife, may have been too pathologically shy to set her niece an example, but, as the King's daughter of 1914–18, Princess Mary accepted her task and its values as she accepted the need of smiling or acknowledging greetings or remembering faces.

'And what would you like for a birthday gift?' the King enquired, shortly before her coming-of-age. It amused the family that the Princess desired neither tiaras nor a pearl necklace but merely permission to work as a probationer at the Great Ormond Street Children's Hospital. She had unavailingly mentioned the project several times already, but now she had her way. To save petrol she drove to and from the hospital in a one-horse Palace brougham but in every other respect took pains to seem an ordinary student nurse, so that patients sometimes asked, 'Is she really the Princess?' As her niece, today's Princess Alexandra, was to do nearly forty years later, she worked her scheduled steady progress through the wards and lecture-rooms. There is the customary story of a sister who stepped in to prevent the royal student undertaking a menial bedside duty but also intercepted a warning Windsor look and desisted. Unknown to the Princess, the question of transfer to the surgical side was put before Queen Mary. 'Why not?' said the Queen, and her daughter served her turn of duty in the operating theatre, 'just clearing up'.

In time, after the Second World War, Princess Mary appeared to some to be an insulated and conventional figure, but the joke rebounds on ourselves: in her twenties, she stepped a little beyond the fussy, conventional standards of her own day like any other young person. On Armistice Day in 1918 she telephoned Devonshire House and asked for the V.A.D. staff to march down to Buckingham Palace and form up in the courtyard. Among the huge crowds surrounding the Palace, 'it was an incredible honour to be with the Guard when the King came out', as Dame Beryl Oliver recalled.

Soon after her twenty-first birthday that year, the Princess had also been appointed Colonel-in-Chief of the Royal Scots, but this could never again be merely a nominal or purely decorative function. In her V.A.D. uniform Princess Mary took the salute of her regiment as it marched through the ruined streets of Ypres, setting a characteristic and enduring precedent for princesses of the future. She was henceforth to be 'deeply involved with the doings and welfare of her Regiments', as her lady-in-waiting of twenty years, Miss Gwynedd Lloyd, has said. And when the present Queen appointed her Major-General in the British Army, the first woman to hold the rank in history, it gave her extraordinary pleasure and satisfaction.

All the royal brothers, young and old, were deeply fond of their sister. As they grew up, she seemed increasingly the very pivot of family life. The King and Queen were not always approachable or, if consulted, their minds seemed to be preoccupied. The brothers were successively in or out of favour with the King, but Mary was always the great mentor, the go-between, eager to further anyone's cause but her own. 'She doesn't confide in me, I don't feel she is happy,' the Prince of Wales—the Duke of Windsor—complained one day to the Queen's close friend, Lady Airlie. More perceptive and sensitive than the younger brothers, he felt that the King liked having Mary at home and did not really want her to marry. On one occasion, he tried to persuade his mother to talk to the King on the topic, but discovered she had done nothing about it. 'I'm so annoyed with her,' he told Lady Airlie, 'that I haven't been near her for over a week.'

The cause of the discussion was probably the latest newspaper rumour, for journalists were always eager, then as now, to forecast whom a Princess would wed. The Earl of Dalkeith, Viscount Althorp and the Marquess of Northampton and others found their names in print as probable suitors, much to Mary's dismay. The problem kept the public in suspense, but appealed equally to scores of people who knew the Princess and were not content to wait on events. When the Marchioness Curzon entertained the King and Queen and their daughter to dinner one night, she decided to entertain the Princess and perhaps satisfy her own curiosity by inviting a number of these eligible young men who she knew. Then after dinner she asked the Princess whom she would like brought to her, and rattled off her list of names, among them Lord Spencer, Lord Northampton and Lord Lascelles. Princess Mary at once answered, 'Lord Lascelles'. Watching them talking together, Lady Curzon quickly suspected romance was in the air.

Gossip averred that Viscount Lascelles and Princes Mary first met on the hunting field, and hunting was indeed one of their mutual passions, but the real links were far firmer, and founded on true family strength. The seventh Duke and Duchess of Buccleuch were among the King and Queen's oldest friends; the King and the Duke had first met as young naval cadets, they had married in the same year, and the Duke's eldest son was soon to marry into the Lascelles family. After the war, Harry Lascelles figured ever more frequently in the Sandringham shooting parties. He was in fact nearly fifteen years older than the Princess: it was almost the story of Looloo and Fife all over again. Then one Sunday in November, 1921, he found himself the only guest at York Cottage, apart from Queen Mary's brother, Prince Algy, and after tea Princess Mary very literally took her fate in her hands by asking him if he would like to see her little sitting room upstairs.

Lord Lascelles needed no second prompting, and they were no sooner behind closed doors than he asked her to marry him. Before giving him an answer, Mary rushed down the little staircase to tell her mother, according to Lady Airlie, and found the Queen resting in kimono and slippers talking to Prince Algy. The conversation went on and on until the Princess could bear it no longer. 'Mama, please' she burst in, 'I must speak to you.' Harry Lascelles was meanwhile still patiently waiting upstairs. Every sound could often be heard through the ceilings of York Cottage. A noisy, laughing procession wended its way to the King's room, with the Queen still in kimono and slippers. The King gave his consent and only then was the embarrassed intending bridegroom called downstairs. 'We then gave Harry L our blessing,' the Queen wrote in her diary next day. 'We were very cheerful and almost uproarious at dinner . . .'

'Mary simply beaming,' she added in subsequent correspondence. 'Such a blessing to feel she will not go abroad.' Three days later, when the engagement was announced, the British public in turn responded, if not with excessive warmth, at least with pleasure and affection. Viscount Lascelles was not photogenic; people had not expected their Princess to marry someone so much older than herself, but then the romantic story of a miser and his sandwiches came to light and instantly draped Lord Lascelles in the necessary mantle of glamour.

For he was the grand-nephew of the last Marquess of Clanricarde who was chiefly remembered in his West End clubs as a miserly eccentric, a lonely figure who would retrieve other members' discarded sandwiches from the waste-paper basket and was widely reputed to rummage for hunks of bread in the dustbins. His family shunned him. One day, touched at the sight of the shabby and lonely old figure, whom he had not seen since boyhood, Lascelles went up to speak to him. Two months later the recluse died, and in a codicil to his will he left his nephew all but a few thousand of his total fortune of two and a half million pounds.

Such a story was, of course, irresistible, added to the announcement of a wedding on February 28th in Westminster Abbey and the promise of the first state pageant since the coronation. The Duke of York (the future George VI) wrote in some excitement to the Prince of Wales, 'As far as I can make out, the 28th is going to be a day of national rejoicing.' Undertaking a tour of India at the time, the Prince of Wales 'missed all the fun', and the Duke of York who was falling in love himself, presently also acquainted his brother with the charming fact that Lady Elizabeth Bowes-Lyon was to be one of the bridesmaids.

'The actual ceremony at the Abbey was beautiful,' he afterwards wrote. 'The streets were overcrowded all along the route of the procession. Mary looked lovely in her wedding dress.' Queen Mary then took up the story in another letter to her eldest son. 'Mary and Harry L drove off at 3.45—Papa and all of us throwing rice and little paper horse-shoes and rose leaves after them. Papa and I felt miserable at parting, poor Papa broke down . . .' The King indeed recorded in his own private journal, 'Felt very low and depressed now that darling Mary has gone' and next day he added 'I miss darling Mary too awfully'.

Princess Mary, Viscountess Lascelles, had indeed been at the centre of her parents' daily life as well as that of her brothers. On the first stage of her honeymoon at Weston Park, the Earl of Bradford's vast and idyllic home in Shropshire, she received with interest the daily 'gate' statistics of the people who had streamed into St. James's Palace to see her wedding gifts and bridal gown.

Even with her wedding she collected funds for her favourite charities and in six weeks over 100,000 people visited the exhibition, with a gain to orphanages, the Girl Guides and an ex-Servicemen's home of thousands of pounds.

## IV

The married couple settled into one of the spare Jacobean mansions of the Lascelles family, Goldsborough Hall, near Knaresborough, where their first son—the present Earl of Harewood—was born early in 1923. Thus was forged Princess Mary's first link with the county that she made so much her own. 'My love for this part of Yorkshire has become such an integral part of my life . . . it would be a great sorrow for me to contemplate making my home else-where,' she once said with obvious sincerity when given the Free-dom of Harrogate.

Goldsborough was inwardly a lovely house of panelled rooms and old oak staircases, outwardly restored perhaps too much in the style of Sandringham, but redeemed by its glorious gardens. These furnished the Princess with another of the rich interests of her life: the grounds had been neglected and presently she was able to write that they were coming on well. If for a time she withdrew a little from public life after the birth of her second son, Gerald Lascelles, in 1924, it should be added that her husband's personality lacked the ingredients of swift public popularity. His tact was such that, when a film production unit made a harmless little picture of the Bramham Moor Hunt, of which he was Master, he autocratically ordered cuts to be made, nor would he permit it to be trade-shown except in the presence of watchful Home Office officials. The Prince of Wales is supposed to have said, 'I get commoner and commoner, while Lascelles gets more and more royal'.

When the glamour of Princess Mary's wedding had been for-gotten, people wondered what she saw in him. The prime attraction was probably a father image that underlaid the shooting and riding, the love of country pursuits, the zest for the turf, the bridge and bezique (although the King himself preferred whist and poker). There were strong elements of physical resemblance; the same gruff intolerant outbursts, though never in either instance directed at the Princess. Yet husband and wife shared, equally, a private and considerable discerning taste in the arts, which George V never had. The planting of trees and shrubs would immerse them in deep discussion, and the problems of farming and the stud farm, first at Goldsborough and then at Harewood, were constant topics of conversation. Both shared a keen and knowledgeable interest in the countryside; and the closest of witnesses, their two sons found home life so happy that on being sent away to prep school, both boys suffered pangs of homesickness deeper than their parents ever suspected.

Lord Lascelles succeeded his father as the sixth Earl of Harewood in 1929. Generations of Harewoods had embellished Harewood House. The new Earl added his collection of Italian paintings and in the family rooms, Princess Mary, the new Countess of Harewood, demonstrated her inclinations towards the then fashionable 'Adam revival'. Their son, the present Lord Harewood, recollects that his parents ran Harewood 'with some degree of grandeur: forty for dinner sometimes in the big dining-room and an indoor staff of twenty-seven, augmented when the King and Queen came to stay'. It was quite in keeping with this atmosphere that on January 1st, 1932, nearly a year after the death of Princess Louise, the New Year's Honours List was headed with the words, 'The King has been graciously pleased to declare that His Majesty's daughter Her Royal Highness Princess Victoria Alexandra Alice Mary (Countess of Harewood) shall henceforth bear the style and title of Princess Royal.'

No doubt the gold plate was brought out at the next Harewood dinner-party, but the new Princess Royal had already resumed a growing accumulation of royal duties as a matter of course. One finds her striking the pattern of the carefully scheduled crowded day that has since become standard routine for the royal ladies. The stress on Yorkshire interests did not diminish her work for the Red Cross, the Royal Air Force Nursing Service, the Girl Guide Movement, or any of her unstinted wider interests. The Duke of Windsor once wrote, 'The word "duty" fell between us'. He was recalling the painful interview when he told his mother and his sister together of his unqualified love for the divorced Mrs. Simpson and his determination to marry her. The Princess Royal sympathized with her brother, but for her henceforth, more than ever, there was always duty, too.

Even in her girlhood, she could seldom be diverted from the appointed tasks of the day. 'When my brothers and I wanted her to play tennis,' as the Duke of Windsor recollected, 'she used to refuse because she had her French translation to do, or hadn't read *The Times* for the day.' The Princess was nearly forty when her father died, and it was a part of her duty that she became her mother's comfort and companion; and her consolation, too, as scene by scene they endured the prolonged drama of the Abdication. With the family at Royal Lodge, they listened together to the former Edward VIII's last broadcast when he was introduced so strangely at the microphone as 'Prince Edward'. Then the Princess Royal diplomatically curtailed the leavetaking, so that she and her mother were the first to leave.

But the die was cast, and his sister was also the first of the family to visit the Duke of Windsor abroad, travelling to Vienna with her husband shortly after that first Christmas. The Duke had taken refuge with friends at Schloss Enzesfeld, and his sister was not only the first visitor from home but also the only one to help lessen the initial shock of exile. Again, years later, when the Duke returned to Marlborough House to see his mother in old age and to sleep under her roof for a night or two, Mary was also there, a sympathetic, understanding and unobtrusive mentor. On his subsequent visits to London, brother and sister invariably dined together, their privacy absolute within the walls of St. James's Palace, where the Princess Royal had moved into the south-facing garden suite as her London home.

Yet her loyalty to her second brother, King George VI, remained absolute. During his pre-war visit to Canada, his two war-time visits to his armies overseas, his 1947 tour of South Africa and again during his illness in 1951, she was appointed a Counsellor of State, the only Princess Royal ever thus to undertake constitutional deputy duties for the Sovereign. Within two weeks of the King's return from South Africa in 1947, a large family luncheon party was held at the Palace to celebrate Queen Mary's eightieth birthday. The Duke and Duchess of Windsor paid one of their fleeting visits to London shortly beforehand, and the Princess and her brother dined together as usual, discussing the party and the plans for their birthday gifts. The Duke had messages he wished passed to old friends and of course to Harry, who was at Harewood suffering from a chill. Yet the Princess Royal was destined not to attend the family reunion, for her husband died with tragic suddenness only two days before.

## V

The Princess Royal had discovered that she was no longer a stranger to anxiety and sorrow. 'I used to lead a sheltered life,' she once confided to a friend, 'but one doesn't any more.' On the outbreak of war, her elder son, George—the present Earl—had not been old enough to join a regiment. He in fact went into action for the first time with the Grenadier Guards in Italy on his twenty-first birthday, and four months later was wounded by machine-gun fire and taken prisoner. The date itself might have sounded a knell to a worried mother, for it was the very day on which her husband had been wounded in France in the First World War and his great-grandfather wounded at Waterloo. The enemy classified her son as a 'prominenti', in effect an important hostage, whose life might be forfeit at any moment: it was small wonder if for a time the Princess Royal suffered from sleeplessness.

Her antidote for anxiety had been to involve herself still more deeply in public service, and in widowhood she filled her engagement-book for months beforehand with the same zealous urge, as if responding to her mother's calm words, 'One must go on'. Once again she began to widen her already considerable list of patronages and presidencies, her offices of rank and her fellowships, from nursing and women's voluntary social work, agriculture and Yorkshire interests to a far wider field. When she agreed to become Chancellor of Leeds University, for instance, she was the first woman to be installed in such an appointment in Great Britain. In 1948, in her wish to carry on her husband's more personal enthusiasms, she had registered her own racing colours, the first royal lady ever to do so, and the precedent had enabled her niece, the then Princess Elizabeth, to register her own racing colours the following year.

The Princess Royal had sponsored Elizabeth at her christening, little realizing that her god-daughter would one day be Queen. Indeed, it was when the young Princess was just thirteen and was staying with the Harewoods at Egerton House, Newmarket, that she noticed the gilt scroll of royal winners under the arch of the stableyard and perhaps first divined the scope of her own future racing interests. The Princess Royal's own racehorses seldom fulfilled her hopes for them and most of the classic prizes eluded her, but she took a lively interest in her niece's successes. Meanwhile, she found herself entering a new phase as the Aunt Mary of the younger generation of royalty and, at about this time, she became aware, also, that her two sons were developing firm romantic interests.

The story has been often told of how Lord Harewood first saw his future wife, the pianist Marion Stein, during an opera interval at Glyndebourne and was introduced to her by Benjamin Britten at the Aldeburgh festival the following year. He courted her during a tour of *The Beggar's Opera* and proposed to her shortly after the curtain-fall of another opera. There were certain difficulties. Lord Harewood was then tenth in succession to the Throne, while Miss Stein's father was a Viennese-born music publisher who had first come to Britain as a refugee. At a small house-party near Amsterdam formed by the Steins, Lord Harewood, Benjamin Britten, Kathleen Ferrier and others, that engagement summer, one guest detected 'a touch of apprehension'.

According to his close friend, Ronald Duncan, the dramatist, 'Harewood occasionally looked worried. His uncle, King George VI, had not yet given permission ... We knew that everything depended on Queen Mary's attitude.' Yet the Princess Royal had come to hold decided opinions of her own in the post-war world; and her son had not faced death during the war without giving her a new sense of the preciousness of life and its happiness. She brought the King round to her point of view and began to prepare the ground with her mother, but less persuasion was needed than she had expected. Lord Harewood returned from Amsterdam and hurried direct to see his grandmother at Marlborough House, and the engagement was announced a few days later.

Aged eighty two, Queen Mary did not feel well enough to attend the September wedding—every other member of the Royal Family was there—but the old lady was at the reception at St. James's Palace. The story was told of the short-sighted author, E. M. Forster, who was asked if he had been presented to Queen Mary and replied that he did not know she was there. The queenly figure in white seated near the middle of the room was pointed out to

Princess Anne with her mother, then Princess Elizabeth, in the garden at Clarence House, 1951.

The young equestrian, aged nine, with her pony, Greensleeves, at Frogmore.

Studio Lisa

The schoolgirl: on church parade at Benenden, 1963.    *Central Press*

Princess Anne's first official engagement: leeks for the Welsh Guards,
March 1st, 1969.

Sheer glamour in white fox, as guest of the Shah of Persia with her
father, 1971.

*Keystone*

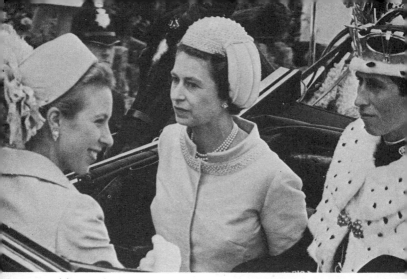

In public, at the Investiture of the Prince of Wales, Caernarvon, 196

*Press Associatio*

In private, a gallop with her brother Charles in Windsor Great Pa

*Camera Pre*

No hands! A mischance at Amberly, 1973: Princess Anne in her
favourite and best-known role.

Central Press

Princess Anne and Mark Philips—a delightfully informal engagement picture.

him. 'Dear me,' said Mr. Forster, 'I thought that was the wedding cake.'

## VI

With a new and unaccustomed chatelaine at Harewood House the inevitable changes were made in perfect agreement. The great Adam mansion in any event had confronted stern economic hazards after the death of the Princess Royal's husband, when Goldsborough Hall and many estate farms had been sold to help pay death duties. Harewood was opened to the public, and the Dowager Countess, the Princess Royal, made her home in one wing, from which she sallied forth, rather like Betsy Trotwood, to retrieve rubbish dropped by the more thoughtless new-style visitors. In 1952 the marriage hopes of her second son, Gerald, then aged twenty-seven, also freshly occupied her affectionate attention. The Duke of Windsor once said that Queen Mary, with her invincible virtue and correctness, looked out as from a fortress upon the rest of humanity; but the Princess Royal had her mother's insight with more than her mother's sympathy.

What did it matter if her future new daughter-in-law, then Miss Angela Dowding, was an actress and a little older than Gerald? What seemed important was that Angela should be the right girl for her son. Their happiness was obvious from the first meeting, and the Princess found herself listening with intense amusement to stories of E.N.S.A. repertory tours with a Jack Hawkins company, entertaining troops in Italy and Egypt, India, Ceylon and Burma. When the engagement was announced the newspapers uncovered the delectable morsel of gossip that the girl who was about to marry King George V's grandson had been born in a semi-detached house in a London suburb . . . but what a pity it was that they never disclosed the real reason. Angela's mother had a rooted dislike of hospitals and nursing homes and hit upon the happy idea of staying in her midwife's little house during the confinement.

After their wedding the young couple set up their first home in a fashionable mews off the Bayswater Road, a circumstance which the Princess Royal must also have reported to Queen Mary with great enjoyment. It was the very house, 21 Albion Mews, which had served as the 'pub' indeed in Margery Sharp's novel *Britannia*

*Mews*. For their second home, too, Gerald was to lead his mother into an amusing adventure.

On the verge of Windsor Great Park there stood the Duke of Windsor's former bachelor home, the deserted Fort Belvedere, a grace-and-favour residence which the Queen had only recently told the Crown Commissioners she no longer required. The grounds were becoming a wilderness of bracken and brambles and the house stood mouldering in decay after more than a dozen years of disuse. Birch saplings rose from cracks in the swimming pool. Beyond the front door was a nightmare of peeling wallpaper and falling plaster. Damp and mould disfigured bedrooms and drawing-rooms. The Princess Royal had but to find out whether the Queen had any objection to Gerald as a tenant, and she was the first to volunteer active help in restoring the garden. For nearly two years the regeneration of this dilapidated scene was one of her staple interests. Regardless of the battle scars she helped disentangle rampant brambles from among the climbing roses and watched each changing vista of progress with delight.

Gerald and Angela had one child, Henry, named after his grandfather, who was born in 1953 only two weeks before the coronation. This was the fourth crowning of close relatives—if we may include Maud of Norway—which Princess Mary attended in her lifetime. For further commemoration, Marion, the Countess of Harewood, also presented Lord Harewood with a son, the second of her three boys, in the coronation year.

Queen Mary had lived to see only her first Lascelles great-grandson, but the Princess Royal found an extended phase of fulfil-ment in the new reign, with its fresh domestic patterns. The present author possesses a set of photographs of grandmama and grandsons at Harewood with a donkey she had given them. There are snap-shots of the four boys with their bicycle and dogs, with the Princess Royal a contented figure in the midst of this family activity. Other photographs show the Princess's remarkable collection of owls—owls in jade or humble pottery, in ivory and metal or in porcelain decked with semi-precious stones—which always made her birthday easy to commemorate. To repay one of his grandmother's gifts a youngster had only to present her with an owl, which he might whittle himself from a block of wood or find in a local shop, to add to her collection. In being closely associated with the city of Leeds, the Princess was amused to discover an owl in the civic coat-of-arms. As patroness of the Embroiders' Guild she was once presented with an embroidered owl, covered in jewels and sequins, and her dining-table was decked with a set of owl mustard pots.

On her breakfast-table, however, was a rival bird, a porcelain parrot, a sentimental reminder of the parrot that had strutted on her father's breakfast-table at Sandringham so long ago. As a senior member of the Royal Family, 'Aunt Mary' came to be more frequently consulted, for her knowledge of precedents and associative details was immense. In the year when Prince Edward was born, the Queen asked her aunt to distribute the Royal Maundy; a delicate compliment, for the Queen Mother was the only other woman to have acted as deputy. An Abbey official who sought to instruct the Princess Royal on the ceremonial found her fully familiar with it. 'I've been reading it up,' she explained, 'to refresh my memory.' It was at least thirty years since she had seen George V and Queen Mary play their part in the ritual, shortly after the traditional royal attendance at the service had been revived after more than two centuries.

The Princess Royal enjoyed undertaking the same tasks and responsibilities as the younger post-war princesses, disconcerting as she may have found some aspects of their world. 'I simply ask myself what my father or mother would have done,' she would say, to solve a dilemma, but the mind boggles at the thought of Queen Mary dancing with the president of an African republic on independence night . . . or of George V in a plane stacked above a fog-bound airport. The Princess had never crossed the Atlantic until she visited the West Indies in 1953. Two years later, when invited to Canada by the regiments of which she was colonel-in-chief, the Canadian Scottish and the Royal Canadian Corps of Signals, she accepted so many extra engagements that the initial arrangements spread into a coast-to-coast royal tour. Both these journeys were made by sea. She recalled her initial distrust of flying with amusement a few years later when she flew by the polar route to Canada in a Yukon aircraft of the Royal Canadian Air Force.

On her sixtieth birthday in 1957, she found herself planning an official tour of Nigeria, and agreeing to an itinerary that might have seemed arduous to someone ten years younger, reading it up so thoroughly beforehand that she knew more about Lagos and Kano than the people who lived there. 'The Princess made a dozen speeches in as many days,' as I noted at the time, 'her duties included the inauguration of two legislatures on behalf of the Queen, opening new universities and factories, hospitals and model market-places.' Then in 1960 came her three-month tour of the West Indies and British Honduras, originally intended as a recuperative cruise aboard the royal yacht *Britannia*, if only she would have made it so. This was followed in 1962 by her visit to preside over the independence ceremonies of Trinidad and Tobago, and the same year saw her tour of Service units in the Mediterranean, with duty visits to Gibraltar, Cyprus, Tripoli and Tobruk.

The millions who thought of the Princess Royal as Yorkshire's Princess scarcely knew of these activities. It was left to an American magazine to style her 'the anonymous ambassador'. Was she attempting too much? In the autumn of 1964 she had no sooner returned from a month's tour of Newfoundland than she flew to Lusaka for a week of exacting functions for the independence ceremonies of the new state of Zambia. With all the tact he could muster, her equerry, Sir Geoffrey Eastwood, mentioned that the Princess had never been afraid of hard work, but his subtle hints made little difference. Meanwhile, as early as 1963, she faced new problems in private life. She must have seen with middle-aged insight that difficulties had entered the Harewood marriage and, although her elder son and daughter-in-law attempted to spare her their emotional turmoil, it was later to be thought a blessing that she did not live to know of their divorce.

That winter the Princess Royal suffered from a particularly heavy cold, but March 28th, 1965, was a day of unexpectedly warm sunshine at Harewood and she suggested a walk to Lord Harewood and two of her grandsons, James and Jeremy. They took the familiar path past the stables and had come in sight of the lake when the Princess murmured, 'I feel rather dizzy,' and suddenly the world and its duties and problems all slipped away. It was twelve years to the very week since her mother, too, had died.

# BOOK TWO

# Princess Anne

'She is thy very princess'
—*Pericles*, Act 5, Scene 1.

# PROLOGUE

# Scene: Nearly the Present

*Through all the changing scenes of pomp and circumstance, no British Queen Regnant has ever first held the title of Princess Royal. No princess of that degree, in other words, has ever succeeded to the Throne. It is as if the monarchy enjoys a built-in equalizing factor; and the fact that the distinction of Princess Royal is conferred for life may seem one of the fortuitous assets of stability.*

*The present Queen Elizabeth II was born Princess Elizabeth of York, eldest daughter of King George V's second son, the Duke of York. With the Abdication of Edward VIII in 1936, her father succeeded as King George VI, when her aunt, Princess Mary, had already held the title of Princess Royal since 1932. Though elder daughter of the King, Princess Elizabeth could not thus be Princess Royal, and her aunt was happily still living at the time of her coronation in 1953.*

*In the play of historic continuity, the Princess Elizabeth and Prince Philip perhaps missed a trick in not inviting the Princess Royal to act as sponsor at the christening of their only daughter, the Princess Anne, in 1950.*

# 1   The Noonday Child

## I

Princess Anne was born nearly at high noon, during the height of summer, in the mid-year of the century—a notable conjunction, surely, for a girl-child of royal lineage, through both parents, of more than a thousand years. On her father's side, she was born a Mountbatten, endowed with the Mountbatten drive and pertinacity and perhaps with their tendency also to carry purposefulness to a fault. She was indeed so truly Mountbatten that she might have begun life as a Miss Mountbatten or styled only with the courtesy title of Lady Anne Mountbatten if her grandfather, King George VI, had not hurriedly amended his own family rules.

Less than two years earlier, and barely a month before the birth of Prince Charles, the King's secretary, Sir Alan Lascelles, had pointed out that under the provisions laid down by George V in reconstituting the House of Windsor in 1917, the styles of Royal Highness and of Prince or Princess passed only in the male line. This would have excluded the children of Princess Elizabeth, whose position as heiress presumptive to the Throne had been neither envisaged nor provided for. By Letters Patent of October 22nd, 1948, King George VI accordingly revised his father's definition; and it must be said that nothing better pleased public opinion in 1950 than the advent of a Princess at that moment in time.

The Monarchy was then nearing one of its high noons of affection and approval. The coming of peace, the romance and Westminster Abbey wedding of Elizabeth and Philip, the Silver Wedding celebrations of the King and Queen (George VI and his Queen Elizabeth) and then the birth of their grandson, Prince Charles, had all brightened the flame of popularity and esteem. The young Philip was astonishingly handsome, 'a heart-throb' as the young people said. After marriage and motherhood, Princess Elizabeth was still charmingly shy and uncertain. In July, 1949, when their infant son was seven months old, they had moved into Clarence House as a home of their own, and it illustrated public interest that a book dealing with the new furnishing and decoration of the mansion enjoyed a wide general sale. The young couple were not averse to illuminating at least this much of their private domestic atmosphere, and when the Princess flew out to Malta to join her husband for their second wedding anniversary, public opinion—and specula-tion, too—was as tender as that of any watchful maiden aunt.

Princess Elizabeth adored Malta. The island gave her the sense of being more a naval officer's wife than a king's daughter, and she revelled in the comparative simplicity and seclusion of the Villa Guardamangia, where the sunny terrace was just sufficiently screened from the constant sea breeze, and she could awake at her husband's side to the sound of church-bells and the distant clamour of the town. Her hosts, Earl and Countess Mountbatten of Burma, Philip's Uncle Dickie and Aunt Edwina, were tactful and con-siderate, and their staff were trustworthy and proof against the flagrant bribes offered by French and German journalists and photographers. The Princess said, ruefully, 'I expect *they* will know before we shall' and by the New Year she felt the happy certainty that a child had been conceived. In the convents of Valetta, young lace workers began putting some of their finest work, caps and collarets, to one side; and much of Princess Anne's layette was indeed to be of Maltese lace.

Back in England, Princess Elizabeth withdrew from public engagements in May, and the Duke of Edinburgh returned from Malta at the end of July in readiness for the event. Looking back to those quiet, confident family days, one remembers above all the crowds that gathered around Clarence House every morning, their numbers growing hourly. They were good-humoured ex-pectant British crowds, each cluster quietly waiting a while at the kerbside, with scarcely a transatlantic face among them, very different from the international tourist throngs of today. They were holiday-makers in London, enjoying 'holidays at home', as the slogan-makers put it, content to wait and watch, men as well as women intangibly in touch with the sentiment and magic of royalty.

If they were patient, the children were encouragingly told, they might see the King and Queen. The King had in fact gone to Bal-moral, but the Queen—the present Queen Mother—had remained to be near her daughter in London. The crowds instantly recognized and gave a cheer to old Queen Mary, waving from her car as she went to call at Clarence House; they saw a puzzled chubby Prince Charles, with nurse and chauffeur, being taken for his airing. All through the sunny week-end, they watched the coming and going of doctors and nurses, and they seemed to gather and regroup from nowhere early on the Monday morning, August 15th, gazing at Clarence House and even scanning the adjacent windows of St. James's Palace. All morning the people waited with a sense of imminent history. Then the sound from across the park of Big Ben striking twelve seemed to coincide with a little cheer from the crowd, and a message spread along the pavements like a bush telegraph, 'It's a girl!'

The news went out on tape to an expectant world within the hour and, simultaneously, the first bulletin was posted at the gate of Clarence House, in secretary Martin Charteris's neat and spaced hand-writing, and signed by the four doctors,

Clarence House,
St. James's
15th August, 1950

Her Royal Highness The Princess Elizabeth, Duchess of Edinburgh, was safely delivered of a Princess at 11.50 a.m. today.

Her Royal Highness and her daughter are both doing well.

    William Gilliatt

    John H. Peel

    Vernon F. Hall

    John Weir.

The crowds pressed forward. They formed a queue—it was an age of queues—to pass before the bulletin board. They were still there, reading, exclaiming, smiling, when the 41-gun salute of the King's troop, Royal Horse Artillery, boomed across Hyde Park, echoed more distantly by the guns at the Tower of London. Meanwhile, Prince Philip had telephoned his own jubilant message to his mother and grandmother at Kensington Palace, 'It's the sweetest girl' and the Queen, on taking her departure, had jubilantly called to the crowds, 'It's a lovely baby!'

Prince Philip had been due for naval promotion and, by happy coincidence, had been gazetted Lieutenant Commander that same morning. Historians did not miss the point that his daughter was the first royal baby to be born at Clarence House since its separation from the adjoining Palace of St. James some 125 years earlier. The young father's next filial duty was to fly up to Balmoral to tell the King all over again that the baby, weighing six pounds, was blonde and blue-eyed and yet 'just like her mother', and to secure his father-in-law's approval for her chosen names. He carried the news, too, of how Prince Charles had received his sister. Not yet aged two, the little boy was taking a most watchful protective interest from the outset.

The names were to be Anne Elizabeth Alice Louise, which the King thought 'unusual and charming'. 'Anne' was chosen less by Stuart predilections than in compliment to Princess Elizabeth's close friend, Lady Anne Nevill. 'Elizabeth' was in token of the baby's grandmother, the present Queen Mother; 'Alice' equally complimented Prince Philip's mother, Princess Andrew of Greece, and Princess Alice of Athlone, and 'Louise' was favoured as a tribute to Earl Mountbatten of Burma, 'Uncle Dickie', whose first name was in fact Louis. The happy chance that three of the names, all except Elizabeth, had been shared by a Princess Royal passed unnoticed at the time. Anne recalls the Princess Royal Anne of Georgian days, the friend of Handel. Alice was a baptismal name of the baby's great-aunt, the then Princess Royal, and the last name was that of Princess Louise, Duchess of Fife. Such links may interest the student of patronymics.

The infant Princess was fourteen days old when, amid the bustle of congratulations, the father registered her birth before Mr. Boreham, the Westminster Registrar, though not without overlooking a small but persistent mistake. The entry requiring the 'name and maiden surname' of the mother was set down as 'Her Royal Highness the Princess Elizabeth Alexandra Mary, Duchess of Edinburgh', thus omitting the maiden surname of Windsor. (Indeed, the same error occurred upon the birth certificate of Prince Charles and escaped the vigilant attention of the King, who had fallen ill at the time.) With more accuracy, the Registrar handed over the new Princess's identity card, MAPM3/96 and the 'child's ration-book' entitling her to the prescribed allowance of bread and milk, eggs and sugar, meat, margarine and butter. The identity card, I am assured, is still carefully preserved in the Royal Archives, but the ration-book long since disappeared, snipped away, coupon by coupon.

## II

The new Princess spent much of the first month of her life in a crib-basket in her father's dressing-room, the nearest suitable room to her mother's suite, a sociable month during her waking hours when the staff came to peep at her one by one, under Nanny Lightbody's watchful gaze. In all her twenty years' experience, from her native Scotland to the Shires, Helen Lightbody said she had never before had a girl baby, a comment capped by a footman who told his family that he had never before seen such a sweet sleeping princess. All the Clarence House duty police came, from Inspector Usher to the youngest constables, usually marching through the hallway in pairs, as if on a particularly dangerous patrol, much to household amusement. Palace jealousies were aroused, in fact, until the clerical staff at the Lord Chamberlain's offices next door were allowed to tiptoe through a pass-door. In that first month, the baby's visitors ranged from old Princess Marie Louise, a link with Jenny Lind and even Disraeli, to the delighted wife of the French Ambassador, who curtailed her holiday in Savoie for the pleasure of cooing in mingled French and English over the cot.

Perhaps Princess Anne may be said to have made her debut to the larger world when Cecil Beaton came to photograph her and we see the newcomer through his discerning eyes and sensitive camera, 'a small baby with quite a definite nose for one so young, large, sleepy grey-green eyes and a particularly pretty mouth . . .' The young mother, eager that everything should be perfect, was willing to pose with her daughter until her arms ached. But the supreme result came quite by chance when Prince Charles, who had been enjoying the fun, wriggled alongside the cot curtains to plant an enchanting and unexpected kiss on his sister's cheek just as the camera clicked. 'It's delicious,' said the Princess, when shown the proof, 'most fortunate in every way!' Throughout the world the photograph was more widely reproduced than any baby picture within living memory. The first news photographs, however, were gained when the baby embarked on her first journey when a month old, a tiny shawl-wrapped cocoon carried in her mother's arms onto the night train to Scotland, an appropriate initial destination for Princess Anne of Edinburgh. The dressing-room and nursery at Clarence House were exchanged for the pleasant and time-worn nursery at Birkhall on the Balmoral estate, the King's first opportunity to see his grand-daughter, 'the new delectable'.

As her elder brother had been, the Princess was christened in the Music Room at Buckingham Palace. The more customary pre-war scene of these ceremonies, the Private Chapel, had been bombed into desolation, but the silver-gilt font, used for royal baptisms since 1840—and incidentally for three Princesses Royal—was brought up from Windsor Castle. It was an October day of misty sun. The then Archbishop of York, Dr. Garbett, presided, and the little central figure wore the traditional royal christening robe of Honiton lace, the underlying satin grown pearly and fragile with age, as one could see, though still essentially perfect.

As usual on these occasions, the gathering was limited to close relatives and friends and family staff. The five sponsors were the Queen (now the Queen Mother); Princess Alice, standing as proxy for her namesake, Princess Andrew of Greece; and the baby's aunt, Princess Margarita of Hohenlohe-Langenburg; with Earl Mountbatten and Andrew Elphinstone. Among the fifty guests, the one comparative stranger was Prince Philip's Maltese steward, Vincent Psaila, alternately beaming and devout and trembling with nerves after the ceremony when presented to the King. Probably the oldest guest was the baby's great-grandmother, Queen Mary, in her eighty-fourth year, whose journals disclose that at any christening she invariably expected the baby to cry. But Anne was calm and sweet, though wide awake throughout, cooing and smiling, a wakefulness sustained during the christening party, when 'baby sister' was naturally the centre of so much interest that Prince Charles was hard put to win attention, now wishing to be beside his mother, now to sit, now to stand, and now seeking a small boy's excuse to leave the room, as Cecil Beaton's enchanting and amusing photographs recall.

Then little Anne settled down to life with 'Nana', to the placid nursery routine, timed to the distant chimes of Big Ben and the pipes of the cuckoo clock. Her mother's laughter, her brother's toy trumpet, the morning strains of the Guards' band must have gradually impinged on her consciousness. When her mother was away in Malta—that first Christmas, for instance—her attentive grand-parents, her aunt Margaret, Nana and the assistant nurse, Mabel Anderson, took over in a quintet of protective warmth. And there was Charles. I leaf through my photographs and notes to discover a picture of the two children in their prams side by side, when Anne was about eight months old. She is in her frilled baby bonnet, Charles with a pram blanket embroidered with hornpiping sailors. And he leans over to take his sister's hand, while she smiles confidently, with some hint at making conversation in her own baby tongue. Late in the summer of 1951 Princess Elizabeth and her husband were to undertake a tour of Canada, and the preliminary family group photographs taken in the garden of Clarence House for the occasion show Anne, at nearly a year old, crawling barefoot across the lawn and reaching to pluck flowers from the border. Charles of course joined her: passers-by in the Mall on the other side of the wall could have had no idea of the pretty scene not four yards away.

The nannies saw that Princess Elizabeth's eyes brimmed with tears on parting from her children for her longer tours abroad, when leaving for Canada in 1951, for instance, and again during the leavetaking of the intended long Commonwealth tour on January 31st, 1952. The King took an ever-increasing interest in his grand-children and went to see them at nursery tea that same day, after visiting the airport in the morning to wave his daughter farewell. It was the last farewell, as we know, for he died a week later in his sleep.

## III

Princess Anne was nearly eighteen months old when her mother became Queen. The daughter of the Sovereign was thus a future 'Princess Royal presumptive', if one may nudge the royal prerogative. Her grand-aunt Mary had of course been Princess Royal for twenty years, and was happily to be with us for many years more, but Anne was now—at that moment in time—second in succession to the Throne. No thought of such matters ever entered her parents' minds in the grief and shock of their hurried return to Britain. The children had been at Sandringham, where Charles at least could dimly understand that his grandfather had gone. Still secure in babyhood, Anne was in her pram in a quiet corner of the Clarence House garden as the funeral cortège passed down the Mall. And shortly before Easter the suggestion that the Queen Mother should have the children at Royal Lodge for a few days was one of the gentle devices employed to draw her from the shadow world of mourning.

Neither the Queen nor Philip wished to leave Clarence House for the cramped and sunless royal suites of Buckingham Palace. They hoped that the Palace could be used for official business while Clarence remained their private residence, but their adviser, the Prime Minister, Mr. Winston Churchill, regarded the Palace move as essential. The royal couple finally left Clarence House on April 10th to spend Easter at Windsor and, as I have said elsewhere,* Edward Halliday's sketches for his *Conversation Piece, Clarence House* captured their last domestic scene in their pleasant home, with Princess Anne alertly building towers with her building bricks upon the floor.

Nanny Lightbody bore with fortitude the responsibility of moving the nursery suite to the Palace, lock, stock and toys. Instead of the Clarence nursery with its fresh white walls, the Palace rooms were in need of new paintwork. The Clarence carpeting nowhere fitted the rooms and had to be made up with odd lengths and patches. It was a case of making do. The Queen laughed at the comparative 'shrinking' of her children, when seen dwarfed in their huge and old-fashioned bath-tub. Yet Anne can have scarcely noticed the change, accustomed to moving from one royal nursery to another. The cabinet Queen Mary had given her for her toys (and, in reality, her more fragile treasures) still faced her brother's slightly larger cabinet across the room. Anne and Charles still had their own child-size play-tables where, already copying her brother's nimble fingers, she could mess with Plasticine to her heart's content. The corgis, like the furnishing, were quickly at home, if not without a misadventure or two in the strange outer corridor. When Charles was absent, Anne still made her pet toy rabbit, Bugs Bunny, the recipient of much conversation and her newly-ordered world remained the same.

When George VI had come to the Throne, a governess had

---

* *The Married Life of The Queen* (W. H. Allen), 1970-2.

instantly instructed his daughters to curtsey to him, but Elizabeth and Philip could not bear such protocol with their own family and it was quickly discontinued. This troubled Queen Mary, who considered that the children should always remain trained in their bows and curtseys and feared they might all too readily forget the old courtly ways. Charles would always bow obligingly. But when the old Queen gently bade her great-grand-daughter, 'Anne, curtsey to me,' the child 'shyly hung her head, scuffed the carpet with her shoe and looked vague'. 'Little donkey,' Queen Mary would say, fondly.

Probably Princess Margaret originally suggested, and Queen Mary certainly encouraged, the game of 'Coronations', which caught the imagination of both children as the preparations for the great event went forward. During 'great-gran's' last Christmas, there were opportunities for dressing up from the deep Sandringham costume chests and back in London the children were taken to see the seamstresses working on the velvet train their mother was to wear. Peeping at the soldiers marching in the Palace forecourt, Anne announced one morning that the Coronation had already begun, only to be loftily informed by her brother that it was just the changing of the guard. Not yet three, Anne remembers the Coronation only with a sense of being closeted without Charles or Nana or Mama, 'the normal sisterly fury at being left behind', she says, and then of 'playing with a lot of invited friends', until her father led her out with Charles onto the Palace balcony, where she waved with a puzzled frown at the great sea of people. 'I was allowed to do that.'

She had already ridden with her brother in the gold Coronation coach, drawn around a courtyard of the Royal Mews during a rehearsal. During June, indeed, she twice stood on the Palace balcony, looking alarmed at the noise and fervour of the crowds, first when her mother wore the crown and then again when the Queen was in red-coated military uniform for her official birthday. On her third birthday Anne was more impressed by the strange need of playing hostess to a number of cousins 'for whom I couldn't have cared less'. The party was in fact staged in the somewhat backstage 'tin wing' at Balmoral, a corrugated iron extension structure with a playroom, where the children could make as much noise as they liked and an old upright piano accompanied ring-o-roses and musical chairs.

Although most of the guests brought gifts, the store of playthings in her nursery cupboard never increased. Toys were regularly parcelled off to children's hospitals faster than new supplies came in. Anne had reached the 'Wait for me!' age of scampering after her elder brother, but she feels sure that Charles looked on while she climbed the trees, a view confirmed in my own memento collection of early photographs. When Charles first rode a borrowed Shetland, Anne was lifted into the saddle and keenly tried to learn how to hold the reins, though so much younger. Her first pony, a strawberry roan named William, was indeed purchased for both children to ride when Anne was barely three, a calculated stratagem to hold their interest while their parents were away on the Commonwealth tour which the Coronation year concluded. Their grandmama also occupied them at this time with a gift of two South American love-birds, which they were permitted to house in the nursery provided they cleaned out the cage themselves. The session with sand, seed and water became a daily chore; and whenever the children went away to Royal Lodge at week-ends, they politely had to ask the nursery footman please to look after 'David and Annie', as the pair were named, as a special favour. Anne took such an interest in 'Annie' that she trained her to come and perch on a stick held out at arm's length, an exercise invariably eagerly practised the moment the children returned from a week-end.

Early convinced that she could thus charm the birds, the little Princess found the budgerigars at Royal Lodge unpromising recruits, though a visit to the aviary remained one of her regular daily pleasures. Life with grandmama in 1953–4 also had the attraction of the Little House, the child-size model cottage in its garden glade, which had been a gift to the Queen as a little girl from the people of Wales. Anne and Charles supposedly looked after the Little House while Mummie was away, sedulously dusting and polishing and serving sponge-cake refreshments to Nana. The panelled living-room was a replica fifty-four inches high and seven feet square, a space into which their grandmama squeezed like an obliging giantess, announcing that she felt as cosy as a rabbit in its hutch. But best of all Anne spent hours pedalling a toy wooden pony-and-trap across the lawns, and loved riding the old rocking-horses that decorate the hallway of Royal Lodge to this day.

The domestic arts seldom held her attention for long. On the other hand, the picture postcards from her parents, arriving in mysteriously sealed envelopes, were carefully kept, useful in geography lessons some years later, and colouring her first impressions of the variety and extent of her mother's realms.

## IV

Life without 'Mummy' was, of course, the unchanging calm and placidity of life with Nana and Mabel. Miss Helen Lightbody, a Scotswoman then in her middle thirties, had begun her unstinted dedication to children with the family of a Jedburgh doctor immediately on leaving school and, after varied experience, had spent six years of nursery responsibility with the two young Gloucester princes, William and Richard. If she seemed a disciplinarian, her strictness was based on her firm belief that royal children, like other children, could be too readily indulged and spoiled. Miss Lightbody ruled the royal nursery indeed with impeccable order: her more serious difficulties occurred with staff who glibly attempted to introduce their friends on visits while the Queen was away. With two nursery maids, and attendant footman—known as the nursery page—a detective on call and, in the Queen's absence, her chauffeur, Mr. Purvey, the nursery was as amply staffed as the nurseries of any earlier generation.

Mabel Anderson, the assistant nursemaid, was also Scottish to her fingertips, the daughter of a policeman who had been killed in the blitz. Her mother came from Elgin and, after the death of the breadwinner, the family had returned there, only just down the road from the commotion of the Gordonstoun rugger field. Like Bobo MacDonald, formerly the Queen's nanny, Mabel's sense of vocation had originated in looking after a younger sister, followed by six years of nursemaid experience and, again like Bobo, Mabel had never lost her inner wonderment at her turn of fortune in working for the Queen. Other nannies have progressed, like Miss Lightbody, by recommendation from one royal household to another. Mabel Anderson had inserted an advertisement in the 'Situations Wanted' column of a nursing magazine and to her astonishment found herself being interviewed by the then Princess Elizabeth a week or two later.

Glasgow-born Miss Catherine Peebles also presided over the

nursery schoolroom, though at first she had little to do with Anne. Recruited from the then Duchess of Kent's staff at Coppins, where she had formerly been governess to the young Prince Michael of Kent, 'Mispy', as the children nicknamed her, would appear for a story-book reading or an elementary drawing lesson on Miss Lightbody's afternoons off. These were the hours when Miss Anderson took charge and, as if aware of a more relaxed atmosphere, Anne occasionally attempted some of her wilder if fairly brief tantrums. She broke rules with impunity in imperiously dragging Charles' most cherished mechanical toys from his personal cupboard, but received one of her first firm spankings after a scene of raging defiance when refusing to put her own toys tidily away.

During the Commonwealth tour, Miss Lightbody and Miss Peebles shared the joint responsibility of writing a report or letter to the Queen once a week on the children and their activities. 'I would like to hear about the little everyday things,' the Queen had suggested, and so the news sped to Fiji and Tonga of Anne's first dancing lesson with Miss Vacani, of a rainy afternoon when she became 'intensively preoccupied' with Plasticine, of the popularity of a washable doll, destined to be prematurely worn out with intensive scrubbing. The children went to Sandringham for Christmas with their grandmother, and on Christmas morning their parents telephoned them from New Zealand. The Queen confessed to her hostess that she found it a great comfort to hear her daughter's rippling laughter on the other side of the world. Perplexed by hearing her mother's familiar yet disembodied voice, Anne thereupon watched the telephone closely for some days. 'That's my Mummy and Papa,' she would say to visitors, pointing at a photograph, and then announce, 'They have telephoned, you know.'

To help disperse the miles, the Queen Mother commissioned the artist, Ulrica Forbes, to undertake some sketches of Anne to send to the Queen, and we pleasantly see the 'most appealingly friendly child' through her intent vision,* 'small yet tall for her age, shaking my hand with a surprisingly firm grip.' These courtesies observed, the little girl asked if she could see into her visitor's handbag and offered in return to show the contents of one of her own, opening

* The author is indebted to the artist's original impressions among her private papers.

## 2  Enthusiasms

### I

A doll's house that seems to have scarcely been used stands on a trolley under dust-covers in one of the storerooms of Windsor Castle, held hostage until some future day when it can perhaps be put on show for charity. Thirty inches high, six feet long, moduled and 'contemporary' with sun windows and a roof-garden, the house is wheeled out on occasion for the amusement of junior second cousins and other little girls who call the Queen 'Aunt Lilibet'. The chromium-plated bath-taps yield real water, a tiny radio in the lounge plays real programmes, there are suites of modernist furniture, refrigerators and a washing machine perfectly to scale. This was, of course, Princess Anne's doll's house. While visiting a London furniture factory when she was a little girl, Prince Philip was told that the workmen would like to make some furniture for her doll's house if they could know the size. 'Unfortunately, my daughter has no doll's house,' Philip replied and, as so often, the original idea grew into an extravaganza of craftsmanship and perfection, a gift for the Princess on her sixth birthday.

Unluckily the project ran into some difficulties of timing. Anne was to celebrate her birthday aboard *Britannia* that year in Scottish waters during a cruise of the Western Isles, and the presentation accordingly had to be made in London in July. The Princess danced with excitement. 'May I please play with it *now*?' she asked one of the donors, and delighted the deputation by remembering of her own accord to shake hands vigorously with each one as they took their departure. For four or five days Nana permitted an hour's *careful* play with the doll's house as a reward for good behaviour. But then 'Daddy's Mummy', Princess Andrew of Greece, arrived at the Palace and the attraction of the new toy faded against Anne's unbounded enthusiasm for her grandmother.

Their affection had been cemented the previous year when Princess Andrew had joined the Royal Family shortly after her seven-

142

tieth birthday, to sail aboard *Britannia* around the coast of Wales and western Scotland. This saw the occasion when Charles first stepped onto the soil of Wales, to build sand-castles, appropriately enough, on the shores of Milford Haven. In Scottish waters, they had all gone ashore to visit the Queen Mother at the Castle of Mey, and Anne had skipped with glee at the thought of taking 'Grandmother' to see 'Granny' in her enchanted castle, where you could feel the power of the sea-wind if you put your hand against the windows. The children accepted the nun-like grey nursing uniform, which Princess Andrew affected, with as little question as they regarded her deafness and gusty manner of speaking, her trick of throwing out words which made each syllable sound important and different. Years later, Anne learned that her grandmother had suffered a life-long speech defect, but meanwhile the attention the old lady paid when a child had something to say, and the need of allowing her to watch one's lips, all heightened Grandmother's engrossing fascination.

Now it was all happening again. On her second voyage on *Britannia*, Grandmother proved that she had lost none of her power of story-telling. The old lady knew more Bible stories, and could tell them more vividly than anyone else. And there were her 'little tales', too, of children in Greece who had been hungry in wartime; Anne could clearly understand that they had to be fed on loaves of bread and cabbages, and that the seeking of every cabbage had become an adventure. Improvising on her experiences while running an orphanage in German-occupied Athens, Princess Andrew found her little grand-daughter older than her years in comprehension.

When the Queen and Prince Philip left the royal yacht for an engagement ashore, Grandmother assumed authority. 'You may be sure I know how to handle children,' she said once, crisply settling a difficulty with Nana. Anne was, indeed, her twentieth grandchild, and it needed only a single reproving glance from her dark brown eyes to establish firm discipline. Whether Nanny Lightbody resented this divided rule is more difficult and delicate to tell, but the atmosphere was not without strain at times. Princess Andrew presently flew to Stockholm to stay with her sister, Queen Louise of Sweden, blandly unaware of any domestic discords, but left behind her a sense of change in the air. Prince Charles would soon be going to school, reducing the need of nursery staff. The

Queen and her husband did not foresee that they would be having more children, and late that summer 'by an amicable agreement' Miss Lightbody resigned.

To smooth the transition, Mabel Anderson had long slept in the night nursery with Anne and had always enjoyed a larger share of her affections. When Philip gave his son swimming lessons in the Palace pool, and Anne perilously insisted on joining in at every opportunity, it was Mabel who obligingly donned a costume and gave her extra tuition. Mabel was the same age as the Queen, establishing an important affinity in the children's eyes, and she managed young Anne with diplomacy when the Princess's fierce insistence on sharing more of Charles's classroom time could have created new stresses. From her attachment to the novel traits of her grandmother, the Princess next swung into an enthusiasm for the governess, whom Charles called 'Mispy' and whom Anne for a time persisted in addressing as 'Bambi', from some fancied resemblance she had found in a movie.

That Christmas, brother and sister saw their first pantomine with the Queen. The occasion found Princess Anne highly sceptical when introduced to Dick Whittington's cat and assured that it was 'a real pantomime cat'. But from this in turn sprang the great dressing-up craze when Anne and Charles missed no opportunity of seeking out discarded clothes and forgotten uniforms in any chest or wardrobe and even beguiled their mother into trying on her old Windsor pantomime costumes. It was like the old Coronation game all over again, except that the mime and make-believe gave Anne a paradoxical and fulfilling opportunity of attracting attention in her own right which she rarely experienced. Relatives say that her father as a boy was a 'loner', and Anne took after him. She confesses that she made a point of disliking most other small girls, as a child, and would fight with the boys, a humorous self-assessment not to be taken too literally.

During the charades fever, when suitable robes and gowns were discovered in every closet, the Princess rehearsed for an imaginary film which, though never actually photographed, had its 'run-throughs' revived by its producer, young Norton Knatchbull, and his father, Lord Brabourne, at every meeting. Norton was just a month older than Charles; his younger brother, Michael, had been born in the same year as Anne. Lady Brabourne had of course been

Patricia Mountbatten, one of Earl Mountbatten's two daughters, before her marriage. Others in the cast, one might recall, were Rose Nevill, born by happy coincidence precisely a month before Anne, and the Phillips and Butter sisters, grand-daughters of Lady Zia Wernher.

From all these families Princess Anne has drawn upon deep reservoirs of lifelong friendship. One remembers Anne and Rose as children at Eridge Castle one day, helpless with laughter after discovering an old-fashioned ear-trumpet and having a wonderful time. As nine-year-olds, both were to be bridesmaids to Princess Margaret, together with Rose's cousin, Angela. In their teens, Angela—daughter of the Queen's close friends, Lord and Lady Rupert Nevill—had her coming-out dance at St. James's Palace—and Princess Anne, having broken her nose while riding to hounds, was out of hospital just in time for the party. But as children their schooling traced different paths, and Miss Peebles found it difficult to find companions of the right age for the Princess when Prince Charles began going to day school.

Several little girls were considered for the Palace classroom, but good behaviour tended to break down when away from obvious adult attention. Play sessions however always ran on happily with the then Dean of Windsor's grand-daughter, Caroline Hamilton, and her friend Susan Babington-Smith. Both were Anne's age, and one afternoon when Miss Peebles suggested a very special toy, the young heads, blonde and brunette, bent over it with serenity. And so Princess Anne's doll's house once more came into its own.

## II

Prince Philip inclines to the theory that his daughter perhaps felt neglected as a child in contrast to her elder brother, hence the competitive instinct, the leadership syndrome, so strongly marked in the quirks of personality that intrigue us today. Her riding success and her defiant fox-hunting are alike both paying old childhood scores. Besides, Anne would always try anything once, a virtue in a princess, whether perilously exploring the dizzy parapets of Windsor Castle or feeding biscuits to a Russian bear, Niki, an intimidating gift of the Soviet leaders, Kruschev and Bulganin. As a very small girl, Princess Anne discovered that the Palace sentries, in their scarlet coats and tall bearskins, presented arms with a tremendous clatter whenever she passed by. Prince Charles had ignored the phenomenon but the Princess could not resist walking to and fro, just as her mother had done as a child, rewarded each time with the same repeated drill, to the sentry's great discomfiture.

Before Charles went to Cheam as a boarder, the Queen and her husband decided to visit the school, and found that their daughter was not to be left out of the expedition. On overhearing that some of the dormitory beds were two hundred years old, she sat on the unyielding mattress with a frown. In the classrooms, Queen Victoria herself could not have scowled more sternly at the stark and ink-stained desks. Anne did not envy Charles his schooling away from home but she missed his company and eagerly travelled in the estate car to meet him at the end of term. Hearing that there would be a visitor's race on sports day, she ran wildly about the Palace gardens in training 'not to let him down', and had the ultimate satisfaction of coming in third. Her brother, a little podgy then, complained that he wasn't accustomed to rich Cheam food. Anne had few food fads and would try any new dish, except peas, which she loathed. The story is that when away from home one day, she found grubs wriggling on her plate and ate them unflinchingly rather than cause any embarrassment at table.

Miss Peebles opened a rich new panorama, however, with her 'girls only' class. Under her tutelage, Anne and her two friends began a series of adventurous and unnoticed explorations of the bustling city around them, to St. Paul's Cathedral and Westminster Abbey, the Tower of London and Hampton Court, to museums and churches and the Zoo, and the governess discreetly steered her young trio away from crowds and the risk of curious onlookers and linked sightseeing with history lessons. Her stories of Queen Elizabeth I served to give Anne her youthful first impressions of her own mother's royal tasks and duties. As the three girls emerged from the Planetarium one day, a small boy in the queue piped up, 'What's the show like?' 'It was wonderful,' Anne replied, fresh from a year's journey around the sun, and then sought a reassurance of her own, 'That's what Mummy would have said, isn't it?'

Then there were regular private sessions at a Knightsbridge gymnasium, and piano lessons with Miss Hilda Bor, music studies not entirely wasted although the Princess describes her present-day standard as 'just tickling the keyboard'. In her eighth year, when the removal of her tonsils and adenoids became necessary, one must put on record that Anne made minor history by being the first member of the Royal Family to have an operation in hospital, taking her teddy-bear, a set of jigsaw puzzles and some books into the Great Ormond Street Hospital for Sick Children. At Windsor, during class holidays, when she sat to Mr. A. K. Lawrence for her portrait, the Queen half decided to curtail the sittings, convinced that her daughter could not sit still for long. But all turned out to be well, and the Queen discovered she had not counted on the youthful help of Prince Charles who considerately came and sat by his sister to help her pose and read aloud an adventure story about Australian bushrangers that held her enthralled.

Certainly, brother and sister find it difficult to recall any crisis of early rivalry. Quarrels flared up but were quickly settled, they seem to have always enjoyed each other's company, and both feel that they share the same wavelength of humour. When they began practising French together, a young Parisienne, Mlle. Bibiane de Roujoux, arrived at Balmoral to guide them into lunch-table conversation and invariably found it difficult to avert a sustained outbreak of giggles. Princess Anne was eight when a professional teacher, Mlle. Suzanne Josseron, came from the Kensington Lycée to take weekly French sessions in the Palace classroom. At about the same time, Anne disconcerted the Queen by slipping into a Cockney accent. Whether this was a side-effect of forming a new Buckingham Palace Brownie pack would appear doubtful, but for a few weeks the Princess's 'allo!' enjoyed an authentic tang of Bow Bells rather than Paris.

The re-establishment of the Palace Brownies had been Aunt Margo's (Princess Margaret's) idea. It extended Princess Anne's acquaintance a little, just as Charles had extended his own social circle at Cheam, and provided some youthful personal satisfaction in proving that she could already tie a reef knot or sheet bend, lay a table for two and fully knew the composition of the Union Jack. Although the newspapers played up the fact that the pack included the daughters of a taxi-driver and an electrician, the group was in fact Caroline Hamilton's somewhat elite pack from Holy Trinity, Brompton Road. Known as the 'Bhams' from their 'Bham Palace' shoulder-tabs, the pack eventually graduated into the Girl Guides' company which created sizzling fry-ups of sausages in Windsor Park, staged nativity plays in the Palace Throne Room and ultimately achieved a Palace production of 'Cinderella' with Princess Anne in the title-role. First night nerves lest Prince Charles should sit in the front row and make her laugh happily proved groundless, and indeed the two did not see one another's theatricals very often.

Sisterly admiration, similarly, was rarely transposed into a key of jealousy, although there were difficulties when Charles first went sailing in the little yacht *Coweslip* with their father. It seemed gravely unfair to Anne to be reminded that she was nearly two years younger than Charles when he was 'really only two inches taller'. But a sailing dinghy from New Zealand was presently introduced onto the placid waters of Loch Muick, near Balmoral, where Anne learned her early sailing craft. Though never allowed to go out alone as a child, a small boat was also moored at Frogmore, which she took keen pride in always keeping shipshape. She could coil rope or correctly fold a tarpaulin while other girls were still dressing dolls. She is remembered, aged nine, hurtling up and down the beach at Holkham with a sand yacht, and capably handling the sail in the breeze, to the astonishment of the craft's seventeen-year-old owner, Prince Michael of Kent.

One of the youthful benefits of an August birthday is that it is usually celebrated on holiday. During the early Scottish cruises aboard *Britannia*, family picnics were often held on deserted islands with only the seabirds as onlookers. They landed one year on the isle of Uist for an anniversary fiesta stage-managed by Martin Charteris and his children, and another time one heard of a birthday celebration upon a 'bleak and totally solitary islet, sadly disrupted by millions of midges'. Later on, Prince Philip instituted a series of summer cruises in the ocean-going yawl *Bloodhound* around the west coast of Scotland, exploring islands and inlets from Arran to Lewis, and Princess Anne said dreamily that she would love to sleep aboard ship for the rest of her life.

Sailing, camping, the enthusiasms succeeded one another as they do with youngsters. Miss Peebles sparked off a tennis fever one year by taking Princess Anne, Caroline and Susan to see the Wightman Cup match at Wimbledon. All three little girls had been having tennis lessons at Buckingham Palace from the L.T.A. coach, Dan Maskell, but now there were visits to Wimbledon (with Prince

Philip adding the attraction of a helicopter flight one day) and tennis with the Nevills at Uckfield, the Knatchbulls at Merstham-le-Hatch, with the Kents at Coppins and with young German cousins at Luton Hoo. Two or three winters saw ice-skating in high favour, with trips out to Richmond ice-rink. The 'disguise factor' of including Caroline and Susan in the little group never failed, and no one who saw a girl in a red sweater taking a tumble or two paid any attention. The rink's usual Swiss-born instructor, who gave Anne lessons, had but recently coached the ladies' figure-skating champion of Europe and a special quality of 'fearlessness' seemed to him remarkable even then in his royal pupil.

## III

One realizes, on looking back, that Princess Anne had the fortune to be slightly ahead of the norm of her age group in acquiring the essential skills of her life style. She would have been nine years old when a visitor to Windsor home park saw her at the wheel of a small blue car, stopping and starting, under her father's guidance. These parental lessons on private roads progressed whenever opportunity offered, and on passing her driving test at seventeen, at the first attempt, she joked about her years of experience. She was ready at eighteen indeed to drive a fifty-ton tank and gleefully to take the wheel of a double-decker bus one afternoon after opening a road transport training centre. At the age of ten she was to be seen briskly driving an elegant little grey pony and trap in Windsor Great Park. The trap, which had once belonged to her great-grandmother, Queen Alexandra, had been brought out of store for her surprise and delight.

The Princess wore her first riding boots when only three, and I have a note of her riding a hunter at five—if for only a few yards—at a meet of the West Norfolk foxhounds. Her first pony, shared for some time with brother Charles, was (as we have seen) a benign and biddable strawberry roan named William, a foundling stowaway of romantic origin. One of his first owners had bought ten ponies in one lot at an Irish fair and, on disembarking from the horsebox, the tiny William had been found among them as an unsolicited bonus. His successor in the Princess's affections was the docile mare Greensleeves, 'very obliging at stopping at roads', as

Anne recalls. Then came Mayflower, a brown mare supplied by the Smith stables at Holyport, where Princess Anne received her first professional riding lessons. But no wild challenge lurked in these placid equine characters, and no one could foresee how vigorously Anne's temperament as a horsewoman was to differ from the Queen's far more restrained enjoyment at the same age.

One of the Princess's most indelible early memories is of her father charging down Smith's Lawn on a polo pony, a recollection so vivid that the thunder of hooves, the uninhibited shouts of the players and her own intense dislike of a cord tied around her waist for safety are all part of the picture. She naturally has no recollection of watching the European Horse Trials at Windsor when aged only four, but at seven she was an excited spectator of the Pony Club gymkhana at Ascot, wildly yelling, 'Oh, come on, come on!' to the young competitors, and impatiently registering her disgust with not a few. At eight she shyly presented the silver trophy for the best harness horse in the Royal Windsor Horse Show. That same year the pulse of minor history skipped a beat, for she was to have attended the Badminton Event for the first time with her mother and instead Prince Charles passed on his chicken-pox to his sister during the Easter holidays at Windsor ... and she had to be content with the screening of a movie, *King of the Wild Stallions*, which he had 'fixed' for her in the throne-room.

Anne was one of the few people to hear, a few hours beforehand, the Queen's tape-recorded message to the Commonwealth Games at Cardiff that announced 'I intend to create my son, Charles, Prince of Wales today.' Sharing the secret and watching the resulting enthusiasm on television, gave the Princess tremendous pleasure, every enjoyable detail enhanced by her affectionate pride. Miss Peebles had primed her in the stories of the Princes of Wales in history and the meaning and dignity of their title. Anne put great thought into devising a letter of congratulation without 'Peebie's' help, but by the time Charles returned from Cheam for the holidays her glow of excitement had diminished.

A little more was heard however of 'I'm nearly nine!' and 'I'll soon be ten,' in her wiles of family persuasion. There is a story that she complained, 'I'm still just Anne' and was told, 'You are *Princess* Anne.' The technique of training a princess to think herself nothing out of the ordinary can indeed clash at times with taking the first steps in royal duty. The sequel nevertheless was that she attended the picturesque Maundy service with the Queen and, like her mother, carried a traditional nosegay of spring flowers as part of the ancient ceremonial. Lisa Sheridan, the photographer, was also asked to make some special studies of the Princess in her everyday activities both at Buckingham Palace and Windsor at about this time and the resulting little book of photographs, *The Queen and Princess Anne* was published 'by authority of Her Majesty The Queen', a rare and exceptional imprimatur.

But the young Princess had shown above all that she could keep a secret, and in 1959 there came 'a stream of secrets', some to be cherished for just a few days, others more difficult to keep to herself. The delightful news that her mother might be having a new baby, the news that cousin 'Pammy' Mountbatten was to marry Mr. David Hicks, the special secret of Aunt Margo and Mr. Armstrong-Jones' engagement—all were confidences that swept her into an exciting crescendo of events. Princess Anne was a bridesmaid to Lady Pamela at Romsey Abbey, 'intent and purposeful' during the ceremony, and radiant with fun afterwards when the lights failed at Broadlands and the wedding reception continued by candlelight. On the February 19th, 1960, when the arrival of the Queen's new baby was imminent, the Princess worked with her school class as usual but was so inattentive that lessons were soon abandoned for the day. She had hoped for a baby brother, and when Prince Andrew was born in the mid-afternoon, her father took Anne to see him within the hour.

Her attitude was delightfully tender and protective. A month or two later, when she was to have a fitting for the lacy ruffled Hartnell dress she was to wear as bridesmaid at her Aunt Margo's wedding, Princess Margaret laughed and said, 'Anne's so busy pram-pushing, we must hope she can find the time!' Presently the pram was exchanged for a little wagon in which she sunnily pulled Andrew around the Palace gardens. In 1961, just before the royal tour of India and Pakistan, the Queen winced at the prospect of not seeing her baby for so long. But Princess Anne had been given a camera by her new Uncle Tony, and one of the royal photograph albums now reveals how enthusiastically she used up reels of film on Andrew and every week meticulously sent off a packet of the best pictures to her mother.

# 3 Benenden

As if for fun in the permutations of coincidence, an augury may be found gleaming strangely in the galaxy of minor royal events shortly before Princess Anne was born. On July 15th, 1950, in the course of a day of mingled duties and pleasures, the then Queen of England, the present Queen Mother, visited a school in Kent and, less officially, the Cazalet stables at Fairlawne, where she inspected some horses she had in training for jumping. The school was none other than Benenden, which was later to claim Princess Anne as a pupil, and the infant Princess made her advent into the world precisely one month later to the day.

If Prince Charles's first step towards his royal future began on the day of his mother's Coronation—the day when, aged four, he thrust up his chin and smartly saluted the crowds from the Palace balcony—Princess Anne's initiation was when she rode in a state landau at the age of eight to watch her mother taking the salute at the Trooping the Colour. Her own more personal first footing in ceremony came the following New Year when she presented the Sunday school prizes at Sandringham, and a month or two later she made a speech to Lady Baden Powell commemorating a half-century of Girl Guides, a speech consisting of a single phrase, 'I ask you to accept this golden candle . . .'

As another of her parents' judicious essays in early training, she read a lesson at the carol service at West Newton Church, no small ordeal even for a self-confident girl of twelve, with all her family listening and her own voice echoing back magnified and shrill from the loudspeakers used for the crowds outside. But this was in the year when Charles first went to Gordonstoun, finding it 'less gruesome' than he had expected, and awaking in Anne all the old impulses of nursery rivalry. She *wanted* to go to boarding school, and the Queen and Prince Philip were in agreement that the broader-based education and the wider circle of acquaintance presented great advantages.

Anne was not the first British princess to be flung into the rush and bustle, the distinctions and disciplines, of a girl's school. Princess Alexandra had gained that particular laurel at Heathfield, on King George VI's direct advice to her widowed mother that she should have 'every chance of being an ordinary child while she could'. Princess Anne was nevertheless to be the first daughter of the Sovereign to break free from the rigid traditional circle of governesses and tutors, and the decision was more difficult a decade or so ago than it seems today. The choice of Benenden was influenced by the considerations that sway most parents: the closeness of friends whom a girl may visit on Saturday afternoons or of relatives to take her out on Sundays. The school was convenient to the Nevills at Uckfield, where the Queen spent so many happy weekends, to the Brabournes near Ashford and quite near for the Queen Mother on her visits to Fairlawne. On the forest uplands that fringe the Weald of Kent, it was reasonably within reach of London and yet sufficiently remote and secluded to deter inquisitive reporters and particularly the insistent photographers of the international press.

Apart from a preliminary visit with her parents during the holidays, Princess Anne had just turned thirteen when launched as a new girl into Benenden. She came down overnight from Balmoral with the Queen, in whose honour the school's teaching staff and three hundred girls were drawn up in the forecourt. A battlemented mock-Tudor pile, once the home of Viscount Rothermere, the place gave an impression of St. James's Palace or Hampton Court, glimpsed at the head of its long straight drive. Shaking hands with some thirty teachers, the new royal pupil must have felt that her reception would never end, and she broke into smiles of relief on hearing that she was one of sixty new girls that term and one of four princesses, the other three being Mary and Sihin of Ethiopia and Basma of Jordan.

The most comforting introduction was to Elizabeth Somershield, a girl of her own age in Guldeford House and the same Lower Fifth form, who was to be her 'house mother'. This is a pleasant Benenden idea for new girls: the 'mother' is usually an arrival of the previous term who introduces her own group of friends and bears the responsibility of helping the newcomer to find her feet. Elizabeth was also one of the three girls sharing

Magnolia dormitory with Anne, the first-floor room so called from the tree that reared its glossy leaves beneath the leaded windows. The Princess was told that there was to be a 'New Girls' Party' the following evening and, as she says, 'I just tagged along'. At the party Anne was to meet Bridget Shearer, another new girl that term, whom she unexpectedly encountered nine years later at Munich, attached to the Canadian Olympics team.

Indeed, Benenden 'seniors' or old girls crop up everywhere and have amusingly spiced royal engagements in Germany, Paris, Hong Kong and Istanbul. The school takes pride in helping its girls 'to realise the value of sound and thorough work' and so they emerge in medicine and the law, in science and on the Stock Exchange, and in practically every testing occupation known to women. Grown up now, they share the same memories, the annual fever of Hobbies Day and Speech Day, in summer the pageant and in winter the rising excitement of preparation for the Christmas close of term, the Carol Service, the ever-changing activities to help local good causes.

But Princess Anne's first impressions were of 'the amount of people and the staggering noise'. The first peal of bells shattered one at seven in the morning, the wild charge to the bathroom was in full swing by five past. Bells rang for appointed purposes throughout the day. Accustomed to silent and empty Palace corridors, the new girl found herself engulfed in chattering streams of girls in the school passageways, and an unexpected meeting with a teacher, Anne remembers, could pulverize her with shyness. Far from quickly forming her own clique, as some reports suggested, the seating at the dining-tables in Guldeford House was changed every few days, so that Anne sat next to everyone in turn and got acquainted equally well that first term with fifty or sixty girls.

Beds stripped before breakfast were made up afterwards: if there had been an Olympics contest in quick bed-making the Princess could have readily qualified. This and the compulsory brisk run down the drive and back helped, Anne said, 'to work off one's breakfast'. New girls were solemnly warned by the more experienced that at end of term they would be expected to sing a song, anything of their own choosing, to Miss Clarke, the headmistress, and the senior girls who took lunch with her at High Table. Most of the innocents shivered at the prospect for weeks.

It was a hoax, of course, which Anne rather wrecked by saying, 'Well, I'll have a go.' Nor was she to be inveigled into joining the Madrigal Club on that account, although Elizabeth Somershield was a member and Anne—with a fairly good contralto voice— later enrolled in the school choir. More in her line, the Princess joined the Badminton Club, for which she eventually served on the committee. She became a leading star of the Dancing Club, specializing in Scottish dancing, and was soon also an enthusiastic exponent in the Pottery Club with Sandra Hacking.

The pleasures of pottery included a barbecue at a kilnhouse where the evening passed so swiftly that, as one of Anne's fellows tactfully mentioned in the school magazine, 'we did not have time to try the electric wheel'. At a school sale of work the Sue Ryder charities benefited handsomely from the brisk demand for models of horses and other pieces signed 'A' and the young saleswomen prudently did not disclose that the potters' group also included an Annabelle, Alison and Antonia.

## II

Princess Anne became immersed and absorbed in the world of school far more readily than Charles and faster than the Queen and Prince Philip had thought possible. The Saturday afternoons with the Nevills at Uckfield grew fewer, except when her mother was there. 'Do you think I can get back early?' she would ask. 'There's a movie, *The Baby and the Battleship*.' Questioned on Benenden cuisine, she could rattle off 'Bones and barley and Ganges mud, dead man's leg . . .', to be interpreted to the uninitiated as hot pot, chocolate pudding and jam roll. Cheerfully announcing that she was about to become a mother, it transpired that there was to be a Christmas party for the babies from the nearby Dr. Barnardo's home, with a schoolgirl mothering each small child. It turned out, however, that first year, that her role lay more prosaically behind the scenes, drudging with the washing-up squad. In her second term, she was a 'house mother' to a new girl, so much a part of the school setting already that two or three days elapsed before the new arrival quite grasped her identity. Like all new girls, the newcomer had talked a great deal of her mother and then realized that her 'house mother' had said very little about her own.

The Princess's teachers found her promising in history, geography and English literature; she enjoyed reading aloud, in which she displayed sensitivity and confidence above average and, thanks to Peebie's firm grounding, she was good in arithmetic. (There was to be no inadvertent cooking of the books later on when Anne took charge of accounts in the domestic science class.) Her practical streak attracted her to physics and chemistry, although she considered herself 'a dud' in the latter, and the flights of higher mathematics forever defied her. The Benenden syllabus embraced French, German, Latin, Greek, drawing, handwork, needlework, public speaking and, in the Sixth Form, committee procedure. Term in, term out, the Queen's daughter could not help but gain considerable personal competence in these studies, apart from the hobby subjects that chiefly interested the press.

Miss Anwyl's handwork class, for instance, was like a toy factory in the winter term in the rush to fill the crates of gifts for the Pestalozzi children's village. The 'Palace', as the well-appointed domestic science lab was nicknamed, saw a fever of cake-baking in all five of its kitchen units just before the Christmas lighthouse boxes were being packed. Benenden has no school motto, no agreement on one having ever been reached except on the basic theme of helping others. From the boat-race mascots made up and sold for cancer research to the income provided for a Tibetan refugee in India, from the 'treats' and financial help to a blind babies' home and the sums raised for the ex-Benenden Sue Ryder charities, Anne learned that every activity possible could be geared to goodwill. All of which was appropriate training for a space-age princess.

The school fees were then £175 a term, and among the optional extra subjects were piano, speech and drama, ballet and fencing. Asked to choose for herself, Anne decided 'I'll take the lot!' but was persuaded to reduce this to pottery and riding, piano and a wind instrument, the oboe, selected mainly because she pretended to consider it unfair that the lady who gave oboe lessons was listed last among visiting teachers. But even with Prince Charles's encouragement, her efforts in this respect faltered after a year or two.

Out of doors, the junior pleasures of the asphalt roller-skating rink were rapidly relinquished. Netball claimed the Princess and then lacrosse, in which she progressed into the second school XII. In her last year the interest of the whole school centred upon the team's fortunes when they reached the finals of the All England schools tournament, won every match in their section and so reached a dramatic crescendo of victory by winning the last match six goals to one. Princess Anne exulted in being unrecognized throughout. Her father greatly alarmed her by promising to make a personal presentation to the team if they won, which would surely have entailed publicity, but he was only teasing and, in the event, a large Easter egg from an anonymous donor was borne onto the field to tremendous cheering.

In summer, Princess Anne played a good game of tennis in the Guldeforde House pairs, but laments that she 'fell to pieces' in more serious matches. Her progress none the less astonished Prince Michael in one of the more serious tournaments at Coppins. Punctual and methodical, as the reports say, Anne spread her activities no wider than any other girl but evinced family talent in marshalling the sixty-minutes-an-hour of her time. There is a story of her elder brother at Cheam, being warned that he might get into trouble with Matron by staying up long after bedtime to finish his chores, and solemnly replying, 'I can't help it. I must finish my duties.' Anne, with her ingrained tidiness, would cheerfully clear up after other girls, 'helping out', as she put it, but unpredictably might equally scowl at the clutter and shrug, 'Too bad. If they can't bother, nor shall I.'

Her parents had expected that boarding school would create a necessary diversity and new measure of freedom in her interests, and were not disappointed. As noisy, casual and, when the spirit moved, mulish as any teenager, Anne 'fratted' and fitted in, though initially not without some deliberate effort. When the Queen attended the school carol service, her daughter's nail-biting and 'nerves' were noticeable. It did not matter so much on Speech Day one year when the Queen came to see a play: Princess Anne played 'Alfred, son of Mrs. Fipps' in Christopher Fry's *The Boy with a Cart* and sank herself, both on and off stage, into the comic elements of the part. Another time, she was unidentifiable in the crowd of seasick animals in a miracle play of the Flood; and her mother was not present, it seems, when the Princess richly clowned and staggered about as a drunken sailor in *Dido and Aeneas*.

Nor did it matter when the Queen or Prince Philip arrived unofficially, inconspicuously parking in the drive like any other parent, to whisk her off for mid-term. As time passed, Anne grew into the habit of writing of the school crowd as 'the rest of us', and the phrase unconsciously disclosed her sense of belonging. 'She's an uninhibited, forthright, friendly person,' typified the general impression. 'She'll always do what she can.' At sixteen, the uncertain newcomer of two years earlier had developed into a much more self-assured young person who could gaily cry 'Watch my halo!' just before a car collected her to take her to Sunday lunch with the Archbishop of Canterbury.

By Benenden tradition, each school house staged a party in annual rota, providing entertainment and hospitality for guests from the entire school and, when Guldeford's turn came up, Anne's advice was evidently sought on sohpisticated royal ideas with the result that 'the early part of the evening was spent playing games of chance and the new wing showed certain resemblances to a casino'. The rival Echyngham House was hard put to it to compete the following year. 'The Hall had been valiantly disguised à la Bonnie and Clyde,' wrote Princess Anne, 'making a bar manned by dollies with maxi-skirts, bright red lipsticks, horizontal headbands and those shoes! The rest of us were ordered to wear necklaces—dresses not needed!' In the holidays she had a free rein in accepting invitations from Benenden parents, and the Benenden contingents were in strength when the Queen gave a reciprocal party for Charles and Anne at Windsor Castle.

Term by term, the Princess had new experiences and exploits to recount with comic emphasis when she came home, her horizons clearly widening as she progressed into the upper forms. The Queen 'had collywobbles' when she heard of the girls going off by the bus-load on Saturday rock-climbing expeditions, with her daughter tackling sandstone rocks fifty feet high. 'I sometimes wonder if rock-climbing isn't a bit more dangerous than is made out,' she said, and Miss Gee, the teacher in charge, made reassuring murmurs. The 'peaks and precipices' were in fact at the Bowles mountaineering gymnasium at Eridge. In climbing kit of anoraks, jeans and gym shoes, the girls were roped together, to climb, to overcome the scramble nets or attempt the hazards and difficulties of the Matterhorn tree. Anne in particular shone with a special proficiency at the outset, in being one of the few girls to know how to tie a bowline.

She passed her test in survival swimming, neatly turning items of underwear into a life-saving jacket while in the water. She reached bronze standard for the Duke of Edinburgh's Award, but declined to try futher and satisfy a school joke about 'wanting a gold medal from Papa'. Alert for any adventurous opportunity, she got to know that direction-finding entailed a night in a youth hostel and that the study of land structure and farming for A-level geography brought a week-end at a holiday camp and being 'let loose on Romney Marsh'. 'We arrived at the holiday camp and a hut known as 'Scarborough' at first sight seemed to be a corridor, but revealed many doors with keys leading to small rooms with wash-basins, double bunks and one-bar electric heaters. What luxury!' the Princess wrote at the time. 'When the excitement was over, there was supper (fish and chips) and the first of the lectures.'

In the morning the schoolgirls visited a farm, only to find the farmer 'called away on business' and so they toiled to the top of a church tower to see what they could through the swirling mist. 'We next did a survey from the coach while eating lunch,' Anne noted, 'and then stopped for refreshments at a café. In the afternoon, we sat hopefully at Lympne airport, waiting in vain for the clouds to lift . . . Airport lounges can be quite fascinating.'

Perhaps one too readily forgets that a daughter of the Sovereign had never before surveyed anything at such matter-of-fact levels. The Prince of Wales, on first visiting the House of Commons, had sat almost alone in the Serjeant-at-Arms' box. Princess Anne went there as a sixteen-year-old with the Advanced Level history group of twenty-four Benenden girls, all equally incognito in blue school uniform. Their mentor, Sir Harry Legge-Bourke, M.P. for Ely, who had offered to show them round was not only the father of Victoria Legge-Bourke, one of Anne's closest Benenden friends, but also a Guards' officer and the author of a standard work on the Household Cavalry. He must have found his experience as escort somewhat trying and, mischievously, since it was St. Valentine's Day, Anne ensured that he was presented with a string of twenty-four blood-red paper hearts as a token of appreciation.

No one paid any attention to the party of school-girls having lunch in the nearby restaurant in Church House among the local office workers or listening to question-time in the Commons. And so, as one of the group recorded, 'We said goodbye to Sir Harry and took the underground to Cannon Street . . . back at Benenden in time for supper.' For Princess Anne it became a notable exercise in royal double identity. Nine months later, wearing a gown of white silk and a diamond tiara, she rode with the Queen and the Prince of Wales in the Irish State Coach to take part in the State Opening of Parliament for the first time, processing demurely into the House of Lords and taking her place in the Chair of State to the left of the Queen . . . but frowning a little, as if she felt the claustrophobia of court life closing in.

### III

When visiting their nieces at Benenden, unwary aunts—though never parents—would sometimes ask if Princess Anne could be pointed out to them, which invariably brought the guarded response, 'She's not around, she's usually off somewhere.' The least sensitive might recognize a loyal brush-off, but the reply was generally truthful. There was seldom a spare Saturday when the Princess and a school friend or two did not head to the village and disappear through the white-painted gates of the Moat House Riding School as if into Arcady.

The stage for this had been set none too soon. Riding was a recent innovation at Benenden, and Cherrie Hatton-Hall had established her school at Moat House little more than three years before Princess Anne's arrival. Winner of such trophies as the Prix Caprilli at Harringay, which she had held two years running, Mrs. Hatton-Hall's invaluable asset was that she remembered as a child being afraid of her first pony and recognized that only skilful instruction had brought her confidence and mastery. Princess Anne was the very reverse, fearless from the outset, and already with a store of encouraging small prizes and rosettes, yet Cherrie felt that she could benefit from a fresh and thorough grounding. But 'don't drop her whatever you do', Miss Clarke, the head-mistress of Benenden, warned Cherrie when briefing her.

Riding on Bandit, a pony then shared with Prince Charles, Anne had made her first appearance in a public competition at the age of eleven and had been given her first 'all round' pony, High Jinks, for her twelfth birthday. She soon won a shared first prize in a pair jumping event at an Ascot gymkhana and then a silver challenge cup for the best under-thirteen rider in a field of twenty. For fun for the children, in that first High Jinks summer, the Queen held a gymkhana for young local competitors in Windsor Home Park and confessed to finding it 'most embarrassing' when the main jumping event was won by her daughter against fourteen entrants.

If Anne now and then gave her instructress an impression of 'thinking she knew it all already', this schoolgirl arrogance could change in a flash to a rueful apology given with a smile just like her mother's. Some twenty girls in their Benenden riding kit came down in the school bus every Thursday afternoon for their seventy-five minute lesson, which began with what were called suppling exercises, touching toes from the saddles without stirrups, before practising circles at trot and canter and then cavaletti. The Princess endured these elementary stages with relative docility although, as Mrs. Pares has said, she 'took a mischievous delight in disrupting her class at intervals, by pinching Jinks behind the saddle so that he bucked!'

But it was with the private or small group sessions on Saturdays that the Moat House amenities were most appreciated, especially with progress in seniority when Anne was allowed to ride over the Hatton-Hall's seventy acres with only her detective, David Groves, for adult company. During her schooldays, the Princess rode nearly every one of the sixty horses and ponies in the paddocks, gaining insight into their individual reactions in a way not always possible with the finely-schooled mounts at Windsor. She can still vividly recall their special characteristics: the skewbald Jester (whom she rode to win in the Benenden show-jumping team against two neighbouring schools), the amenable Dumbell, the skittish Roulette, Copper, Dinah, Punch, the bouncy Jiminy and the rest. It was with Jiminy, crossing a field, that she lost her balance, lurched forward on his neck and broke a bone in her little finger. 'Oops, there goes my finger,' was all she said and, white-faced, 'endured the pain pretty well' while taken up to London by Mr. Groves to have it set.

The Queen allayed Benenden anxieties by promptly sending a message that no real harm was done and that the accident would no doubt do the Princess good. And indeed Anne's interest in the finer arts of schooling a horse developed rapidly, until she presently rode in a school quadrille team for the Benenden Fête, the rehearsals

—the school magazine reported—'involving endless patience, collisions, practice, rhythm and effort, as Virginia Witty, Grizelda George, Princess Anne and Caroline Brown found to the cost of their nerves'.

Cherrie Hatton-Hall's regular tuition was undoubtedly responsible for the good seat and balance, allied to improving judgement and horse-sense, so evident when the Princess began her advanced coaching under Alison Oliver in 1968. Yet Anne could be 'cussedly stubborn', as Mrs. Hatton-Hall once said in her reminiscences, and rough edges were not smoothed nor high standards attained without occasional conflict. An acute crash hat crisis, for instance, occurred behind the idyllic pastoral scenes of the Benenden pageant. In her role as a messenger to Queen Elizabeth I, Anne had to gallop into sight to announce the coming of the Queen. The ground was rough and potholed and a fall could have meant serious injury. It was only prudent to require the Princess to wear a hard cap beneath her feathered Tudor bonnet . . . and she flatly refused.

No other girl would be riding in two hats, no one else was asked to look so silly, she stormed, and it was useless for the producer to point out that the other girls were merely walking their horses. The Princess jutted out that firm Victorian lower lip of hers and took the argument to her house-mistress, only to hear that she must be sensible and do as she was told. The riding teacher was asked to take up the issue but found she could not cope with this mood of outright—and right royal—rebellion. 'I won't do it—I'll phone Mummy!' the Princess threatened, fully convinced that she was being unfairly mollycoddled. In the end she phoned Mummy and put down the telephone crestfallen. 'If you've been told to wear a cap, you jolly well will have to wear a cap,' the Queen had said. And that was the end of the matter. The minor role played by Anne and High Jinks in the pageant was a considerable success and, of course, the peak of her hard cap was never noticed.

Eventually it fell to Anne to write the annual riding report—thinly disguised in the third person—in the school magazine. 'The individual Combined Training was won by Princess Anne with J. Macalpine second and A. Bidgood third. Very well done everybody!' Then the regal commentator could not resist mentioning a more pressing topic, involving her own début in a contest at national levels. 'Last year we did a Quadrille on Open Day and this year C. Brown, L. Greer, J. Lloyd and Princess Anne are off to Clapham Common to try their luck against eighteen other Quadrilles with the hope of qualifying for Wembley . . . It won't be quite the same thing as the Church Fête!'

In the event, Court mourning for her great-aunt, Princess Marina, compelled the Princess to withdraw from the opening rounds, although the formalities were relaxed in time for her to ride, in gorgeous Georgian costume, in the finals at the Horse of the Year Show. The team had qualified among eighteen other quadrilles and Anne ecstatically dreamed of winning. The Wembley audience numbered thousands and nerves were taut. At Benenden, a cross-country event had once been lost 'thanks to one miserable girl who went on the wrong side of the flag at the last fence' and in the complicated formation dressage at Wembley there was similarly one miscreant in what seemed a disastrous finish, or so the Princess decided. In the wreck of her hopes, her indictment of the offender, delivered in ringing tones and salty language, could be heard far beyond the changing room.

The team in fact came in second, and Anne regretted her outburst afterwards. But her rage had been no less incandescent both with her horse and herself when, riding with the Oxford University Draghounds one Easter, she had fallen at the last fence and broken her nose. Her choice of words was so explicit that the master of hounds thought she was only shaken and it was a day or two before Anne had learned she would have to undergo an operation. What really worried her was not the risk to her looks but the prospect lest the injury should wreck a projected visit to Jamaica for the Commonwealth Games. But that is a later story.

## IV

School life, family life and the texture of royal events usually blended far better than anyone expected. Benenden was sufficiently close to 'Aunt Margo and Uncle Tony' in their hideaway Sussex cottage near Nymans for Anne to go to Sunday tea. Close enough to Uckfield, similarly, to have her official sixteenth birthday photographs taken—weeks ahead of the event—in the Nevills' drawing-room.

That was the year when Anne rode with the Battle riding club in a pageant commemorative of 1066, and Guy Nevill, then at Kent University, was in the audience with his sister Angela. A few days later, Guy took part in a fierce Norman jousting display, this time with Anne among the spectators. Lord Abergavenny's place, Eridge Park, was also within Saturday radius for visits to Anne's special friend of her own age, Guy's cousin, Lady Rose Nevill, and the band of young people would gather around the swimming pool in the June sun. Out of term time Anne watched the Eridge Horse Trials two years running and at a party afterwards there occurred the first casual, scarcely remembered meeting with a young Sandhurst cadet named Mark Phillips.

With Prince Charles aboard *Britannia*, during the summer holidays, Princess Anne also took part in the two-day visit to the Home Fleet in the Clyde, when the Queen inspected the lines of fighting ships and 'little ships', and her daughter 'thoroughly enjoyed the fun' of visiting frigates and destroyers, exploring below decks, clambering up and down the companionways, 'good training in more ways than one', as Charles said, with a glance at sisterly puppy-fat.

A surprising array of attractive engagements, could, indeed, be fitted into holiday schedules and the Princess remained unaware of how much adult planning had gone into these happy overlaps of pleasure and pomp. Brother and sister were invited to Athens for the wedding of King Constantine of the Hellenes and Princess Anne-Marie of Denmark, to whom Princess Anne was to be a bridesmaid while Prince Charles and Prince Michael of Kent were 'crown-bearers' to the groom. But first Prince Philip flew Charles and Anne from Balmoral to southern Germany for a festive series of family meetings with their aunts and cousins of Hesse and Hanover. In Greece, the wedding preliminaries were bright with balls and beach parties, feastings and fishing trips. The wedding service, a ceremony of great splendour in the cathedral of Athens, took place on Friday September 18th and, on Monday the 21st, Anne was back at Benenden, back in the crowd, for the first day of term.

Princess Beatrix of the Netherlands had similarly wished to invite Princess Anne to be a bridesmaid but unwarily fixed her wedding for March 10th, when not even the nuptials of a Crown Princess could interrupt school routine. The tenth was in fact a

Thursday, the riding day at Benenden, and while the wedding-cake was cut and the champagne glasses clinked in Amsterdam, Anne and her riding friends feasted at that most attractive of establishments, the mobile fish-and-chip shop in the village.

'Variety,' Prince Philip once observed, 'is the spice of everything', a precept certainly followed whenever he had a say in devising his daughter's holiday fun. Flying her to Liechtenstein for her first winter sports holiday, he piloted the Andover aircraft from London, pretending to be heading for Zürich, for instance, but then surprised her by landing in Paris, with time for a sightseeing whirl through the city and dinner at a bistro on the Left Bank before they caught the late night Arlberg express. The ski-ing itself was marred by the attention of massive contingents of the European press. 'They didn't tell me about this,' Anne remarked, ruefully, 'at my ski school in London.' The following year, she quietly joined a group of Benenden girls for a package winter-sports holiday at Davos and revelled in their complete anonymity.

Her mother and father could, similarly, not have made a more imaginative or alluring decision than to include her in Prince Philip's trip to Jamaica to open the Commonwealth Games. The programme included an extra-mural incognito stopover in New York and a reunion in Kingston with Prince Charles, who flew in after his two terms in Australia at Timbertop, and at all the social events centred on the Games Princess Anne found herself pleasantly holding her own in a jamboree of some of the most toughly disciplined yet sturdily individualistic young men and women in the world. For side attractions there was all Jamaica to explore, shooting the rapids of the Rio Grande on a raft and swimming amid the smooth long breakers of the Carribbean.

The Princess found, I think, that she could seldom enlarge on such pleasures, the carefree side of royal duty, among her schoolfellows. She could 'get by' only by narrating the comic side, and only then with her most trusted Benenden friends. Gone, now, were the unselfconscious days when she licked ice-cream with a Benenden cluster outside the village store or suggested that a take-off of Trooping the Colour would be marvellous for a gymkhana. The real event was still a giggle backstage, 'Papa had to give Mummy's horse a jab in the rump with his sword when it wasn't doing what it was told.' But in her last year at school one of her mistresses particularly noticed 'the public person taking over from the schoolgirl, conscious of the fact that she was Princess Anne'.

In 1968 she was also now endowed with authority as Captain of House, as well as an elected member of the Upper Sixth. Suddenly that summer the G.C.E. examinations were hanging over her and, like other lordly Six Formers she left school still not knowing whether she had gained her A-levels pass. (She in fact passed in history and geography, with a special Merit in an optional extra geography paper.) Just before the irrevocable end of term, the Queen, with the Duke of Edinburgh and the Prince of Wales, visited Benenden on 'Hobbies Day', to watch the Hobbies Entertainment—which ranged from piano solos indoors to Princess Anne in the Quadrilles outdoors—to take sherry with the staff and to dine with 'the Upper Sixth, the Council and the Founders'.

Presenting the prizes, the Queen could not fail to notice that none had been won by her daughter. But Princess Anne that last year had conscientiously attended lectures on the care of the old and the care of the environment, on occupation therapy and teaching and aspects of social work, on industrial management and local government finance. She had learned something of the practical careers that others would follow, from jobs in the War Office to town-planning and nursing. She had been trained in committee work, had taken part in mock elections and had become versed in the activities of a social service group in London to which many Benenden Seniors (old girls) are dedicated. There had never been better training for a Princess, a presumptive Princess Royal.

## 4  Hopeful Venture

Just at the time when Princess Anne stepped from the world of school, one of the Queen's racehorses, a colt by Aureole named Hopeful Venture, brilliantly won the rich Grand Prix de Saint-Cloud. It was notably the first win ever gained by a horse in the royal colours upon French soil, and every member of the royal household found it amusingly propitious for Princess Anne in her own hopeful venture into the adult world. She made her social début at one of the last Palace garden-parties of the season, a 'decisive eye-catcher' in her blue-dotted white mini-coat, as one guest noted, and celebrated her new freedom by attending the Royal International Horse Show with her parents. A hopeful venture, indeed, that she spent nearly every evening that week following the show-jumping fortunes of David Broome on Mister Softee, Harvey Smith on O'Malley and Marion Coaks on Stroller. The phrase was repeated about the Palace until everyone tired of it and, the Princess blushed deeply, a year later, on being complimented that her first year in the public eye had been a hopeful venture in every way.

She wanted 'just to do nothing', she told a friend, freed from Benenden discipline, but in fact her fleeting last weeks of being seventeen were devoted to her twin enthusiasms of riding and sailing. The Queen found occasion to visit Cowes that summer for the first time since her Coronation year; Prince Philip sailed in the tiny *Coweslip* while Anne supposedly 'crewed' in the Bermudian sloop, *Sea Wraith*, obligingly scrambling about to distribute sandwiches and open beer-cans. The town was crammed with French, Belgian, and Dutch sailors who wolf-whistled the slim blonde in her Holland cap, impartially unaware of her identity. And she was the belle of the crowded Royal London ball, partnered by a sufficiency of young naval officers, as well as the unquenchable Uffa Fox, with his shouts of 'Starboard!' to all who threatened their course.

But the real sailing came later, when *Britannia* had once more set out to round northern Scotland and rendezvous as usual with the yawl *Bloodhound*. Once again there was the familiar fun of exploring unknown coasts and inlets or revisiting old ones, and the lark of going ashore in the early morning to beg water at crofts and farm-houses, trying out outlandish accents or wild excusses. The game never palled for Charles and Anne of seeing who could remain 'incog' longest: points were lost at any gleam of recognition in an inquiring glance. Then there was the deeply enjoyable experience of sailing in small craft off the Moray coast. 'The silence is blissful after you switch off the engine', wrote Princess Anne. 'The only sound is the rush of water, relaxing and hypnotic, the gentle creak of the rigging and occasional flap of a lazy sail. It gives me an utterly detached sensation that I have only otherwise experienced on a galloping horse—a feeling of contentment, of being in the hands of the fates or the elements.'

She had tried to set it all down only a few months earlier in 'a spot of fine writing' in the orange pages of the school magazine. 'If it is blowing then sailing becomes a fight, a battle against all that the wind and waves can throw at you ... Then nothing can touch you in your determined fighting of the elements, your feeling of supreme confidence and light-headedness when the wind and sea die down and you have won your personal battle, no matter how small ... You become a part of your ship, testing your skill, not against anyone else's but against nature, your ideals and the person you would like to be.'

We may see now that the essay was full of character, and the Princess had incautiously ended, 'Sailing on a sunny day, with a fresh breeze blowing, with maybe somebody you really care for, is the nearest thing to heaven anyone will ever get on this earth—certainly the nearest I will ever get.' Which, of course, set nearly every newspaper wildly guessing at the 'somebody', while totally overlooking the young man on whom she had rather a 'crush' at the time, her second cousin, Prince Michael of Kent. As we may perhaps tell, he could not be on board for her eighteenth birthday and Anne then had to be told of the serious illness of his mother, Princess Marina, who died a little more than a week after the Royal Family had arrived at Balmoral. Then, in September, Princess Anne heard with great sadness of the sudden death of her governess, Miss

Peebles. Within the month all three young people of the Royal Family—Charles, Anne and Michael—thus attended two funeral services in St. George's Chapel, Windsor Castle, and that autumn the Princess was indeed in solemn mood as she surveyed her future.

There had 'never been a thought', as Anne said later, of going on to university, although the newspapers were full of surmise at the time on whether she had sufficiently qualified by her two A-level passes in history and geography. Egged on not a little by Michael, who talked enjoyably of the days when, at her age, he had gone to Tours to study French, she had perhaps day-dreamed of becoming a student at the Sorbonne with Emma Soames.

It was six years since the Princess had visited the Loire Valley for a week or so to help improve her French. She had at first tried to face the rather frightening crowds, only to be finally daunted by the sightseers who appeared whenever her hosts, the Marquis and Marquise de St. Genys, attempted to take her beyond their gates. She had passed her G.C.E. in O-level French but still felt 'cramped and awkward', with none of Michael's genuine linguistic ability. But now grown-ups noticed, not without sympathy, that she no longer wished to leave London. Prince Michael was working at the Ministry of Defence and possibly Anne saw herself in a slightly romantic role to her bereaved cousin, a companion to help him through the sadness of his family loss.

The Princess's decision to take a 'crash course' at the Berlitz School of Languages in Oxford Street that autumn was characteristically her own. The Queen and Prince Philip were to pay a visit to Brazil and Chile in November and Anne persuasively argued that the course—'total immersion', as one ad-man called it—would keep her more than busy in their absence. The course required her to study French from 9 am to 7 pm for six weeks, with a 90-minute break for lunch, and an additional study of French literature as homework. The more intensive of the lessons lay in private conversational tuition with two tutors. It was tough going, but Prince Philip, a good French spokesman, was more than satisfied on trying her out on return. A Palace car usually put Anne down or called for her at the Berlitz door but the Princess also renewed some previous experiments in avoiding attention and occasionally went shopping with Mabel Anderson or some other companion in crowded Oxford Street itself. It made good copy the following year, and went down marvellously well, when she gave a speech to open the Festival of London Stores and confessed that she had shopped at Selfridges and Peter Robinson and Dickens and Jones, and had been 'tempted into Fenwicks by way of being stuck in Bond Street traffic jams on the way back from my language course'.

But meanwhile 1968 was, of course, the year of the Mexican Olympics, when Britain's Three-Day Event team won the gold medal for the second time, and the Queen Mother attended a cocktail party to honour the riders at the Whitbread cellars in the City of London. She took Anne along with her to meet the victors—Major Allhusen, Jane Bullen, Richard Meade, Sergeant Jones and, with them, their young reserve rider Mark Phillips. The following month, the Queen gave a reception to all the British Olympic personnel, a crowd of over 300 to fill the Throne Room. It is said that one of the young athletes cheekily sat on the Throne itself—and it seems equally certain that Anne sought out Jane Bullen, Mark Phillips and Richard Meade to talk of Eridge, Crookham and Badminton and all the intense kindred enthusiasms that now filled her horizons.

## II

Within the span of that first winter at home, the Queen initiated Princess Anne into the rituals of regimental dinners and receptions, the pomp and sparkle of State banquets, the good graces of world film premieres, the solemnity of services of dedication, and much more. As an earnest of the future, the Princess skipped up to Balmoral with her father just before Christmas for a few days to follow his small family shooting party with her own gun-dog across Gairnshiel. Taking up both the 'duty' and the social side of the day-to-day royal round was like stepping into a second skin. 'It's all perfectly simple,' she said, when a journalist enquired about the presumed difficulties of taking up a schedule of royal engagements practically from scratch.

The impetus value of a royal patronage came under discussion, her personal dilemma framed in her question, 'Won't I be just a figurehead?' It seemed to Anne after her five years away at school that people could not really know much about her. The Princess received no press clippings and, apart from a marked paragraph or illustration passed to her by a Palace secretary, she only casually saw the references to herself and had no idea of the real force of her public image. Far from considering that her life was spent in 'a glare of publicity', as journalists claimed, she felt herself so far only on the fringe of the arc-light 'though maybe it will come to me yet'. She did not like being 'fairly constantly slated' as an outdoor type: it was just that she was lucky to have had the opportunity to ride or sail. Charles advocated going on the air to help iron things out, getting the questions set up a bit. Anne considered there might be an easier way and found it with the aid of Bill Heseltine, the young Australian who had recently been appointed Press Secretary to the Queen.

A press reception was vetoed as too formal and unwieldy, and the two press cocktail parties ultimately given at the Palace early in 1969 were quite without precedent. A glass of 'coke' in her hand, the Princess circulated among the guests, almost inviting questions yet adroitly sidestepping the more candid probes which might have embarrassed anyone less poised or quick-witted. Many of the journalists had expected someone shy and inexperienced, over-swaddled with equerries. Instead, they found the sparkle of a debbie eighteen-year-old with, as one summed up, 'a clear sense of humour ... the ability to appear utterly relaxed ... a nice uncomplicated young woman'.

The Queen had intended that the Princess should undertake her first solo engagement on April 25th with the undemanding opening ceremony of a Young Farmers' club centre in Warwickshire, but Prince Philip contrived to push his daughter in at the deep end. As Colonel of the Welsh Guards he had been invited to take the salute and present the traditional leeks at the regimental St. David's Day ceremony. Instead he found himself 'obliged to fly to Ethiopia' ... and so Princess Anne stepped into the breach, clearly not unprepared with her natty green coat and half-military millinery, and coping with drollery, charm and confidence with the absurdity of handing vegetables to tough troopers. As a run-up to his Investiture, the Prince of Wales had also recorded his first radio interview that same day, and brother and sister compared notes when dining together that evening. Said one of the elders, 'They were clearly enjoying themselves.'

Although their paths were obviously diverging, their affectionate rivalry and interest had never been stronger. Anne rocked with laughter in the Cambridge audience when Charles clowned amiably through the Trinity College revue. Charles went off to Sweden for a ski-ing holiday with Prince Carl Gustaf that March, while Anne tried her freshly accomplished French and her more rusty winter sports skills with a group of friends at Val d'Isere. When Charles began his Welsh university term at Aberystwyth and could be mischievously described as 'still at school', Anne launched her first ship, the largest tanker ever built in Britain, 'and for a starter,' she said, 'that's not bad'. Earlier she had also carried out her first full day in the provinces, thrilled and enthusiastic for weeks afterwards in describing her impressions of the Rover factory at Solihull. In the meantime she had also devoted herself, with keen anticipation, to her preparations to accompany her parents to Austria on her first State Visit. Deep was her disappointment when she fell ill with influenza on the very eve of the journey, and had to be left behind. Prince Charles is supposed to have sent her an ironic 'Get Well' card and perhaps did so in fun, but the firm reality was that he cheerfully telephoned her from Cambridge full of brotherly commiseration.

Happily, the Princess rapidly recovered, and flew out to Vienna only two days late, radiantly announcing to Lady Margaret Hay, 'Well I've made it!' 'Only just!' came the reply with a gesture at the lowering sky, and then the heavens opened, thunder crashed and the rain pelted down as the royal cavalcade of cars splashed its way from airport to city. Although in time to join her parents for an intended slow drive round the Ringstrasse, she could have seen little in the rain, and at the Rathaus luncheon she concealed her disappointment by apologies at bringing 'the unromantic English weather' with her. But her own personal moment came that afternoon, after a Commonwealth reception, when she arrived ready in riding kit at the celebrated Spanish Riding School, which her parents had visited earlier.

On this occasion, the platoon of international photographers marred none of her enjoyment. The head of the school, Colonel Handler, had known that she would wish to ride one of the stallions but said he was 'amazed' when, after a hurried briefing she began to get the timing right and achieved a *passage* and the *piaffe*, a trot performing without gaining ground. 'Haven't you come to photograph the horse?' she called to the clustered cameramen, amused that they seemed to be frantic with excitement. But what equally astonished Colonel Handler, proving her mother's long memory, was when she pleasantly told him, 'I hear this isn't the first time you've seen me riding a Lippizaner,' and reminded him that he had been present at the Buckingham Palace riding school when she had been lifted onto the back of a Lippizaner for a moment as a three-year-old child.

The entire State Visit had a reassuring edge of familiarity. The Princess found her suite at the Hotel Imperial like a waltz-time movie set, white and gilded with vistas of gleaming parquet and plump baroque cherubs, but there was 'honest school soap' in the bathroom and she was the first to discover that a mysterious electric switch amid the towels and the crystal heated the marble tiles of the floor. The visit embraced a tour of the Tyrol, and visits to Salzburg and Graz. But it was in the children's village at See-kirchen, chummily having tea with the orphans, that Anne gained the quite unexpected and individual triumph that placed her picture in newspapers and magazines throughout the world. The camera caught her in a moment of utterly relaxed enjoyment, for it was just like visiting the Sussex Pestalozzi village near her old school, as if Benenden had provided a dress rehearsal in her role of being royal.

III

At a press conference held at the Earl Marshal's court shortly before the Investiture of the Prince of Wales, a Dutch journalist enquired if Princess Anne would be created Princess Royal upon the same day. Garter King of Arms responded that they were concerned only with the Investiture and that he regretted he had no other informa-tion. In retrospect, it would appear that the impeccable royal sense of occasion faltered for once, when the iron was red-hot for a new-minted title. The Queen's advisers recognized that sufficient heraldic chi-chi had been deployed already and yet probably missed an in-valuable opportunity. At Caernarvon that summer, a slender figure in pale blue, the Princess shared the acclaim of the crowds. Through all the long ceremony, she had felt 'most moved' at the moment when her brother passed from her view to be presented to the people as Prince of Wales and she heard the roar of cheering from the Castle Square. She knew that he merited the affection, and she strangely shared that day his sense of being set apart.

Few people just then would have regarded her as curiously isolated within the royal orbit. In the tempo of the generations she remained an only daughter and had no close girl cousins of her own age or just a little older. There was at that time no other prominent teen-age princess in Europe, none at all events so close to a throne. Even the young Queen Anne-Marie of the Hellenes, seldom mentioned in newsprint without being 'youthful' or 'little', was four years Princess Anne's senior. Princess Alexandra was widely thought to be Anne's mentor in the A to Z of fashion, although the age difference of fourteen years must alas have set her firmly within a staider generation. The Queen's dresser, dear old Margaret Mac-Donald, gave the benefit of her long experience for the St. David's Day outfit of Anne's first official engagement, ideal at the time although it seemed singularly dated three months later. But Anne essentially had to find and set her own distinctive fashion style.

Princess Alexandra, in fact, introduced her young cousin to the sympathetic wholesale house of Susan Small, whose chief stylist, Maureen Baker, was later to design Anne's wedding gown. Anne followed the well-trodden family trail to Norman Hartnell, with the difference in routine that she went to his salon personally to select a dozen dresses or more. These were then submitted to the Palace where Anne and her mother viewed them together 'to come to a mutual agreement'. The Queen's influence was tactful: she expressed preferences but never opposed anything her daughter really liked. For two or three years, all the Princess's 'official' clothes were thus discussed in some detail beforehand. But conscious that she had to exercise and train her own individual dress sense, the Princess watched the dress pages with more attention than some young girls, and went shopping with friends, flicking through the rails at Fortnum's, watching a dress show at Belinda Bellville's or delving into Chelsea to visit the ever-promising salon of Nora Bradley. 'It's always a total mystery to my why I am described as a fashion leader,' she once said, with a self-deprecating smile. 'Clothes are part of the job—if you can call it a job.'

It was the definitive era of the mini-skirt, phase one, when her own age group were similarly trying to set their own style, do their own thing, friends like Sibilla Dorman, with whom Anne and

Charles spent a swimming and sailing holiday in Malta that summer, and Sandra Butter, Lady Zia Wernher's grand-daughter, then embarking into dress design as a professional career. The interest of the Nevill cousins, Angela and Rose, simmered just then around a boutique in Wilton Mews in which Lady Rupert Nevill had an interest and, in Paris, Emma Soames—daughter of the then British Ambassador Mr. Christopher Soames—was at the threshold of her job as an assistant fashion editress of the French *Vogue*. And perhaps in passing we may note the dance at the British Embassy given for Emma and her brother Nicholas the week-end before Prince Charles's investiture. Princess Anne, Princess Alexandra, Mr. Angus Ogilvy and Prince Michael all flew over in the same plane. The Embassy garden was spangled with dreamy lighting for outdoor dancing in the warm June evening. Anne asked the guitarist to play *Beggin'*—'Beggin', Beggin' you, Put your loving hand out baby'—and everyone in the dancing throng was enjoying themselves too much to heed the tinkling cymbals of any romantic surmise that mistakenly preoccupied some people just then.

## IV

Anne's own group of friends never lacked for talk or laughter in the 'flat' as Princess Anne disarmingly called her three-roomed suite overlooking the Palace gardens. At the head of a remote nook of corridors, and originally shared with Prince Charles, it underwent only a very gradual change of atmosphere until long after Charles had moved into a suite on the Mall frontage of the Palace, leaving his sister exclusive possession. 'There'll be more room for my ponies,' Anne had said, meaning her amusing framed drawings of frisky, long-legged colts and her collection of horses in crystal, bronze, porcelain and pottery that filled every spare display shelf.

A man from the 'pubs'—the then Ministry of Public Building and Works—had flattered her a little by asking for her specifications for repainting, and found Anne content with 'something light and bright . . . much the same as now, really'. She made do with much of the furniture, both trad and contemporary, which Charles had left behind, but introduced one of the first pictures she had ever acquired—the wide horizons of a Seago landscape. After reading a book about her parents' happiness aboard the S.S. *Gothic*, used in 1953 for a Commonwealth tour which the Princess was too young to remember, she discovered that the liner's royal furnishing was still in store, including her mother's divan bed of rose-patterned chintz, and nothing would content her until she was allowed to have it, a link of sentiment perhaps with all the happy hours she had herself spent at sea.

Princess Anne's last days of 'being blissful eighteen' were rounded off with a family holiday cruise to the Shetlands and Norway in the royal yacht *Britannia*, and although a cold confined her to her cabin for a day or two she recovered in time to visit her Norwegian cousins, King Olaf and the newly-wed Crown Prince Harald and his attractive brunette wife, Princess Sonja, whom she had last seen during their English honeymoon. Her nineteenth birthday was spent amid the unalloyed happiness of the yawl *Bloodhound*, with her father and Prince Charles and six friends—Nevills and Knatch-bulls and Kents—who remained unobserved by the world, as on her anniversaries for years past. Among other commemorative symbols, her personal standard was flown for the first time at the masthead, a richness of red, gold and white, itself unnoticed save by the few as the yachting party explored the fiords north of Bergen. And yet the occasion had a farewell poignancy, for this was to be last royal cruise of the *Bloodhound*, Prince Philip having decided on grounds of expense that the time had come to sell the yawl and rely in future on chartering a suitable successor.

Much as she disliked her father's decision, Princess Anne could only accept it. Among her birthday gifts was a sumptuous loose-leaf engagement book, tooled and embellished with her name and title, to replace the civil service issue she had used previously. All her public engagements of the past six months had been in a sense impromptu and unexpected. The lady-in-waiting who accompanied her—usually Lady Susan Hussey—belonged to the Queen's rota and, always conscious of critical voices, the Palace was at pains to point out that the Princess's clerical assistant was not in fact her private secretary. The new book had three columns for morning, afternoon and evening. 'We'll fill it up,' said Anne, as if still the small girl ready to try everything.

At nineteen the Princess had a bank account at Coutt's but still found it needful to watch her parental dress allowance. 'I'm afraid it's over my limit,' she would say, declining a purchase. At that moment in time, she had no Civil List allowance of her own, but was due to receive £6,000 a year on coming of age at twenty-one. On New Year's Day, 1970, however, the provisions of the Family Law Reform Act came into force and unexpectedly brought her a windfall. The coming-of-age was now at eighteen, instead of twenty-one, and the first quarterly warrant of £1,500 was paid into Princess Anne's account shortly afterwards. A Palace accountant pointed out that this was a 'gross'. From that moment, she discovered, she was also supposed to contribute to the cost of official cars, and in fact staff salaries and expenses soon outran the balance until, in 1972, after the Select Committee enquiry into royal costs, she received a Civil List increase to £15,000, rising to £35,000 on marriage.

Princess Anne's personal standard, with its silver-white label and red heart above the basic Royal Arms, was publicly flown early in September, 1969, when she opened a road transport education centre in Shropshire and incidentally drove a double-decker bus along some of the training roads. This experiment at the wheel she equalled a month later, driving on the slippery skid pan after opening the police cadet training school at Chelmsford, and 'undertaking every manoeuvre,' as an official said, 'that we would have expected the Duke of Edinburgh or Prince Charles to try'.

Then came the Princess's somewhat dramatic visit by helicopter to to a North Sea natural gas drilling rig, competently clad in a red trouser suit as if for any emergency, ready to scale any catwalk or make a conspicuous splash if swept overboard. In a spirit of enquiry she in fact made an unscheduled scramble into one of the survival capsules and now keeps a plaque of compressed salt from below the ocean bed, carved in her profile, as a memento. The next day, she flew to Germany to visit her regiment, the 14th/20th King's Hussars. She had assumed the colonelcy-in-chief, her first, three months earlier, and was now scheduled to receive a civic welcome in the Paderborn town hall, attend a mess dinner, to take the salute at a regimental parade the following morning and drive a Chieftain tank. Unscheduled—and a surprise to those present—was that she replied to the mayor of Paderborn in German and not only drove the fifty-ton Chieftain for three miles up and down the rough practice grounds after a short briefing but also appeared to set a new speed record.

'I'd love one for Christmas,' she said, but what she got was a diamond brooch subscribed by all ranks and the gift of appropriate number plates for her car—1420 H—which the Hussars had acquired from, among other previous owners, a dairy milk float. Staying with her aunt and godmother, Princess Margarita, at Langenburg in southern Germany that week-end she hilariously recollected the escort horse that had reared in terror at the sight of her personal standard, and she found the newspapers staging their own field day with pictures of her firing a Sterling sub-machine-gun—she placed five shots within three inches of the target centre—and firing an automatic from the hip, equally creditably. Warning her that she would be asked to try out a machine-gun, Prince Philip, Prince Charles and Prince Michael had ludicrously enlarged its terrors until, thorough in everything, she had taken some basic coaching from all three.

These were early highlights of her twentieth year. In that same season, she also undertook solo official visits to Bristol, Manchester, Bolton and elsewhere, until the phrase 'The Princess Anne left Heathrow Airport, London, this morning in an aircraft of the Queen's Flight to visit ... Upon arrival Her Royal Highness was received by H.M. Lieutenant for the county...' began to threaten the *Court Circular* with monotony. The Princess named and launched the hovercraft *The Princess Anne* at Dover, sat to Terence Cuneo for her first adult portrait and accepted her first presidency: to head the Save the Children Fund. She 'received purses' at the Albert Hall, was chief guest of honour at a Mansion House lunch and engagingly visited children's homes, schools and housing schemes. She prettily unveiled plaques and laid foundation stones. She looked wryly flattered on learning that her presence at an agricultural show had doubled attendance. At Kensington Palace old Princess Alice of Athlone, who could remember the patterns of royal behaviour over eight decades thought it quite extraordinary that the young Princess was doing so much so well.

Princess Anne found press attention to her 'private' riding activities less easy to endure. In planning a full programme of show-jumping and eventing, the enthusiasm of the sponsors often had to be kept on a tight rein. On the line to the organizer, a cool-voiced lady-in-waiting would enquire if the Princess could take part 'without a barrage of press and publicity'. At Taplow and Downlands, Wylye and elsewhere, it had to be understood that 'advance publicity might deter the Princess from arriving'. At the Everdon Horse Trials, the name Miss J. Smith appeared on the programme, a stratagem justified when the Princess Anne 'took over' Royal Ocean but then chanced to be spectacularly thrown, happily with little resulting publicity. The Princess made new riding friends who knew when to shield her at times from an embarrassing camera. She liked the free and easy ways of the riding fraternity, the recognition that others could have nerves as well as oneself, and the ready avenues of wider acquaintance on a new proven footing of equality.

She had admired Richard Meade from her early teens, for instance, when he had seemed assured of a place in the Tokio Olympics team only to take a penal dive into the Badminton lake upon Barberry which brought an end to his dream. In 1969, the year after his Olympic Gold was secured in Mexico, he was a guest at Windsor for the Ascot house party, as if in compensation for another ducking at Badminton when Barberry lost his bridle in the lake. Mr. Meade went out of his way to inspire the Princess with confidence. At the Eridge Horse Trials, when he won the Advanced Class, Anne was third in the Novice Class on Doublet.

It was a misfortune of those early trials that the Princess often found that her prize money cheques were made out to the Queen as owner. 'I didn't see a penny,' she claimed, with mock despair, after some £20 had thus been diverted by mistake. In October, 1969, she competed in the Combined Training Championships at the Horse of the Year Show, gloomy at finding herself retired with thirty faults in the show-jumping and finally reduced to ninth out of eleven starters. But by the end of the following year she had qualified for the Badminton Three-Day Event and suddenly the future glowed with challenge. In public and private life, she had sailed through a series of hopeful adventures, a hopeful venture indeed.

## 5   Princess of the Seventies

### I

Until 1970 Princess Anne had followed the Queen's overseas tours by news reports, phone calls, letters, her mother's amateur movies and everybody's conversation, in that order, with no real sense of personal involvement. Then the Queen and Prince Philip undertook to commemorate the 200th anniversary of Captain Cook's voyages by a two-month tour of New Zealand and Australia, following 'roughly in his footsteps' and Anne found herself enmeshed in a high-pressure tour that even hardened Palace officials termed 'one of the most difficult yet, physically'. In Australia itself the royal group—which also included the Prince of Wales—were to have 235 engagements in 35 days, compared with 97 in 38 days on their visit of seven years earlier. The route lines on the wall charts looked tangled and intricate, causing one secretary to jest, 'If you lose the book (the itinerary) you'll be on a desert island for life.' And Anne was once again 'flung in at the deep end', into a plan that, as she said at the time, 'made me lose sleep for excitement'.

To a friend she also expressed the less cheerful prospect, 'I hope we won't be stuck in a lot of stuffy town halls' and the family no doubt discussed this deterrent at the breakfast-table. The Queen was troubled by ancient and perennial complaints that she met too many officials and did not meet the people, although 'officials' are obviously always the people's representatives. As if by bush telegraph, New Zealand High Commissioner staff in London knew months beforehand that an indignant young voice at the Palace had asked, 'Why not go out and meet the crowds? Why on earth *not* get engulfed?' And when the royals arrived in Wellington and promptly 'went walkabout', the effect of the Queen's orange coat and of Anne's lemon outfit was as deliberate as R.A.F.—or N.Z.A.F.—markers flung into a stormy sea, and Anne impetuously headed into the crowds ... determined that nothing should mar a technique she had evidently suggested and polished with unstinted confidence.

Summing up at the end of the tour two months later—not to add her subsequent Canadian travels to the North-West Territories and her visit to Washington that summer—one realized that no teen-age princess had ever before travelled so far or so variously or faced such sustained exposure to the public eye. The Princess shrugs and says, 'Well, you know, I simply tagged along.' Yet it was highly skilled tagging, requiring constant adaptability and watchfulness in support of her parents. Royal tours can be too readily taken for granted. The Australians complained that she did not smile enough and Anne tried to put it simply, 'It's difficult to keep the smile bright when you're fourth in line.'

Having expected the tour to be 'pretty demanding', she approached each task with the willingness of Doublet facing a five-barred gate, and every resulting pleasure—and the pleasures were innumerable—seemed a bonus. A week-end away from wintry London, and with a day lost into the International Date Line, there was the air-travel conjuring trick of being in the South Seas, downing her first bowls of traditional kava, first on Fiji, then on Tonga, awaking to a serenade of nose-flutes . . . and trying not to tread on the children's fingers when they unexpectedly wanted to stroke her wet-look shoes. There was the yuk-yuk Tongan feast of sucking pigs that she had seen time and again on the Windsor movies but the films lacked the mingled scent of hibiscus and basted crackling that confirmed the reality. (The autocratic King Tauf'ahau had ordered a special issue of postage stamps which included the glamorous Snowdon photograph of Princess Anne.) And then in Wellington, apart from the welcoming carnival of small boats, the crowds were smaller and quieter than she had expected. The 'hurrahs' of popular description were in fact 'oo's' and 'ah's' and scattered cries of 'Hi, Annabelle!' But there were less comfortable manifestations; the pressing groups of a hundred or more filled with an urgent wish to shake hands, the sudden outbreaks of 'touching' fever.

Flying to South Island to spend their first week-end on a sheep station with the Acland family, Charles and Anne described to their hosts the entirely new physical sensations of the walkabout 'like being at some enormous party', and they argued the good sense of safety precautions that still gave enhanced pleasure to the crowds. Riding in the rain, they only later heard that their parents, sailing aboard *Britannia* to South Island, had unexpectedly encountered fantastic gales, causing the royal yacht practically to stand on end in a walkabout of its own. So the tour went on, undamped by the persistent wet weather. Anne reckoned one evening that she had established a record mileage, sploshing around the agriculture showgrounds near Christchurch. While the Queen and Prince Philip often followed their separate schedules, Prince Charles and Princess Anne pursued their own programmes of junior events, such as a lunch with all the prefects of local schools or a reception of youth organizations, all with walkabout trimmings. There had surely never been a royal tour so diverse in the events it offered the local people.

The sparse earlier crowds of the tour were replaced by multitudes, lured from their television sets by the chance of talking to the Queen or of persuading Anne to admire one's string of kids. As one correspondent said, the effect was electric, people strained to have a natter. And the effect on the royals was scarcely less stimulating. At dinner everyone had a different crowd story to tell. In Auckland Princess Anne happened to tell one woman, 'I'm used to the rain,' and heard the phrase repeated and repeated to the back of the crowd like an echo. 'Used to the rain! Used to the rain!', surprisingly culminating in a terrific cheer. One of the equerries asked afterwards, 'What on earth did you say to them?'

Meanwhile, Australia loomed to Anne as something tougher and more intimidating, despite Charles's reassurances that one 'played it along'. The chief difference was that the 'walks round the town hall' were stepped up to a far more vocal audience. The wind blew and the wolf-whistles shrilled. In Sydney, on the second day, the press decided that Anne, wrestling with the streamers of her turban, had asserted, 'I can't see a thing in this bloody wind!' Or was the expletive something firmer and worse? Cooked up as it was, the absurd controversy seasoned the tour with Australian relish. Reactions could be foretold. If Anne looked bored during a tour of a power-station, succumbing at last to turgid explanations, one could put that down to inexperience. When a Canberra student in outlandish drag thrust a bouquet of weeds into her hand, Anne played it along, to resulting cheers. If a crowd looked baffled at being hemmed behind a hefty barricade, the Princess copied her mother in going as close as possible to the rails, often worrying the police by her apparent disregard of crowd pressure hazards.

There were danger-spots, such as Collins Street, Melbourne, where two people in fact died in the crush, unknown to the walking royals, and dozens were taken to hospital after one wild jostle to get within talking distance. Anne dropped any show of enjoying herself when she noticed a small boy, lost and wailing and at risk of being trodden underfoot, and rather commandingly stopped the fiesta until policemen made sure he was safe. Trivial in itself, this incident in turn made news around the world.

Behind the public scene there was also a congenial string of happy private social events, part fixed up by Prince Philip through the Michael Parkers and other friends, part through the solid acquaintance that Prince Charles had established during his two terms at Timbertop, the outback colony of Geelong grammar school. To see Timbertop, before Charles flew home to resume his studies at Cambridge, was Anne's unquestioned 'must', and they went up from Melbourne to a week-end of riding and exploration in the gum forests in company with Charles's old school friend, Stuart Mc-Gregor. Nevertheless, the new generation of Timbertop boys seemed rather vague about the visitors.

'You're welcome, Margaret,' said one, until Princess Anne explained her identity. After Charles had returned to England and the Princess was on her own, she quietly spent a week-end with a Queensland farming family, helping in a sheep round-up before returning in time to join her parents aboard *Britannia* for a cruise in the Great Barrier Reef. It would be diverting at some time to record the ever-varying scenes in which the Queen has celebrated her birthday. Her forty-fourth anniversary was spent in a light-hearted picnic on an uninhabited island which her daughter and husband helped to find, during which the Princess explored the coral reef so energetically that she returned to Canberra with her legs scratched and bruised —and Bill Heseltine, the Queen's press secretary, felt called on to deny that she had been badly bitten by mosquitoes.

But this was merely to put the rebuttal before the bites. In the Canadian North-West Territories two months later the swarms of 'skittas' and black fly were ravenous, and the Queen and her daughter wore trousers in self-defence. Thereupon, as a sidelight to fashion history, the correspondents in Yellowknife conscientiously recorded that the Queen of Canada had officially appeared for the first time in a trouser-suit.

## II

In a jovial aside to Commander Fulford, the naval doctor on the tour of the North-West Territories and Manitoba in 1970, Prince Philip asserted that all his family at least made excellent guinea-pigs in the physiological effects of climate. Through two months of midsummer, Princess Anne undertook engagements that included trips to Germany and Glasgow, Dusseldorf and Durham, and then from London in July they all dropped suddenly into the ice-fringed airport of Frobisher Bay. Amid the welcoming band of airmen, Eskimoes and government folk, Anne discovered herself instantly cast in an unofficial role as visiting commandant of the Eskimo girl guides and it was noted that she had in fact carefully chosen a sable hat to help dress the part.

Her father had been enthusing on the lonely attractions of the Canadian Arctic for years. To sleep the first night in a new-built hotel, its modern elegance still smelling of cement, to breakfast on fish that Prince Charles had literally caught through a hole in the ice, to try an impromptu walkabout in the Canadian Legion Club as the high-spot social centre in town, to fly on to Resolute Bay and to lodge the following night in a schoolhouse, can all be inferred as lively reportage for Princess Anne's personal journal.

Joining the tour from Ottawa, Charles had brought along a girl of Anne's own age, Premier Trudeau's niece, Jocelyne Rouleau, so that the three young people formed their own lively trio when 'off duty'. In Yellowknife they touched down suddenly into a temperature in the seventies—'out of parkas into lightweights,' as Charles recommended when the plane radio gave the ground temperature figures, and a light-hearted barbecue occupied the long evening of the twenty-four-hour Arctic day. 'Loud cheers for P.A., particularly, wherever we go,' wrote one member of the royal retinue. The royal visitors stayed up into the small hours to see the midnight sun, only to sight but a dismal gleam behind the rain-clouds. Flying south again, into the scorching heat of the Manitoba centennial celebrations, Mary Dawnay, the lady-in-waiting, had cause to smile wryly when she opened some mail and had to pass the Princess a query on the forthcoming 1971 visit to Kenya, then in the planning stage.

'For me, it's a super pleasure trip,' Anne had told a group of hipster youngsters, when asked about her Canadian impressions. While the Queen and Prince Philip bore the brunt of the Manitoba official ceremonies, inspections and luncheons, Anne and her brother snatched carefree leisure from the side excursions, a canoe jaunt along the Red River, a prairie horse show at Swan River, a helicopter swirl along the shores of Duck Bay. But in Brandon the heat was still more intense, and some of the all-seeing news scouts considered the Princess 'sombre', a criticism that was to seem like the first cloud in a summer storm. As its climax, the intensive programme promised Anne the silver lining of her first experience of the United States, in the shape of a 'a very private visit' to Washington at the behest of President Nixon's two daughters, Tricia and Julie. But privacy is relative and unguaranteed, especially for a royal princess's first visit to a feminist republic.

Prince Philip had cautiously hinted at the possibility of not getting very far, not seeing very much, through the predictable cordons of police and the voracious wolf-packs of reporters. Like any father, he may have wondered whether Anne had paid any attention. Her first stings of disillusion may have come in the adulatory atmosphere aboard the presidential plane that flew the royal visitors from Winnipeg. Then the strains of *Rule Britannia* and the fanfares of herald trumpeters greeted them on the lawns of the White House. Casting a trained eye over the phalanx of press, TV crews and other onlookers, Charles' equerry, David Checketts, estimated their number at several hundred. And there was President Nixon himself, with microphones ready, waiting in the stifling heat to recite a speech of welcome stiff with State Department compliments. The perceptive journalist who said that Princess Anne could not conceal 'a mood of incredulity and vague discomfort' seems to have misinterpreted her wry sense of humour.

Anne's happier anticipations of the American scene were promptly realized however when she and Charles zoomed over Washington in a 'chopper' an hour or two later for a barbecue at Camp David, the presidential retreat in Maryland, with Tricia and Julie Nixon, Julie's husband David Eisenhower, his sister, Susan, and others in a pleasantly young and friendly group. While most of the youngsters went swimming, the Princess was content none the less to sit in the shade of the patio. With motherly intuition, Mrs. Nixon saw that she was exhausted and marvelled at her resilience. Later in the evening they 'took in' the Lincoln Memorial and the moonlight view from the top of the Washington Monument, among other sights, not omitting some walkabout questions to people in the eternal crowds. A reporter seized his opportunity to ask questions of his own, and Anne said with a smile, 'I don't give interviews', a remark that sounded stiff and sour when reported in print, torn from its context. That night she slept at the White House in the four-poster bed in the Rose Room, 'where her mother and grandmother had slept before her', as Mrs. Nixon mentioned next morning.

'But not Queen Victoria?' Anne teased her.

'No, but she gave us a desk made from the wreck of the British ship *Resolute*.'

'There's a coincidence,' said the Princess. 'We were in Resolution, scene of the shipwreck, only last week!' and was on her marks for the rest of the day. They made the obligatory tour of the Capitol and the Smithsonian Institute, where they found the moon astro-nauts Neil Armstrong and Frank Bormann waiting to show them round and answer questions. 'But I could ask you questions all day,' the Princess told Bormann. Lunching on the presidential yacht *Sequoia*, they sailed down the Potomac to Mount Vernon, but Princess Anne first took time off to transfer to one of the Coast Guard speedboats with Mary Dawnay and streak up and down the broad waters, the breeze wonderfully refreshing.

On the visit to Mount Vernon itself, the Princess faced one of those ordeals that she dreaded. George Washington's homestead is elegant and charming in exterior, but it would take the brush of Hogarth to delineate the terrible scrimmage of cameramen and commentators in its small domestic rooms, a jostle so unseemly that even the calm Squadron Leader Checketts felt called on to cry, 'Let's have some dignity!' Yet these were mere incidents, after all, probably less jading than the handshaking of the long reception lines at the British Embassy tea-party That evening the Princess and her brother slipped away from the White House to pay an im-promptu visit to an open-air concert in Lafayette Park. The orches-tra rose to the occasion by playing the Pomp and Circumstance march and the audience rose similarly in a storm of welcoming applause. At the ball at the White House later that evening, Princess Anne danced into the small hours . . . and yet was up at nine a.m. for a day of high-speed—but mercifully less official—sightseeing with Tricia and Julie. 'It's just that I can't get used to twenty million reporters at my heels,' she had ruefully apologized, and they successfully took in the boutiques of Georgetown, an art gallery and a baseball game before rejoining Charles to catch the B.O.A.C. night plane home.

## III

If the milestone of a twentieth birthday should seem bright with auguries, Princess Anne's anniversary was indeed fittingly ornamented. The royal yacht *Britannia* was once again cruising off the west coast of Scotland, and the Princess's birthday cards were appropriately delivered by helicopter. The guest list included Princess Alexandra, with her husband, Angus, and her younger brother.

But Anne sometimes withdrew from the family group to do her 'little jobs': she enjoyed working for an hour or two in the calm of her state-room, with the radio jingling, and the gentle tremor of the ship in smooth passage. Books on Kenya were piled with her riding magazines, and riding event entries shared her cramped desk with the itinerary proposals for her first solo tour.

One of the most minor events of the year, a return to Benenden to open a new wing, blended with the serious business of having a score of years to her birthday to give pause for thought. She could consider herself somewhere midway between leaving school and getting married; and having accepted the presidency of the Save the Children Fund she soberly asked herself if she were doing enough. The Prince of Wales was planning to spend a few days on African safari early in 1971. 'Why not come along?' he offered. Prince Philip suggested that the best way to publicize any organization was to make a film about it, and the two ideas coalesced. When the B.B.C. agreed to make a television safari film for the popular Blue Peter children's programme, Anne remarked that all the television cameras in North America had at least got her used to 'being followed around with one, if it would do any good'. The New

Zealand Save the Children organization just then reported an immediate increase of membership for the Fund as a result of the Princess's interest. And so a dual project was agreed, not for one film but ultimately two, both to further the S.C. work and funds.

Charles and Anne flew out to Nairobi together in an R.A.F. plane on February 6th, 1971, the date itself not insignificant for it was nineteen years to the day since their mother had been staying up-country in Kenya at the Treetops lodge on that morning of destiny when she became Queen. At Nairobi brother and sister then parted company, the Princess wasting no time in beginning location work with Valerie Singleton and the film unit. 'We hadn't been filming a couple of minutes before we knew that if the film was a flop it wouldn't be Princess Anne's fault,' said the producer, Edward Barnes.

One of the essential sequences of the film was set in the Starehe Boys' Centre where waifs are given practical help when they wander in from the bush. No longer overconscious of the cameras, Anne found it very like being a house mother again. On seeing her in a cotton frock, the boys of the school could scarcely believe she was Princess Anne. Children usually disbelieved her on that score, though the boys knew her at once when she wore a gold-and-white gown at a school entertainment. Trailed by the film unit, she made a sentimental journey to Treetops. As her mother had done, she sat on the balcony, her Pentax poised for the animals who might visit the water-hole in the forest clearing below. Another evening, the dialogue of a riding sequence was being planned when the Princess surprised Val Singleton by talking about her ambitions as a three-day event rider. There was no limit to what one might do, one might be chosen for the team to represent Britain in the Olympics.

Anne was thinking ahead to the Crookham and Rushall Trials as the highway to Badminton and to her own confident prospect for April when the film would be shown. When April came she was already concerned with the production of her second film, its scenes ranging from her Palace apartment to a play centre in Islington, a picture which in the event was screened at the 650 Save the Children Fund club branches throughout the Commonwealth. Meanwhile, the world had already noticed how a certain Lieutenant Mark

Phillips of the 1st Queen's Dragoon Guards increasingly preoccupied her in friendly rivalry and at the Rushall Horse Trials he came superbly first on Great Ovation, an eight-year-old he had been thinking of selling the previous year. Princess Anne was fourth on Doublet, the splendid jumper of South American stock which her mother had given her at Christmas, and now the challenge was definitive. 'See you at Badminton, then,' she said, looking Mark straight in the eye.

Even the supercilious who pretend to regard royalty as of little account were infected with the enthusiasm of that unforgettable Badminton three-day event, shared with millions, as it was throughout, by television and all the public media. On the opening day Princess Anne led among the twenty-five entrants who had completed their dressage, and the next day Mark Phillips alone managed to get in front of her with a difference of only seven penalty points. Subsequently he maintained his lead across the thirty-three fences of the rigorous cross-country course, while Anne lapsed to fourth on timing. On the third day, one show-jumping error reduced the Princess to fifth—Doublet's hind leg having splashed the water—and Mark Phillips was the immaculate winner. That night he partnered Princess Anne, with the Queen and Prince Philip and other guests, at the Duke and Duchess of Beaufort's victory dinner at Badminton House. Despite her measure of defeat, the Princess was radiant. She had not only creditably ridden against the best event riders in the world but was now at least in line for a team place in the European Championships ... and perhaps even the Olympics beyond. And was there, too, in her heart some inkling of a future celebration at Badminton House ... the happiness of her betrothal just two years ahead?

## IV

More than in other occupations, the working members of the Royal Family live in three time dimensions, the past of ineffaceable record, the present of diversion or duty and their ever programmed future. With the plaudits of Badminton still ringing in her ears, Anne launched her first naval frigate *Amazon*, seizing the opportunity in her speech to say that she had no sympathy with Women's Lib and that Amazons in any case had been at their most formidable on horseback. Next, she paid a brief Save the Children visit to Norway and then in May joined her parents for the intensive 1971 centenary visit to British Columbia. All that apparently remains now of the exuberant '4,500 miles in 10 days' are the sound-tapes of bands, speeches and cheers, the news reports and photographs, the local television films and the irrepressible itinerary:

'Princess Anne to fly to Totino to open the Pacific national park, to receive a horse's head carved in driftwood...Drive to Kelowna. Flight to Vancouver.' And next day, 'Princess Anne lays stone of CBC building, lunches at University of British Columbia, rejoins Royal party by helicopter...' But at this juncture in the programme the Princess sought the sanctuary of *Britannia* with what was politely called 'a stomach upset' and Prince Philip deputized for his daughter. The following week she felt direly unwell again, missing that colourful presentation of Duke of Edinburgh awards in Victoria, the wonderful State dinner at Government House...

Packed royal schedules seldom allow for illness. The show must go on, and the wish 'not to disappoint' dominates everything. While Anne winced and attempted to keep her discomforts to herself, the early summer none the less saw an increasing number of engagements cancelled or curtailed. On July 8th the Princess had planned to attend the wedding at the Savoy Chapel of her close, friend, Fiona Phillips, Lady Zia Wernher's grand-daughter—no relative of Mark—and at the last moment she pleaded a headache. But this time the doctors were summoned and later that same day the Palace announced that the Princess had undergone an emergency operation for the removal of an inflamed ovarian cyst from which a haemorrhage had occurred. Better this unusual candour than the whispers that might have run rife otherwise. But what of the Princess's European riding hopes, which suddenly seemed threatened with disaster?

Visiting Anne in the Edward VII Hospital for Officers, her trainer, Alison Oliver, was prepared to commiserate, convinced that her protegé could not be ready for the next necessary riding trials at Eridge. Instead she found the Princess sitting in a chair, already making plans for a crash get-fit course of walking and climbing at Balmoral. On the twenty-first 'anniversary of her birthday', as the *Court Circular* never fails to state with precision, the local folk at Thurso sang 'Happy Birthday' as the Princess Anne came ashore from the royal yacht to lunch with the Queen Mother 'and other members of the Royal Family' at the Castle of Mey. The following day she flew south to ride, under Mrs. Oliver's watchful eye, for the first time since her operation.

The Eridge trials opened only five days later, and the Princess led on Doublet in the dressage and show-jumping on the first day, six points above Mark Phillips. On the second day, Mark was still lying second across country near the end of the course when Doublet unaccountably stopped and Anne fell at a trappy watersplash that put her out of the running. The rest is a matter of equestrian history. Although left out of the official British team for the European Championships, Princess Anne was invited to compete 'as an individual', as Miss Gordon-Watson had done two years earlier, and accepted with spectacular results.

When the Marquess of Exeter suggested that the Queen might care to spend the week-end at Burgley and watch the events, H.M. replied, 'There's nothing I'd like better.' Great Britain won the team championship with less than half the penalty points heaped on Russia, who came second for the silver medal. And against seasoned competitors from nine countries, Princess Anne won the European individual gold medal, finally sailing over fence after fence against the clock in a faultless clear round. She was the first member of the Royal Family ever to hold a European equestrian title, and almost danced with delight. Buoyantly voted Sportswoman of the Year by newspaper readers and elected Sports Personality of the Year by B.B.C. television viewers, these polls faithfully reflected the public view. Here was a Princess who proved her skill and prestige against all other exponents and provided, as world champion racing driver Jackie Stewart said, 'a terrific image for her country'.

## V

And so, after our quest of the princesses of five centuries and more, one comes to the princess of the seventies, the young woman moving towards her mid-twenties, photogenic as princesses should be and yet with persuasive symptoms of deep and lasting strength of character, autocratic at times as only princesses can be, self-confident and yet often self-deprecating. 'If you stop having nerves, you're not doing the job as well as you should,' she says. A Princess Supremo, if one may judge by the space admiringly accorded her in the news-papers, a coverage in column inches and glowing adjectives far exceeding the space ever accorded to the Queen as Princess Elizabeth, or to the Princesses Margaret and Alexandra at the same age. Her prestige is a phenomenon. When a Gallup poll sought to list the world's most admired women, at the time of the Queen's Silver Wedding, the Queen topped the poll for the third year running, while Princess Anne 'appeared from nowhere' to come third behind the Queen and Mrs. Golda Meir.

Popularity is like a robe of office to a princess, its sheen attracting ever wider attention when one's unfolding personality seems fresh and new, its embroideries of news and gossip irresistibly fascinating to the watching world. It is a garment, this popularity, that can last for life in the constancy of public affection and esteem and yet may quickly grow threadbare and even shabby if worn without an inner dignity.

In one aspect of modern popularity, the global strategy of public relations, Princess Anne is already astonishingly experienced. Since her twenty-first birthday, she has shone as the most-travelled member of the Royal Family other than Prince Philip, not only often accompanying her parents on their joint travels but more recently crossing novel and more distant horizons on her own. Her father once described her a chameleon, from her frequent changes of mood and style, but in travel Princess Anne sometimes seems a lively fire-cracker fizzing among the schedules. Thus in the autumn of 1971 she flew with her father to Teheran for the 2,500th anni-versary celebrations of the founding of the Persian Empire, and in the following week joined the Queen and the Duke of Edinburgh for their State Visit to Turkey. With a quick change at Zurich airport, a week-end was spent with cousins in southern Germany, and then a flight direct from middle Europe to Hong Kong enabled her to visit her regiment, the 14/20th King's Hussars and to see the local work of the Save the Children Fund, and much else be-sides.

This meteoric jag needed fast camerawork and fast reporting: Anne riding Alvane, the Shah of Persia's finest horse; Anne at the tented city of Persepolis, eclipsing the glamour of a dozen assembled queens and princesses in a dazzling hooded coat of white Arctic fox (made, as it happened, from the skins presented to her the previous year in Manitoba). And then Anne gravely listening with her parents to love-songs in a former Turkish harem, and Anne again, shopping for Christmas gifts in a Communist store in Hong Kong, hunting for a lost ear-ring in the matting of a Saladin armoured car and, incidentally, blithely demolishing six targets with her accurate shellfire on an Army range. . . .

One could alight on a hundred incidents equally capsuled yet completely reflecting her pep and buoyancy. For a month in 1972 she took part in the tour of Thailand, Brunei, Sarawak and Malaysia with her parents, her impressions distilled in scores of Pentax shots of golden spires and flag-decked elephants, dancing girls and floral barges, a dream of oriental splendour and a nightmare of security against terrorist guerillas. Yet she checked out of the tour in a punctual and feverish anxiety to resume her Badminton event training in England, and was back in the saddle, exercising Doublet not twelve hours after her plane landed. Within a few days, it was part and parcel of the same swift transition that she acted as a Counsellor of State for the first time, standing even protocol a little dizzily on its head. When abroad for any length of time, the Queen appoints two members of the Royal Family to act as Counsellors to transact the routine business of the Crown in her absence. Princess Anne had been absent with the Queen and yet now was at home to represent the absent Sovereign.

The Council was held at Clarence House with Queen Elizabeth the Queen Mother, and it aptly fell to her grandmother to teach her the use of one of the stranger tools of the royal craft, pricking with the traditional steel bodkin the names of those nominated by the Queen as High Sheriff for each county as inscribed on a vellum roll. Queen Elizabeth I, legend tells, had no pen at hand when the roll of names was brought to her one day and took up her needlework bodkin instead, and so it has been ever since. One gathers that under the not unamused eyes of Mr. William Whitelaw, Mr. Julian Amery and other members of the Council, Anne performed this curious task to the manner born. Her future duties might include presiding over a Council and receiving new ambassadors. But for the moment it was pleasant to join her grandmother's luncheon-party at Clarence House, to be complimented on the morning's role and to talk enthusiastically of future plans.

Doublet, she felt, could be good enough for the Olympics, and 'a good show' with him at Badminton might bring her into selection for the Munich Games. He promised well in the Crookham trials and all her hopes were pinned on him exclusively. Indeed, she had no other horse of qualified experience. Alas, the Badminton event was less than a week away when Doublet suffered a strained tendon and had to be withdrawn.

It was a bitter blow, skimming away Anne's rosy Olympic ambitions at a stroke. Many another rider might have almost abandoned riding for weeks, in sheer disappointment. But when Badminton began Anne skipped the opening day rather than fill time as a passive spectator, and was already schooling the Queen's horses, Columbus and Collingwood, with Mrs. Oliver at Winkfield Row.

Time indeed was too precious, and too demanding, to be wasted idly. In May there occurred a tour of the Channel Isles when, for the first time, Princess Anne was the principal passenger of the royal yacht *Britannia*. In June she visited Monaco, ostensibly to attend a concert at the Monte Carlo Opera House in aid of the Monaco Red Cross but in reality also to spend a few hours of 'stunning sightseeing' with Prince Rainier and Princess Grace, before flying to Seville to be principal guest at the wedding of Prince Alexander of Yugoslavia, whom she had first met as Charles's contemporary at Gordonstoun. Here, too, Anne touched an aspect of the fine feather-edge of diplomacy. On the death of his father, King Peter, Alexander had refused to assume the role of a pretender king in exile and thus, freed of a diplomatic impasse, the way was clear for the Queen, the Duke of Edinburgh and Princess Anne to pay a State Visit to Marshal Tito in Yugoslavia that autumn. Alexander and his bride, Princess Maria Gloria of Orleans Braganza, were still on their honeymoon, in fact, when they heard that their sunny wedding in Seville smoothed the way indirectly for the first visit of a British monarch to a Communist country.

Walking through the streets of Belgrade in 1972, Princess Anne did not realize that, within the year, the way would be clear to journey deeper through the Iron Curtain into the republic of the Ukraine and perhaps to defend her European riding title in the ancient capital of Kiev. But the deep shadows of Ekaterinburg were dispersed as readily in the hot sunshine of Ethiopia, in the course of her solo visit to the Emperor Haile Selassie. During the naval week at Massawa, Anne stepped onto the deck of the Soviet destroyer *Skritnit* on a polite visit of inspection and the white-capped sailors accorded her perhaps the first applause of royalty heard under the Russian flag for more than fifty years. Bluff Admiral Kruglakov explained that his ship was faster than the Princess's horses. 'You think so?' said Anne, with a blissful smile.

First attempts and first achievements are foundation assets of popularity. If Princess Anne's official visit to Ethiopia and the Sudan received exceptional press coverage, she also earned it as the only presumptive Princess Royal to have led her entourage on a mule-back safari over the remote mountains that are called the Roof of Africa, to pitch camp at 13,000 feet, and to photograph the rare Walia Ibex in the lost world of the Simien ranges, 'three most incredible days', as the Princess said. 'Credibility was indeed strained,' wrote one member of the expedition, 'by the sight of Mary Dawnay riding the jagged trail with a Harrod's green shopping bag on her pommel. David (Chief Inspector David Coleman, the Princess's detective) supposedly brought up the rear. But he was followed all the way up the mountain by a mule train of wild-looking characters who turned into white-coated waiters at the wave of a stick.' 'If you think we're nuts,' said Princess Anne calmly, watching one of the cameramen scrambling alongside, 'I think you're balmy, too!' But she invited, 'You'd better come in and look,' when they grew hysterical at the sight of her tent, pitched at the wildest heights of the expedition and furnished within minutes by carpets, camp beds and sleeping bags, with pristine sheets and pillows.

Advised to have medical checks before setting out, her chic and select retinue gasped in the thin and icy air and not a week later they were sweltering in the heat and humidity of Khartoum. One recollects that Anne herself was seized with 'African tummy' and yet, though feeling shaky, she fulfilled the round of garden parties, charity balls and special visits that protocol required before leaving Addis Ababa. In Khartoum, as Maurice Weaver wrote so ably, the Sudanese government were clearly aware that mad dogs and Englishmen go out in the noonday sun and had arranged that the siesta hours should be thoroughly occupied with a visit to a youth centre and a garden party. Next day the schedule included the Khartoum College of Nursing, a flight of 200 miles to study the

Gezira irrigation scheme, visits to two schools and a youth folk display, tea with the Sudanese Women's Union and finally dinner with the Foreign Minister.

Successful as the tour was in fostering goodwill, it further highlighted Princess Anne's salient characteristic in determining to do a job well, no matter at what cost to herself, even in personal hazard. She was fully aware of security risks in the troubled Sudan —where only the week after her visit diplomats were kidnapped and murdered by terrorists—and had shrugged with one of her rueful, half-wilful smiles. 'Once she sets her heart on a plan, nothing will dissuade her,' a close personal friend has noted. When Anne flew out of Khartoum on Saturday night the temperature had touched 107°F, and her plane touched down at Heathrow just before dawn on a chill February morning. Whereupon she surprised everyone very much, except those who know her best, by driving straight from the airport to breakfast with Major and Mrs. Peter Phillips, at their home in Great Somerford, Wiltshire, where their son, Mark, was home on leave.

## VI

Occasionally, amid the trivia of everyday royal events, there occurs some small circumstance to which one needs must pay close attention. In their Silver Wedding year, the Queen and the Duke of Edinburgh had occasion to pay a sentimental visit to the Royal Naval College at Dartmouth, and an officer thought it 'strange to see Princess Anne in tow, in view of her growing independence'. Sailing for Scotland a week earlier than usual, the Queen and her husband paid an official visit to the Isle of Man from the royal yacht *Britannia*, and daughter and parents found themselves in the highly unlikely situation of travelling together in a horse tram. But when the royal party disembarked at Aberdeen on August 8th it was noticed that the Princess 'had already jumped ship'.

By then, in fact, she was in Yorkshire, paying a visit to the Duke of Norfolk's eldest daughter, Lady Anne Fitzalan-Howard, at Everingham Park, where an alluring set of cross-country horse trials was held the following day. In one sense, it was equally no coincidence that Lady Anne's aunt, Lady Katharine Phillips, lived at one of the nearby farmhouses of the Everingham estate and happened just then to have her young nephew, Mark, as a house guest. The Duke of Norfolk's sister, one should explain, had married Mark's 'Uncle Joe', Colonel Joseph Phillips. The stage was truly set for a musical comedy plot. Within the week the Queen also came south to York to stay with her old friends, Lord and Lady Halifax, at Garrowby Hall, to attend the Knavesmire race-meeting on Princess Anne's birthday, the 15th, and all the more to enjoy the novelty of finding herself a guest at the birthday party at the Hall that evening. The local gossips could guess that the son of the house, Lord Irwin, danced with the Princess, but the birthday girl in fact conferred her dancing and conversation on Mark Phillips for most of the evening.

The Queen looked on with that detached amusement of hers. Young Mark probably still seemed one of Anne's ever-changing enthusiasms, though the friendship had been progressing for some time now and few young people seemed to find so much to say to each other. In their remarkable—indeed, unprecedented—press and television interview in the Palace gardens after their engagement, Anne and Mark were to confess that their romance had deepened 'after Badminton', without precisely mentioning which Badminton. It was, one thinks, the 1972 event, from which Anne had to withdraw Doublet with such disappointment while Mark on Great Ovation went on to win the leading trophy for the second year running. Anne's sense of 'a total muck-up' in the sudden quenching of her prospects for the British Olympic team at Munich could only be compensated for by her buoyant interest in the team itself, perhaps not least when Mark was selected. The team were guests at the Ascot week house-party at Windsor and the Queen herself decided to go to Munich and see how they fared.

As it turned out, that plan was cancelled by family events. But Anne followed her father to the Games, on her feet with excitement for most of the three days while she watched Richard Meade, Bridget Parker, Mary Gordon-Watson and Mark Phillips, beside herself with wild joy in seeing the team at last win the gold medal. 'There's a moment in sport when the enjoyment wears off because of the pressure put on you to be successful,' the Princess had said. 'That is the moment to stop and make sure in your own mind what sport is all about.' And what was it about? It concerned the personal achievement of winning and the enjoyment of good fellowship, the satisfaction of ever-widening experience as well as the proving of one's own ability. And it concerned the enchantment of unexpectedly falling in love.

The comparative lull after Munich was however quickly filled with Princess Anne's hopes of defending her Raleigh trophy at the Burghley Three-Day event, especially in competition with Richard Meade, who had taken the Olympics individual equestrian gold medal. Declining an invitation to sleep at Burghley House, she stayed at the George Inn in Stamford, decisively preferring the good company of other competitors to more formal surroundings. She had chosen to ride the Queen's big and powerful grey horse, Columbus, and was well up with the leaders in the calm dressage phase, only to suffer another dire catastrophe to her hopes the following day.

On the steeplechase course Columbus proved too much for her, simply that. On the second circuit she realized that he was running away with her and that she was no longer fully in control. The Princess had little option but to pull him up and withdraw, almost in tears at abandoning her chance of the finish. Columbus was a big double handful of a horse, as the experts agreed, better for a young man than a girl. 'Let Mark have a go', said the Princess, in effect. The Queen obligingly loaned him the horse and, with Columbus, Mark increasingly discovered his own new world. Anne in return tried out Mark's horse, Persian Holiday, finding a holiday from royal environment every time she stepped into the solid middle-class atmosphere of the Mount House at Great Somerford.

The young couple almost mischievously seized every opportunity of meeting, usually with the excuse of discussing one horse or the other. One of the reasons why Mark's parents, Anne and Peter Phillips, had moved to the Mount House from Tewkesbury when Mark was nine was because the out-buildings gave such scope for the children's ponies; they never dreamed that they had thus fostered a future royal courtship. And in the later summer of '72 a neighbour who chanced to see Mark strolling round the stables with a young blonde took her merely as one of his sister Sarah's friends. For a few blissful months, indeed, the smoke-wisps of rumour conveyed nothing of the real strength of their friendship.

The contemporary popularity of Princess Anne carries with it the deep public wish for her success and fulfilment and lasting happiness, a desire so tangible that impatient imagination gradually leapt ahead of true event. The Princess and the dragoon, as one writer put it, figured so often in friendship and riding rivalry that romantic speculation soon became inevitable. In many ways it was fortunate that Lieutenant Phillips, as he was, was soon transferred to Catterick Camp. Out of metropolitan sight is out of metropolitan mind and Anne knew from the Duchess of Kent that Yorkshire pays high regard to commonsense reticence. The Princess was welcome at Garrowby Hall, whenever she wished, and at Catterick an Army officer's wife had the surprise of her life when her husband mentioned, 'My dear, I rather think that Princess Anne would like to stay with us the week-end after next.' Mark's commanding officer, Colonel Maurice Johnston, has remarked that he was in the picture from the start. And Princess Anne gained sharpened insight into the life of a young Army wife: waiting for your man to come off duty and then all the more intensely enjoying his company.

Looking back, the remembrance of the six week-ends in Yorkshire will always glow for the young couple from the year before their wedding. Life was suddenly a cinerama of hunting and hunt balls, dances and lonely unobserved moorland rides, of laughter and happiness, idyllic even to loopy attempts one day at Appleby to hold hands unnoticed after a picnic lunch at a gamekeeper's cottage. When Prince Philip went up to Balmoral for a few days' shooting, Anne accompanied him, an exceptional departure from routine, as if she were seeking 'a talk with father' when she could count on finding him contentedly undisturbed and in his most genial frame of mind. Whether Mark then joined the party is unknown from Balmoral records, and public attention was sufficiently distracted just then by the indignant furore that raged around the Princess's fox-hunting.

## VII

The Duke of Windsor had once asked Princess Anne why she did not hunt since she was so fond of riding, and she had replied in two words 'Blood sports!' Fondly remembering his own hours of enjoyment in the hunting field, and his sister's, too, the Duke had responded with equal brevity, 'A pity!' The hunting fraternity might deem it a pity, too, that he did not live to see his grand-niece at a meet of the Zetland and then with the Bedale Hunt and again with the Cheshire Hunt, the Beaufort and the Cottesmore, week upon week. The first news of these outings broke across the front pages with untimely coincidence on the very day of the Queen's Silver Wedding.

Some wondered what the eighteenth-century caricaturist Gillray might have made of the flouting of the President of the World Wildlife Fund by his daughter's pursuit of the last of Britain's larger carnivores. The abolitionists' phrase about the pursuit of the uneatable by the unspeakable became inconvenient when the pursuer was Princess Anne. The argument plunged the English into one of their typical convulsions of self-examination. One royal hunt was a news story after half a century of careful avoidance of blood sports; two and more expressed wilful defiance of the larger weight of public opinion. And then again, this seemed a not uncharacteristic echo of Mountbatten stock, and some considered it admirable and typical of her generation that the Princess should question old taboos and test controversial prohibitions for herself.

More important to Anne was perhaps the novel excitement of keeping up across unknown and unpredictable country, over no matter what obstacles—and particularly keeping up with Mark. Especially Mark, who had proposed that inaugural day with the Zetland in the first place. Notably Mark when she stayed with his people at the Mount House again, when he was home on leave, and all the old fox-hunting prints about the house conveyed a timeless new meaning, emblems of the fun they had following the hounds of the Beaufort Hunt, twice in five days. The fox was however no longer the only fugitive. Anne and Mark were now the quarry of all the world's news cameras.

The popular press leapt—stronger than Columbus at any fence —at the prospect of a 'soldier boy' taking his girl home to see his parents. In the New Year of 1973 the flow of gossip deepened into an irrepressible flood when Mark spent his first two January week-ends at Sandringham. Outside the gates the reporters watched the pair riding into the wintry fog and, when Mark left to join his regiment in Germany, the Princess could not resist teasing the press-men, 'I'm on my own today. A pity, isn't it?'

Glancing over the papers her sense of humour nevertheless lapsed at times into burning indignation. Mark's light parting kiss on the quay at Harwich was exaggerated beyond measure in cold print. Mark had planned an Olympic team reunion at Somerford during his first week-end leave from Germany, only to find news-print hints of a stolen week-end. It had seemed fun to Princess Anne to rush home from the Sudan and straight to breakfast at the Mount House, and then drive direct with Mark to a training session at Mrs. Oliver's. But morning by morning the stables were besieged increasingly by the reportage hordes and the quiet Berkshire lane became a focus of expectation for a news-hungry world. Half in anger, more in dismay, Anne asserted one day that there was 'no romance and no grounds for these rumours of a romance'. Mark begged the reporters to remember that they were making the horses nervous. Indeed everyone was becoming nervous, including perhaps the Queen's press secretary, Mr. Ludlow, who resigned on 'a difference of opinion' a week or two later.

Then two hearts at a gallop met their own coincidence shortly before Badminton, when the Princess was thrown and trampled on by Mark's horse, Persian Holiday, and, at the Rushall Trials the following day, Mark was unseated, half rolled on and knocked out by the Queen's horse Columbus. He had been unable to hide his concern on hearing of Anne's accident, and Anne was white-faced as she rushed to the first aid tent for news of Mark. Happily no bones were broken and both laughed ruefully at their bandaged arms. It remains only to be said that Anne, riding the Queen's com-paratively inexperienced Goodwill, came eighth in the three-day Whitbread event at Badminton, while Mark faced a final day of total disaster. Columbus threw him twice, including a ducking at the lake, Great Ovation went lame and when he continued with Columbus it was too late for retrieval. But he had already twice won the trophy, he had known the victor's laurels and he won the hand of his fair lady. On May 29th there came the not unexpected announcement in the *Court Circular*, 'It is with the greatest pleasure that the Queen and the Duke of Edinburgh announce the bethrothal of their beloved daughter the Princess Anne to Lieutenant Mark Phillips, the Queen's Dragoon Guards, son of Mr. and Mrs. Peter Phillips.'

## VIII

Casual and candid, quick-witted and quick-tempered, careless of speed limits in more ways than one, wilful yet self-questioning, Princess Anne once said of one of her more tepid royal duties, 'When you are doing it, you think to yourself, "*Why*? Why do I do this?"—and afterwards you realize it is well worth while.'

Anne hurriedly left her family engagement luncheon to fly by helicopter to a Riding for the Disabled school and watch a group of handicapped children proudly riding their ponies. Into the subsequent week of official duties in Germany she slipped a magical week-end with Mark at her Aunt Margarita's astonishingly romantic Langenburg Castle. Amid her wedding preparations there were scheduled engagements in Liverpool, Birmingham, Chepstow, Huddersfield and Beverley, to name a few which had been arranged months beforehand.

And before the first fitting of her wedding dress, that dreamy gown by off-the-peg designer Maureen Baker, there ensued her major riding adventure in Kiev. In defending her European equestrian title in the 1973 three-day-event in Russia, she was in fact the first British royalty to set foot in the Soviet Union since the Revolution. The Princess played it cool. But there came the debacle of the second jump on which one third of all the competitors came to grief: an obstacle of stout poles nailed together six feet in depth and over a ditch, approached down a hill with a final mud slide, and as one commentator said 'like a Cossack battle assault course rather than a sporting event'. Anne took a heart-thumping somersault and decided to retire, presently crying in private against Mark's comforting shoulder.

With sixty penalty points against her for the fall, there was clearly no point in risking her horse Goodwill further. Bruised but unperturbed, she was riding again within the month and won the Spillers combined championship of dressage and show-jumping at the Horse of the Year Show. And so to wed ... at Westminster Abbey on November 14th, a date doubly happy in choice, for it was also Prince Charles's twenty-fifth birthday. Again, Anne introduced new notes in the tested pattern of royal weddings in electing to have only two bridal attendants: her youngest brother, Prince Edward, and her cousin, never more delectably pretty, the nine-year-old Lady Sarah Armstrong-Jones. The wedding-night destination moreover remained a secret, until it was divulged the following day as Thatched House Lodge in Richmond Park when the happy pair were already flying on their way to the Caribbean.

It was the ordinary British Airways scheduled flight to Barbados, and with the surprised passengers delightedly drinking a toast to the young couple we reach our happy ending—and the happy beginning. In retrospect, the fates already seem to have scripted the first year of marriage in contemporary tempo, swinging from romance to nightmare danger, from domestic bliss to disciplined achievement, weaving plot and counter-plot at a pace strangely characteristic of our time.

In Bridgetown harbour Rear-Admiral Trowbridge of the *Britannia* was supposedly under orders to take the honeymooners cruising wherever their fancy dictated. 'We shall be bored stiff', Anne had said mockingly. In reality, rain lashed the royal yacht and the seas ran high. It seems probable that a secret passenger was aboard, for at the weekend Princess Margaret mysteriously appeared on the isle of Mustique to open up her hideaway villa, and for a week or two the newly-weds disappeared as completely as they could have wished. Then in effect they embarked on a second-phase working honeymoon, leaving the royal yacht for official flying visits to Ecuador, Colombia, Jamaica, Montserrat and Antigua.

They found themselves 'riding the Equator' at a ranch nine thousand feet up in the Andes, dancing in a fiesta in Quito and bargaining for ponchos at an Indian village where a carnival loudspeaker announced that 'the Queen of London and the Prince Phillips Marks' had arrived. And while the London crowds were still filing past the mounds of wedding gifts on public view at St. James's Palace, the Princess found herself unexpectedly in the role of a worried young wife while her husband was laid up feverishly ill with a bug in the Embassy in Bogota.

He quickly recovered, of course. Captain Mark Phillips, as he had recently been promoted, slipped effortlessly into his hitherto unforeseen public role. His smile was a tonic, agreed the Jamaican Press, when he first toured a hospital. He 'beamed happily' at the crush of would-be partners at the Kingston ball. He 'smilingly shook a thousand hands' at an Antigua garden-party. As her last official function before her wedding Princess Anne had opened the

Motor Show and a day or so after their return home she and Mark
were principal guests at a banquet for racing driver Jackie Stewart.
Their combined public appearances were henceforth to have a
certain elan.

They spent their first married Christmas with the Queen and
Prince Philip at Windsor and their first married New Year with
Mark's parents. Three weeks later they were in the Middle of the
light-hearted confusion of wives, babies and ranks on a Canadian
Servicemen's plane bound for Ottawa. Mark had meanwhile taken
a brief tank instructor's course, and the Queen had invited them to
accompany her 1974 tour of New Zealand, Australia and the
Pacific isles, as if extending the spirit of their honeymoon. Stopping
off for three days at Government House, Ottawa, they tried the
toboggan slopes and a snowmobile run, and paid the first royal
visit to Quebec since the separatist terrors. Toronto, a little jealous,
asked if the couple could pay a visit to open the Agricultural
Winter Fair on November 15th. 'Wonderful!' said the Princess.
'We can fly over the day before—November 14th—our first
wedding anniversary!'

As an Army wife, Anne thinks of herself as ready to pick up and
go 'moving on', as Mark says, 'where the Army sends me'. More
by luck than apparent influence, however, Mark was posted for
three years as an instructor at the Royal Military Academy, Sandhurst, and offered an empty house in the grounds that, as Anne
confided, 'seemed just made for us'. Oak Grove House was in fact a
dilapidated Regency house at a 'Colonel's rental' of £400 a year,
and remarkable for the large number of very small rooms con-
tained within the limited space—three reception, five bed, two
bath—but the couple greeted it with enthusiasm.

The furnishing problems pursued them to the Commonwealth
Games village in Christchurch, where they admired stools 'that
might match our Orkney chair' and while buying souvenirs at a
native market in New Guinea they puzzled over the size of local-
made doormats. Meanwhile, at home, the police worried over the
security difficulties of Oak Grove, the surrounding trees that could
conceal a gunman, a nearby public path that might tempt intruders.
Anne's attitude was fatalistic, 'not to worry . . .' Were there not
risks anywhere?

When danger materialized, it came unexpectedly, on a prosaic

March evening, in the fantastic kidnap attempt in the Mall. 'So unbelievable,' as Anne says, 'that one doesn't really believe it happened' ... the sudden shots, the splitting glass, the gunman attempting to open the door of the car, and Inspector Beaton, her bodyguard—shot three times—collapsing in the road. Then the incredibility of looking down the barrel of the gun, Mark holding her fast while her assailant seized her other arm, and the absurd forgotten phrase from Nanny Anderson rising to her lips, 'If you stop now, we'll say no more about it.'

Yet more remarkable in perspective in that unwary unsought moment was the gallantry of the Londoners who came to her aid, heedless of personal safety ... the Dulwich journalist who confronted the attacker only to receive a bullet in his chest, the office cleaning manager who 'had a go' with his fists and interposed himself as a shield, the passing motorist who blocked the kidnapper's car and, when the firing ceased, the woman passer-by who asked, 'Are you all right, love?' And the young South Londoner, awarded the George Medal for his heroism that night, who attempted to explain his own courage, 'I have a wife and two kids but my life means nothing compared with the Princess's ...', words of deep sincerity and loyalty to shame the detractors of the monarchy.

In the Princesses Royal of the past our own Princess Anne may find no single common factor, save a share of ancestry. One is irresistibly reminded of another Abbey bride of over fifty years ago, the only daughter of the monarch, the Princess Mary, subsequently a Princess Royal, who similarly seized whatever freedom was possible to a princess in her day and yet yielded whenever necessary to the ingrained demands of duty. One is reminded, too, of the Princess Royal Charlotte, with her 'boundless charities' and her deck of cards stacked against Napoleon; of the Princess Royal, Empress of Prussia, wishing 'to push on ... to try and add my little might to all great and good purposes, for the inward satisfaction'. And retrospect drifts back to the Princess Royal Anne of Georgian days, hurtling over fences and ditches and yet in middle life adding her strength and expertise to the prudent management of a nation.

As her only daughter moves into married life, it is still for the Queen alone to decide whether the style and distinction of Princess Royal should be revived or disregarded. Is there some argument that the form has become superfluous, a mere decorative device, archaic as the gage of the King's Champion or the obsolete technique of walking backwards? On the other hand, the style has never lacked popular acceptance. With few exceptions, the Princesses Royal have carried a sustaining tradition through the centuries. Far from losing significance, the role has added purposive strength and renewal to the Monarchy, and perhaps a new era of princesses truly royal has already begun.

# Bibliography

The author's primary reference materials have included the Calendars of State Papers, Domestic, for the respective years, particularly in the reigns of James I, Charles I and Charles II; the *Dictionary of National Biography*, *The Annual Register* and *The Times*. The following books are also given in sequence of narrative, rather than alphabetical order:

*The Royal House of Scotland*—Eric Linklater, 1970
*Lives of the Princesses of England*—M. A. E. Greene, 1855
*Lives of Four Princesses of the House of Stuart*—Agnes Strickland, 1872
*Five Stuart Princesses*—Robert Rait, 1902
*Mary Tudor*—Beatrice White, 1935
*Mary Tudor*—M. G. Brown, 1911
*Elizabeth the Great*—Elizabeth Jenkins, 1958
*Queen Elizabeth*—J. E. Neale, 1945
*Elizabeth of Bohemia*—Carola Oman, 1964
*Henriette Maria*—Carola Oman, 1936
*Her Majesty*—E. Thornton Cook, 1926
*Royal Daughters*—E. Thornton Cook and Catherine Moran, 1935
*The Court at Windsor*—Christopher Hibbert, 1964
*The Windsor Tapestry*—Compton Mackenzie, 1939
*Heirs to the Throne*—Annette Joelson, 1966
*Diary of Samuel Pepys*—Various editions
*Diary of John Evelyn*—Various editions
*Charles II*—Sir Arthur Bryant, 1955
*James II*—F. C. Turner, 1948
*Orange and Stuart*—Pieter Geyl, 1969
*William Prince of Orange*—Marjorie Bowen, 1928
*Lives of Hanoverian Queens of England*—Alice Greenwood, 1909
*Six Royal Ladies of the House of Hanover*—Sarah Tytler, 1899
*Memoirs of Court of England*, Vol 4—J. H. Jesse, 1901
*A King in Toils*—J. D. Griffith Davies, 1938

*Diary of Lady Cowper*, 1720
*Frederick Prince of Wales*—Averyl Edwards, 1947
*Handel*—Herbert Weinstock, 1946
*George Frederic Handel*—Paul Lang, 1967
*George Frederic Handel*—Newman Flower, 1947
*Concerning Handel*—William G. Smith, 1948
*Lord Hervey's Memoirs*—Romney Sedgwick, 1952
*The Four Georges*—W. M. Thackeray, 1866
*The Daughters of George III*—D. M. Stuart, 1939
*Six Royal Sisters*—Morris Marples, 1969
*Autobiography of Mary Granville*, Mrs. Delaney, 1862
*Diary & Letters of Madame D'Arblay* (Fanny Burmey)—ed. 1904
*Hanover to Windsor*—Roger Fulford, 1960
*Victoria R.I.*—Elizabeth Longford, 1964
*Vicky*—Daphne Bennett, 1971
*Queen Victoria's Sister*—Harold A. Albert, 1967
*The Prince Consort*—Roger Fulford, 1949
*Dearest Child*—Roger Fulford, 1964
*Queen Victoria's Relations*—Meriel Buchanan, 1954
*The Kaisers*—Theo Aronson, 1971
*Queen Alexandra*—Georgina Battiscombe, 1969
*Life with Queen Victoria*—Marie Mallett, 1968
*King George V*—John Gore, 1941
*Queen Mary*—James Pope-Hennessy, 1959
*Lady Lytton's Court Diary*—ed. by Mary Lutyens, 1961
*A King's Story*—The Duke of Windsor, 1960
*Thatched With Gold*—Mabell, Countess of Airlie, 1962
*King George VI*—J. W. Wheeler-Bennett, 1958
*Anne*—Judith Campbell, 1970
*Princess Anne, Champion of Europe*—Bernard Foyster, 1972
*The Queen and Her Children*—Lady Peacock, 1961

# STAR BOOKS

are available through all good
booksellers but, where difficulty is encountered,
titles can usually be obtained *by post* from:

Star Book Service,
G.P.O. Box 29,
Douglas,
Isle of Man,
British Isles.

1 or 2 books – retail price + 5p. each copy
3 or more books – retail price post free.

Customers outside Britain should include 7p.
postage and packing for every book ordered.

If you have enjoyed this book you will also like:

# JIMMY YOUNG
## Jimmy Young

The stories are outstanding. How our Jim got to where he is, and why. J. Y. is a winner, he's still winning, and now he wins new friends with the paperback edition of the hardback smash bestseller. *40p*

# MY LIFE AT CROSSROADS
## Noele Gordon

The faithful millions who never miss a programme of the phenomenal ATV Crossroads series can now meet head on the woman behind Meg Richardson who has captured their hearts. *45p*

# LIBERACE
## Liberace

Master of music, money and — for millions all over the world — a man of irridescently good manners, Lee Liberace has never swerved from confronting and triumphantly overcoming the problems of success. The most splendid and one of the most fascinating figures of the concert halls continues to splash hard-earned fame upon adoring audiences. Here's sweet talking and lots of it from a magical star. *75p*

If you have enjoyed this book you will also like

# BRANDO
## Bob Thomas

Sex hero? Surrealist daub? Great artist? Man of integrity or sham? Whatever you think, here is the real Marlon. How he arrived, stumbled, and re-emerged white hot to cauterise the wounds inflicted by the venom of his critics.

*80p*

# MARY PICKFORD
## Sweetheart
## Robert Windeler

"'Actresses should realize when they deliberately choose a public career they have no right to disappoint the public — and no right to privacy. As a toy of the public, that's part of the price." Strong words from the girl whose smile "made you hear the angels sing". This is Mary Pickford's story, full of romance, accomplishment, glamour, and tragedy. An extraordinary evocation of a unique era.

*75p*

# THE STAR
# ILLUSTRATED HISTORY
# OF THE MOVIES SERIES

The final word on such unforgettable
legends of the screen as:

# HUMPHREY BOGART
# KATHARINE HEPBURN
# CLARKE GABLE
# BETTE DAVIS
# MARLON BRANDO
# MARILYN MONROE

**Each book 60p and lavishly illustrated**